Robert H. Ferrell is Professor of History at Indiana University. He is also the author of *American Diplomacy in the Great Depression: Hoover-Stimson Foreign Policy, 1929-1933; American Diplomacy* (Norton); and *Foundations of American Diplomacy*.

Raymond Aron   *On War*   N107
_____   *The Opium of the Intellectuals*   N106
Julien Benda   *The Treason of the Intellectuals*   N470
Marc Bloch   *Strange Defeat: A Statement of Evidence Written in 1940*
   N371
Jan Huizinga   *In the Shadow of Tomorrow*   N484
John U. Nef   *War and Human Progress: An Essay on the Rise of
   Industrial Civilization*   N468
José Ortega y Gasset   *The Revolt of the Masses*
Bertrand Russell   *Freedom versus Organization, 1814-1914*   N136
_____   *Power*   N479

Peace

IN THEIR TIME

The Origins of the Kellogg-Briand Pact

BY ROBERT H. FERRELL

The Norton Library

W · W · NORTON & COMPANY · INC ·
NEW YORK

TO MY FATHER AND BROTHER

AND TO W. R. CASTLE

Acknowledgment

Many individuals have made this book possible. I am greatly indebted to William R. Castle, who as assistant secretary of state in 1927–29 had much to do with negotiation of the Kellogg pact; Mr. Castle most kindly permitted use of his hitherto unpublished voluminous diary.

The essay was originally written as a dissertation for the degree of doctor of philosophy at Yale. William Weed Kaufmann's suggestions and encouragement were very helpful. Hajo Holborn with patience and thoroughness aided toward understanding the European context of the Kellogg-Briand Pact. Harry R. Rudin first called my attention to the "new diplomacy" of the post-1918 era; it was his view of the origins of the Kellogg pact which led to this present study. Samuel Flagg Bemis has helped in so many ways that it is impossible to enumerate them; the essay would have progressed nowhere without his friendship and criticism.

The editor of the Yale Historical Series, Lewis P. Curtis, made many excellent suggestions in preparing the manuscript for publication. Miss Jane Hartenstein of the Yale University Press likewise read the manuscript with a keen eye for error. It has been a pleasure to work with the editor of the Press, Eugene Davidson.

Contents

Chapter One: ARMISTICE 1918

The "war to end war" came to an end on November 11, 1918. Never was there such a celebration. In Paris, the capital of the victorious Allies, cannon opened the day with a booming salute to victory. With one accord the populace turned into the streets. Throngs of people jammed the boulevards from sidewalk to sidewalk. One almost could have stepped down the middle of the Champs Élysées on the shoulders of the happy, shouting crowd. A great mass of people gathered in the Place de la Concorde, where the statue of the captive City of Strasbourg after forty-seven years shed her crape and mourning wreaths, and took on instead the tri-color of France. Premier Georges Clemenceau declared to his rejoicing countrymen: "Le jour de gloire est arrivé!"

There were similar scenes in London. As soon as the armistice news became known, a huge mass of humanity began to converge toward Buckingham Palace. The crowd flowed over the Queen Victoria Memorial. Small boys perched themselves on the lap of the statue. All eyes looked toward the Palace, where scarlet cloth and gold draped the balcony above the main entrance, sign that royalty would appear. The waiting crowd was becoming restless when the king in naval uniform, the queen bareheaded, the Princess Mary, and the Duke of Connaught stepped out on the balcony. Cheer after cheer rent the air, flags and handkerchiefs waved, and the Memorial became a pyramid of fluttering color. The massed bands of the guards struck up "God Save the King," then the national anthems of the Allies. The crowd finally broke up and poured back into the London thoroughfares to the tune of "It's a Long, Long Way to Tipperary." For the rest of the day London gave itself up to celebration.

In the United States the real armistice was an anticlimax. False rumors of peace had prematurely touched off a boisterous revel on November 6. Many people, hearing that the armistice rumors were spurious, declared they would continue celebrating until the actual end of the war. When the final news came on November 11, all New York let loose. The canyons of Manhattan filled with so much wastepaper that the National Board of Fire Underwriters became seriously worried. Impromptu parades started up everywhere, with opprobrious effigies of Kaiser Wilhelm as the center of attraction.

In Washington President Woodrow Wilson hastily assembled the Congress, and there followed a memorable scene. At two minutes past one o'clock the chief executive appeared at the House chamber escorted by a committee of senators and representatives. "The President of the United States," shouted Joseph Sinnott, sergeant-at-arms of the House, as Wilson entered through a doorway to the left and rear of the rostrum. In an instant the entire company was on its feet, cheering. "It is not now possible," Wilson said, "to assess the consequences of this great consummation. We know only that this tragical war, whose consuming flames swept from one nation to another until all the world was on fire, is at an end . . ." [1] In his own heart and mind the president was resolved that this victory should, if possible, be a victory over war itself: out of it would come some sort of international constitution for keeping the peace of the world.

In Berlin, the capital of the defeated Hohenzollern Empire, there was a different scene. A revolution of the proletariat was on foot. The Soldiers' and Workers' Council issued a communiqué announcing that "Great joy and enthusiasm prevail everywhere." [2] But there was reason for doubt. The German people could not have been joyful on the day when so many of their dreams collapsed and when so much that was long familiar disappeared. Great joy and

1. New York *Times*, Nov. 12, 1918.
2. London *Times*, Nov. 12, 1918.

enthusiasm probably were not much in evidence except among the stalwarts of the revolutionary movement itself. Undoubtedly, however, millions of tired German soldiers looked forward on November 11, 1918, to returning home, and to living in peace the rest of their days.

People everywhere on November 11, 1918, were sick of war and glad of peace—boisterously glad in the Allied capitals, at least hopefully relieved in gloomy Berlin. Peace at last was a reality, a much-blessed reality. Peace felt good indeed after four long years of frightful war. It was a day of glory all over the world, glory in hope of universal peace.

Perhaps the Armistice would actually mark the dawning of a new warless era for the human race! It was incredible to think that the nations, having found peace after so much travail, would lose it. Although Wilson very cautiously advised his listeners that "It is not now possible to assess the consequences of this great consummation," it was rather Lloyd George who voiced the deep spirit of November 11 when he emotionally told the House of Commons: "I hope we may say that thus, this fateful morning, came to an end all wars." [3]

I

The popular desire for peace, of course, did not first arise during the Great War. People have wished for peace ever since human beings started fighting each other—and that, we may rest assured, was a very long time ago. Popular longings nevertheless rarely became articulate until fairly recently in the modern era, during and after the period of the French Revolution when thrones and altars at last began to shake and fall as the people arose to take over their governments.

The French National Assembly invoked international peace in 1790. It wrote into the Constitution of France a solemn pledge:

3. *Parliamentary Debates, House of Commons,* Nov. 11, 1918, quoted in Harry R. Rudin, *Armistice 1918* (New Haven, Yale University Press, 1944), p. 385.

"The French nation renounces all wars of conquest, and will never use its forces against the liberty of another people." [4] Here at long last was response to yearnings of millions of the downtrodden French peasantry. Although it is sadly true that after this noble renunciation the French nation turned all Europe into a twenty-year battleground, popular aspiration for peace unrelentingly continued in strength and voice during the wars of the Revolution and Napoleon.

After Waterloo and prior to August 1914 the main cause of war in the Western world was the desire for achievement of national states in central and southeastern Europe, thus completing the work begun in France in 1789. During the nineteenth century the great powers busied themselves principally in oversea expansion or in industrial growth. The century 1815–1914 was a relatively peaceful century compared to the Napoleonic conflict which had gone before. But although there was no general war among the nations of the world, war still remained recognized as—to use Clausewitz' phrase—an "instrument of policy."

Plans for peace nonetheless seemed almost unnecessary until the European alliance system began to tighten up visibly near the end of the century. Oddly enough the remarkable French Foreign Minister Théophile Delcassé, foremost apostle of *revanche* and destroyer of the work of Bismarck, was one of the unintentional mentors of the peace movement, for Delcassé's skillful construction of ententes and alliances helped create an ominous war psychology in Europe, alarming men of good will and turning their thoughts toward planning more actively for peace.[5] These humanitarians addressed their efforts to the Peace Conferences at The Hague and to the promotion of arbitration treaties among the nations.

It is a fairly well-known story that the First Hague Conference originated not in the idealism of the Russian monarch who pro-

4. For interesting details of this renunciation, see Albert Sorel, *L'Europe et la révolution française* (8 vols., Paris, 1885–1904), II, 84–91.

5. Delcassé was foreign minister during the years 1898–1905. Although he returned to the Quai d'Orsay during the World War, it is his earlier work for which he is remembered. For an excellent biography of this French statesman, see Charles W. Porter, *The Career of Théophile Delcassé* (Philadelphia, 1936).

ARMISTICE 1918 5

posed it, but in the difficulties of his finance minister, Count Witte, who was having financial troubles in bringing the Russian artillery up to date.[6] The tsar's invitation to the powers proposed two topics for discussion—reduction of armaments and peaceful settlement of international disputes. The first proved to be a complete fiasco. The second resulted in establishment of the Hague Permanent Court of Arbitration, setting up rules for voluntary arbitration of international controversies.

The Second Hague Conference of 1907, called at the behest of President Theodore Roosevelt after the Russo-Japanese War of 1904–05, was no more successful in clinching the cause of general peace than its predecessor. Already a European armaments race was in full swing, and—the new world peace movement notwithstanding—experienced diplomatists knew that the year 1907 was no time for disarmament. Sir Edward Grey frankly told the House of Commons: "The difficulty in regard to one nation stepping out in advance of the others is this, that while there is a chance that their courageous action may lead to reform, there is also a chance that it may lead to martyrdom." [7] The Second Hague Conference's two most important acts were (1) the Porter Convention, which prohibited forcible collection of international debts except under certain conditions,[8] and (2) the decision to create a tribunal to adjudicate violations of sea law in wartime—an international prize court —thus necessitating codification of belligerent and neutral rights

6. E. J. Dillon, *The Eclipse of Russia* (New York, 1918), pp. 269–278. See also Thomas K. Ford, "The Genesis of the First Hague Peace Conference," *Political Science Quarterly, 51* (1936), 354–382. Ford argues that Witte worried over money for artillery because he wanted to spend available money on the navy; and so he favored the conference idea if it might prevent expenditures on artillery.

7. E. L. Woodward, *Great Britain and the German Navy* (Oxford, Oxford University Press, 1935), p. 134. The German kaiser declared that King Edward VII, during a visit to Germany, had described the disarmament discussions prior to convening the Second Hague Conference as "humbug." After this disclosure Wilhelm attended the wedding of Fraulein Bertha Krupp, where he announced that "To you, my dear Bertha, God has ordained a magnificent sphere of influence." *Ibid.,* pp. 125–126.

8. If the delinquent state refused arbitration or, after arbitration, refused to abide by the award.

and duties; but the resulting Declaration of London never achieved enough ratifications to go into effect. The Second Hague Conference, hailed by peace-lovers throughout the world, actually produced not plans for peace but rules for war.

Nor did peace advocates get any further by their promotion of arbitration treaties. France and Great Britain in 1903 dubiously furthered the cause of peace by bringing forth a new model formula for such pacts. This famous formula agreed in advance to arbitrate disputes but excluded from arbitration all questions affecting the vital interests, independence, or national honor of the contracting states, or disputes involving third parties. This was the formula used by Secretary of State Elihu Root in a set of well-known and much-admired bilateral treaties between the United States and other powers. In diplomatic practice these treaties meant that states refused to arbitrate the very questions which led directly to war. As instruments of peace the numerous arbitration treaties concluded on the Anglo-French pattern were of negligible value. "I only went into them," President Theodore Roosevelt told his friend Sir Cecil Spring-Rice, "because the general feeling of the country demanded it." [9]

The peace movement in the United States did not place all its hopes on the Hague Conferences and on the growing network of arbitration treaties.[10] Workers for peace sought to advance the cause through the manifold activities of privately organized peace societies. These societies already had a long history. The New York Peace Society and the Massachusetts Peace Society had been organized after the Napoleonic Wars. The American Peace Society established itself a few years later. By the middle of the nineteenth century there were no less than fifty distinct peace societies in the United States. But these were all genteel organizations—quaint, old-fashioned, somewhat stodgy. After the turn of the twentieth century there appeared two lusty new institutions: the World

9. W. Stull Holt, *Treaties Defeated by the Senate* (Baltimore, Johns Hopkins University Press, 1933), p. 212.

10. The nations of the world, before the end of 1914, had concluded more than one hundred treaties containing the Franco-British formula.

Peace Foundation and the Carnegie Endowment for International Peace. Andrew Carnegie, enthusiastic founder of the Endowment, gave the express commandment to "hasten the abolition of international war, the foulest blot upon our civilization." [11] Such new organizations, cooperating with invigorated old-time peace societies, began to work tirelessly for abolition of war. To describe their activities there soon arose a new word, "pacifism." [12]

Thus the years passed and the work of the peace movement grew more and more impressive. In Europe the nations were building up armaments, but there was no war.[13] In the year 1913 the nations dedicated a magnificent Peace Palace at The Hague, built by Andrew Carnegie [14] as a home for the Permanent Court of Arbitration. In the United States there was a brand-new navy and some imperialistic accomplishments in the Caribbean and Pacific, but most Americans believed the world was better off—and even more peaceful—because of the Philippines, the Canal, and the new navy. Perhaps they were right. In the languid summer days of June 1914 profound peace hung, with a great stillness, over all the world.

Then, suddenly, in an instant, all Europe burst into flames.

11. Nor was Carnegie satisfied even with abolition of war: "When . . . war is discarded as disgraceful to civilized men . . . the Trustees will pleas [Carnegie simplified spelling] then consider what is the next most degrading remaining evil or evils whose banishment . . . would most advance the progress, elevation and happiness of man, and so on from century to century without end, my Trustees of each age shall determin how they can best aid man in his upward march to . . . perfection even here in this life upon erth." Andrew Carnegie to the trustees of the proposed Carnegie Endowment for International Peace, Dec. 14, 1910. For text, see any of the Endowment's yearbooks.

12. Norman Angell, "Pacifism," *Encyclopedia of the Social Sciences,* XI, 527–528.

13. Other than fighting in obscure corners of the globe: the Transvaal, Manchuria and Tsushima Straits, Tripoli, the Balkans.

14. Andrew Carnegie gave $1,500,000 for building the Palace. All the great nations contributed gifts—clocks, gates and railings, paintings, candelabra, etc. Speaking after the ceremonies of dedication, August 29, 1913, Carnegie movingly described "the greatest of all causes, the abolition of war," and "the killing of man by man, the greatest of all crimes." *A Manual of the Public Benefactions of Andrew Carnegie* (Washington, 1919), p. 276.

II

To Europeans and Americans alike, outbreak of World War brought almost complete astonishment. In the New World particularly hardly anyone was prepared, mentally, for such a tremendous catastrophe.

Decades of peace, which peace leaders everywhere had heralded as a New World Order of Concord, proved mere prelude to war. The international peace fabric, with its solemn peace conferences, its network of arbitration treaties so laboriously constructed, all vanished when Austrian guns flashed and boomed before the Serbian city of Belgrade.

In Europe initial astonishment rapidly gave way to surging patriotism. Young men en masse flocked to the colors. The war, they thought, would end quickly with victory. But in the United States astonishment changed to revulsion as the American Government hastily declared neutrality.

American feeling toward the World War altered only slowly as, after the initial rush of the German armies into France, fighting bogged down into a war of position. Most Americans, including President Woodrow Wilson, persisted in believing that their country should remain neutral—a Refuge for Civilization driven from the Old World to the New. Pacifism was popular. Even ex-President Theodore Roosevelt at first was content with neutrality. But as he began to feel the realities of the threatened balance of power he compared the then-current pacifist song, "I Didn't Raise My Boy to Be a Soldier," with "I didn't raise my girl to be a mother." His published speeches and articles during this period bear the title *Fear God and Take Your Own Part*.[15] At first he received little support from the great majority of Americans.

The war in Europe gave a new impulse to peace organizations in the United States. They worked feverishly to keep the country out of war and, if possible, to end the war itself. There arose a National Peace Federation, advocating "continuous mediation." Two of the nation's leading feminists, Miss Jane Addams and Mrs. Carrie Chapman Catt, formed the Woman's Peace Party to "enlist

15. (New York, 1916).

all American women in arousing the nations to respect the sacredness of human life and to abolish war." [16] Several American peace conferences met during the spring of 1915, among them a notable convention at Philadelphia which established a League to Enforce Peace. This latter was at once a new peace organization and a new proposition: a group of leading Americans proposed that in the future the nations of the world *enforce* peace.[17]

Then there was Henry Ford's "Peace Ship." This odyssey had its beginnings when a Hungarian pacifist, Mrs. Rosika Schwimmer, and the youthful secretary of the Chicago Peace Society, Louis P. Lochner, went to Detroit and persuaded the multimillionaire automobile manufacturer to support the National Peace Federation's proposal for continuous mediation.[18] Accompanied by Lochner, Ford then proceeded to Washington to see President Wilson.[19] Said Ford to Wilson: "I have today chartered a steamship. I offer it to you to send delegates to Europe. If you feel you can't act, I will. . . . I shall take a shipful of American delegates to Europe." Wilson, who had received his conspicuous visitor with every courtesy, suddenly grew cold and formal, and Ford and Lochner soon found themselves outside the White House grounds.[20] Never-

16. Marie L. Degen, *History of the Woman's Peace Party* (Baltimore, Johns Hopkins Press, 1939), p. 41.

17. See Ruhl J. Bartlett, *The League To Enforce Peace* (Chapel Hill, N.C., 1944). The League desired that all justiciable international questions not settled by negotiation should, "subject to the limitations of treaties," be submitted to a judicial tribunal; all other questions not settled by negotiation should be submitted to a Council of Conciliation. Signatories would use economic and military forces against any one of their number who violated the above procedure. Codification of international law meanwhile would take place via periodic conferences.

18. Years later Mrs. Schwimmer and Lochner again achieved fame, the former when in 1929 she was denied American citizenship for refusing to bear arms, and the latter as head of the Berlin Bureau of the Associated Press, 1928–42, and later as translator and editor of the late Joseph Goebbels' diaries.

19. Ford always was open to new ideas and disdained old ones. "I don't read history," he once remarked. "That's in the past. I'm thinking of the future." Louis P. Lochner, *America's Don Quixote: Henry Ford's Attempt To Save Europe* (London, K. Paul, Trench, Trubner, 1924), p. 18.

20. Ford's only comment was: "He's a small man." For this interview of Nov. 23, 1916, see *ibid.*, pp. 24–25.

theless, Henry Ford's steamship, the *Oscar II*, ridiculed by newspapermen as the "Peace Ark" and the "floating Chautauqua," sailed forth to Denmark. Many unsophisticated Americans undoubtedly sympathized with the voyage and the passengers. But instead of "getting the boys out of the trenches by Christmas" Henry Ford, having departed for neutral Copenhagen on December 4, 1916, sailed secretly for home on the day before Christmas.

Woodrow Wilson meanwhile had been re-elected president of the United States on campaign slogans such as "He kept us out of war," and "War in the East; peace in the West; thank God for Wilson!" These were such slogans as to hearten American peace workers. But Wilson had quietly changed his views from a year before when he had told the world that "There is such a thing as a man being too proud to fight." In 1916 he began to advocate "preparedness," and while this proposal was not antithetical to peace yet it did look in the direction of war. The New York social worker, Miss Lillian D. Wald, together with many other workers for peace, sought to counteract Wilson's new advocacy by raising the specter of militarism.[21] But it was easy to advocate preparedness and, at the same time, be against militarism. At the end of 1916 the American peace movement was running into difficulty.

It is impossible to assess the influence of the preparedness campaign on the martial spirit in the United States. Undoubtedly preparedness did the peace movement no good. Yet one safely can risk the generalization that at the beginning of 1917 Americans as a whole did not want their country to enter the European war. Only after Wilson's postelection efforts at mediation had failed and after German resumption of unrestricted submarine warfare, the publication of the Zimmermann letter,[22] and the Russian Revolution of March 1917, did war gain in popularity. Even then there was stubborn opposition. When Wilson proposed arming the American merchant marine for defense a small group of "willful

21. Miss Wald headed the American Union Against Militarism.

22. In which the German secretary of state sought to coax the Mexican Government into the war (not yet declared) against the United States, offering Mexico her "lost territories" above the Rio Grande.

men" in the Senate resolutely filibustered against it. When he finally asked Congress for war fifty members of the House of Representatives and six senators held out to the end for peace.

III

War, at first, was almost exhilarating. To the home front it offered parades, campaigns, drives, a wide variety of buttons and badges, and, of course, higher wages. To new citizen soldiers going overseas it offered adventure, a sort of Grand Tour under highly dangerous circumstances.[23] At first, only at first.

As for President Wilson, it has been said that the war for him was no adventure and that he went into it not in the spirit of a knight entering the lists but in the spirit of a policeman entering a barroom brawl: he was there to break it up. There was some truth in this. Wilson however made a superb war leader and infused into the American people a will-to-win hitherto unmatched in American history. Although in 1916 he had solemnly declared that "force will not accomplish anything that is permanent," a year later he was demanding "force to the utmost, force without stint or limit, the righteous and triumphant force that shall make right the law of the world." [24]

Under such inspiring leadership Americans embarked on their first "total war." Everyone helped with the fight, for a World War's front was everywhere, not merely in the trenches in France. War no longer was a simple matter in which Sir Galahad unhooked his armor from the wall, mounted his charger, and in forty or fifty minutes was answering the summons of his liege lord. Nor was total war at all comparable to eighteenth-century war, when—although war already had become something of a science—the army "represented a nation only as a football team represents its college." [25] Even the coming of the "nation in arms" in the days of Carnot,

23. This was the delightful description given to the Russian soldiery of the second World War, in Alexandra Orme's *Comes the Comrade* (New York, 1950).

24. Speeches in New York, June 30, 1916, and in Washington, Apr. 6, 1917.

25. Preston W. Slosson, *The Great Crusade and After: 1914–1928* (New York, Macmillan, 1930), p. 31.

Napoleon, and Scharnhorst, while requiring many citizens to fight in the army yet did not require transformation of national economies into machines for war. Only with the World War did total war arrive.

But this World War, we must not forget, was also a "war to end war." It was Armageddon, so people said, the final battle of the nations. To idealists world peace was its objective. Peace indeed became the official raison d'être of the American war effort. As Wilson said when he introduced to the world the Fourteen Points, "The program of the world's peace, therefore, is our program." That program, he added, was "the only possible program." [26] Peace leaders in the United States and abroad, although busy with war work, thus considered it almost a part of their contribution to the struggle that they should help prepare plans for peace.

It is no exaggeration to say that where there had been relatively few peace schemes before the World War, there now were hundreds and even thousands. Especially in Europe, as the war lengthened into terrible years of trench warfare, did seekers after peace find unexcelled opportunity in the Allied countries to evolve plans and to espouse them before war-weary populations. A telling argument, frequently employed, was that peace had broken down in 1914 because there was no established system for settling international disputes: the Hague Tribunal hardly entered into the thoughts of diplomatists in the hectic days of July 1914, and obviously the old Concert of Europe had proved too flimsy an institution to survive great international crises. And so it came about that thoughtful statesmen together with millions of peace-desiring folk everywhere were pondering plans to insure world peace, to prevent a repetition of the July 1914 catastrophe.

Then came the victory. The guns on the western front ceased firing.

26. Address to Congress, Jan. 8, 1918.

Chapter Two: THE SEARCH FOR PEACE:

THE ADVOCATES

T he years following the 1918 Armistice have re-
ceived many appellations: the interbella period,[1] the Long Armistice, the "twenty years' crisis," [2] the Washington Period,[3] the Aspirin Age,[4] the "After" years,[5] the "Fool's Paradise of American
history." [6] Although there is something to be said for each of these,
the present writer would prefer to call the decade after the 1918
Armistice "The Search for Peace." If one word was repeated more
often than any other during the years after the poignantly memorable Armistice, that word was "peace." Peace echoed through so
many sermons, speeches, and state papers that it drove itself into

1. Samuel Flagg Bemis, *A Diplomatic History of the United States* (3d
ed., New York, Henry Holt, 1950).

2. E. H. Carr, *The Twenty Years' Crisis: 1919–1939* (London, 1939).

3. This refers to the years after the Washington Disarmament Conference
of 1921–22. S. F. Bemis, "The Shifting Strategy of American Defense and Diplomacy," in Dwight E. Lee and George E. McReynolds, eds., *Essays in History and International Relations in Honor of George Hubbard Blakeslee*
(Worcester, Mass., Clark University, 1949), pp. 1–14.

4. Isabel Leighton, ed., *The Aspirin Age: 1919–1941* (New York, 1949).

5. Preston W. Slosson, *The Great Crusade and After: 1914–1928.*

6. "Never did the Western Hemisphere seem safer, a paradise of peace.
Perhaps it would be more accurate to call that period the Fool's Paradise of
American history." S. F. Bemis, "Shifting Strategy," *op. cit.* During this era,
writes Bemis, American foreign policy had five postulates: isolation, anti-
imperialism, disarmament, neutrality, pacifism.

the consciousness of everyone. Never in world history was peace so great a desideratum, so much talked about, looked toward, and planned for, as in the decade after the 1918 Armistice.

Diplomats labored for months at Versailles, seeking in a League of Nations and other arrangements a foundation for peace. Statesmen in following years met at Washington and Geneva to talk disarmament. At Geneva in 1924 they examined—and rejected—a far-reaching protocol of peace. They later concluded at Locarno in 1925 a more limited pact to guarantee peace along the western borders of the new German Republic.

While diplomats thus worked arduously for peace, organizations of private citizens sought to help in the great cause. Sometimes the labors of these two groups complemented each other. Sometimes citizens and diplomats—much to the disgust of the latter—found themselves proceeding in opposite directions. The "intrusion" of public opinion into foreign policy nonetheless was a notable fact of the period after the 1918 Armistice, which professional diplomats had to reckon with whether they liked it or not.

This intrusion occasionally resulted in a more open, more "Wilsonian," sort of diplomacy, but not infrequently the result was a diplomacy more obscure, roundabout, and veiled than ever had occurred before the first World War. Diplomats in the old-fashioned days of Bismarck and Delcassé had called an alliance an alliance, but after the World War (caused, many people believed, by alliances) the word "alliance" went out of fashion. New words appeared. Diplomacy of the 1920's dealt in nonaggression treaties, pacts of guarantee, protocols, pledges of perpetual friendship. All because public opinion associated the word "alliance" with the word "war," rather than "peace."

This extremely sensitive peace-consciousness did not mean of course that people were at last ready to renounce war altogether. There were revisionist nations in Europe—Germany, Italy, Hungary—and the peoples of those nations were becoming ever more strident in their demands for change, peaceful or (they hinted) otherwise. Then there were countries such as Czechoslovakia and Poland, born out of the World War, whose peoples could hardly subscribe to a belief that nothing good ever came out of war. Even in nations where desire for peace was strongest—the great powers of the status quo, France and Britain, which had suffered terribly in the World War—young men again would have flocked to the colors if national existence itself were at stake. And in the United States, where nearly everyone wanted peace, most Americans like Europeans still would have fought for great questions of national honor, interest, independence, and freedom as understood in Anglo-American constitutional history.

This was the climate in which diplomacy had to be conducted. Peace, in general terms, was the great popular desire; and many diplomats held office by will of the people. There indisputably was a "peace psychology" among the citizenry everywhere. Citizens were even forming new organizations, and invigorating old ones, for the express purpose of propagating peace on earth and good will among men.

What, then, was the general outline of this citizen campaign for peace? What was the pattern, if any, of the organized peace movement during the twenties?

Briefly, peace organizations in Europe, while usually much smaller and less influential than those in the United States, were in general agreement as to their objectives. The leading societies all supported the League of Nations. Whatever seemed to bolster the League and the cause of peace—Washington Conference, for example, or the Locarno treaties—they likewise supported. In the United States, however, although there was much more powerful peace organization, there was much less unanimity as to program.

The numerous American peace societies believed themselves confronted by four peace issues: the World Court, the League of Nations, disarmament, and militarism. While generally agreeing on the desirability of American adherence (albeit with "appropriate" reservations) to the World Court, most of them accepted the League of Nations only with uncertain enthusiasm. And as for disarmament and militarism, while peace groups ostensibly agreed on the desirability of the former and the evils of the latter, they disputed disarmament's particulars and militarism's aspects. It is safe to say that by the spring of 1927 no one peace formula had appeared in the United States capable of uniting enthusiastically all the various American peace groups. Only an exceptionally astute individual, with an exceptionally astute formula, could ever have brought about such a union.

I

Although there were peace societies of various sorts in all the European countries, yet aside from certain societies in Britain, France, and Germany, the organized peace movement in Europe was of very modest proportions. Even the British, French, and German peace societies were not as large or important as one might have expected, considering popular interest in peace.[7]

There were several reasons for this. Establishment of the League of Nations had realized the hopes of a large section of European peace workers. The League carried on all its activities in the name of peace, and to many persons this made private peace societies superfluous. Then again, it is probable that Europeans were not as organization-conscious as, say, Americans.[8] Another reason for weakness of the peace movement in Europe was the long and ardu-

7. There is no one book which gives a satisfactory account of the peace movement in the 1920's. Arthur C. F. Beales, *History of Peace* (New York, 1931) and Merle Curti, *Peace or War: The American Struggle 1636–1936* (New York, 1936) are extremely general for this period and in fact treat the years 1918–28, when the peace movement reached its apogee, as a sort of "epilogue" (Beales' word) to the story of peace. To obtain material for this present chapter I have had to rely largely on my own investigations. This involved much reading of pamphlet material and study of the office files of peace organizations in the Swarthmore College Peace Collection at Swarthmore, Pennsylvania. Often it was necessary to search in rather obscure places to discover an organization's membership, budget, program, and influence.

The number of European "peace and kindred organizations" as listed by the National Council for Prevention of War (Great Britain), *Peace Year-Book: 1929* were as follows: Austria, 16; Belgium, 11; Bulgaria, 8; Czechoslovakia, 10; Danzig, 2; Denmark, 10; Estonia, 4; Finland, 4; *France, 38; Germany, 19; Great Britain, 63;* Greece, 3; Holland, 13; Hungary, 7; Ireland, 5; Italy, 5; Latvia, 4; Lithuania, 2; Luxemburg, 1; Norway, 9; Poland, 13; Portugal, 4; Rumania, 4; Russia, 2 (both expatriate); Spain, 2; Sweden, 9; Switzerland, 20; Turkey, 1; Ukraine, 1 (expatriate); Yugoslavia, 4.

8. See Arthur M. Schlesinger, *Paths to the Present* (New York, 1949), chap. ii, "Biography of a Nation of Joiners," pp. 23–50.

ous acquaintance of Europeans with war; such familiarity did not lessen desire for maintenance of peace, but it did tend to produce a certain sophistication, unfriendly to radical solutions. For these reasons the organized peace movement in Europe never gained much strength.

At the head of the various national peace societies stood the Bureau International de la Paix, a coordinating agency with headquarters in Geneva. The bureau during the twenties was a decaying organization, managing to stay in existence chiefly because of money from a Nobel Peace Prize award in 1912.[9] It conducted its business through a council, but though council meetings occurred twice or three times a year, only two times since 1920 was there a quorum. The average attendance of the fifty members in the years 1920–28 was fourteen. Replies to circular letters sent from the bureau to council members averaged ten.[10]

Of the national peace organizations, the strongest by far were the British League of Nations Union, the German Friedensgesellschaft, and the French Ligue des Droits de l'Homme. In France the Ligue by 1927 had over 120,000 members in more than 600 sections. The Ligue championed the League of Nations. In addition it took great interest in Franco-German rapprochement. Friendship between the two Rhine countries, the Ligue held, would prove one of the greatest of all factors for world peace.[11] The Deutsche

9. Expenses in 1924, for example, were $8,773; receipts, $7,158. *Comptes du bureau international de la paix pour 1924* . . . (n.p., n.d.), Swarthmore College Peace Collection (hereafter cited as SCPC).

10. "Confidential Memo. No. 1 on I.P.B.," Oct. 9, 1928, manuscript in SCPC. The American compiler of these doleful statistics, one Benjamin Gerig, in 1928 was undertaking to breathe some life into the nearly deceased Bureau International de la Paix.

11. In the field of Franco-German rapprochement there also labored the Paneuropa Union, an organization for European federation led by Count Richard N. Coudenhove-Kalergi. Coudenhove had impressive qualifications for heading such a movement: he was a Czech citizen living in Vienna, born of a Japanese mother and an Austrian father; his forbears were Venetians and Greeks. Of a somewhat messianic nature, he promised perpetual European peace as one among the many blessings which would follow upon European federation ("Once Pan-Europe is created—a state without boundaries, without oppression, without wars—then astounded Europeans will suddenly realize

Friedensgesellschaft, founded in 1892, was the oldest and largest
of German peace organizations. It had 28,000 members as of 1927,
and 250 local groups. That same year the DF's executive chairman,
Dr. Ludwig Quidde, received the Nobel Peace Prize.[12] Like the
French Ligue des Droits de l'Homme, the DF concerned itself
chiefly with the League of Nations, envisioning in the League the
most promising path toward permanent world peace. The British
League of Nations Union in 1928 had a total membership of 477,-
984 in 2,760 branches and 649 junior branches.[13] The union in
1928 spent over $200,000 advancing the cause of the League of
Nations in particular and world peace in general.[14]

There were other, smaller organizations in France, Britain, and
Germany, but they were not of very great importance. Many were
international in membership. Among them were the War Resisters'
International, Fellowship of Reconciliation, Women's International League for Peace and Freedom, and Oxford Group movement. The War Resisters' International and the Fellowship of
Reconciliation were out-and-out pacifist groups. The Women's International League inclined toward pacifism, for its president and
mainstay was Jane Addams, the uncompromising pacifist of Hull
House, Chicago. The Oxford Groups were the spawn of another
American, Dr. Frank N. D. Buchman, known variously as Frank
or "F.B."; Buchman's organization was predominantly religious,

that Europe is the long-lost paradise." *Paneuropa,* 2 [April 1926], 15). His
movement achieved a short-lived importance when Aristide Briand in 1929
made an effort toward European union. For details of the Coudenhove program see issues of his movement's monthly, *Paneuropa,* and also Coudenhove's
autobiography, *Crusade for Pan-Europe* (New York, 1943).

12. Dr. Quidde shared the 1927 prize with Professor Ferdinand Buisson of
Paris, president of the French Ligue des Droits de l'Homme.

13. In 1928 there were League of Nations societies in thirty-nine different
countries, linked together by the International Federation of League of Nations Societies. The British League of Nations Union was by far the largest.

14. The British Union provided 4,180 meetings with speakers during 1928.
The Union's publications had varying circulation, a monthly with 95,000, a
monthly *News Sheet* with 60,000, the *League News* (for children) 35,000. LNU,
Annual Report: 1928.

seeking—as one devotee put it—to establish a Dictatorship of the Holy Spirit: each Oxford Group member endeavored to follow his own lights, and these lights frequently shone toward pacifism. All of these international groups—WRI, FOR, WILPF, and the Oxford Group movement—were rather small during the twenties in numbers, influence, and budget.[15]

Peace sentiment in Europe seems to have preferred to attach itself to other than propagandistic organizations. Trade unions

15. Each member of the WRI took the following pledge: "War is a crime against humanity. We therefore are determined not to support any kind of war and to strive for the removal of all causes of war." The WRI in 1930 had 40 sections in 21 different countries, and members in 53. The International itself for the year ending Mar. 31, 1927, spent £596, with income of the same. In 1928 the WRI in the United States had 6 affiliates: Association to Abolish War (400 members), Women's Peace Society (2,000 members), Women's Peace Union, World Peace Association, FOR (4,500 members), War Resisters' League (400 members). (Membership figures from NCPW, *Organizations in the United States That Promote Better International Understanding and World Peace* [Washington, 1927].) In England the WRI affiliated the No More War Movement (5,000 members) and The Young Anti-Militarists. WRI, *War Resisters in Many Lands* (Middlesex, England, 1928?).

The FOR was as much a service organization as peace organization. It undertook various projects such as aid to children and to stricken areas. The British FOR had 7,584 members in 1927. NCPW (GB), *Peace Year-Book: 1927*. The American FOR in Jan. 1928 had 5,551 members; the 1927 receipts were $29,801.90. "Minutes of executive committee," Jan. 5, 1928, FOR-US files, SCPC.

Jane Addams bore the brunt of financing the WILPF. Of receipts of $11,752.20 for the international office in 1928, $6,000 came directly from the WILPF's American section, and this was called Miss Addams' Contribution. WILPF files, SCPC. The American section as of the annual meeting in 1927 had a total annual income of $18,039.02, 6,300 members, and a staff of three. "Annual Report of the Executive Secretary," WILPF-US files, SCPC. The British section of the WIL had 3,500 members in 1927. NCPW (GB), *Peace Year-Book: 1927*. In 1928 the British section had a budget of £2,239. WIL-GB, *Yearly Report: 1928*. According to NCPW, *Organizations in the United States*, the WILPF had a total membership of approximately 50,000.

For the Oxford Group movement, see Allan W. Eister, *Drawing Room Conversion* (Durham, N.C., 1950), and especially Walter Houston Clark, *The Oxford Group: Its History and Significance* (New York, 1951).

were strongly pacifist, and there was a revival of the prewar belief that a general strike could paralyze any warlike manifestations by national governments.[16] Many of the postwar political parties, moreover, were intensely peace-minded. The British Labor party, the Herriot Socialists in France, and the Social Democrats in Germany made perpetuation of peace a key item of their political faith.[17]

It is true of course that announced programs of labor organizations and political parties did not always mirror the thoughts and interests of all their members. There could not have been anything like unanimity when in 1920 the International Miners' Congress at Geneva, representing 1,500,000 workers, declared for resistance to war; when in 1922 the International Trade Union Congress at Rome, representing 24,000,000, made a similar declaration; or when in 1926 the British Labor party at Margate, representing 5,000,000, voted against war.[18] Yet undoubtedly there existed strong antiwar sentiment among European workers and labor parties.

The trade unions and political parties had many other aims besides peace, aims which were on a national and even local level and which occupied most of their time. Only organizations specifically organized for peace could so dedicate all their activities. During the postwar years in Europe such groups for several reasons [19] were not strong. The three largest devoted themselves to promoting the already established League of Nations. For new ideas and vigorous action in behalf of them it was necessary to look elsewhere than in Europe. Leading all the nations of the world was the organized peace movement in the United States.

16. A general strike in Germany in 1920 had defeated the Kapp Putsch.

17. Because of the peculiar class- and interest-structure of European political parties, it was much easier for them to take a clear-cut, detailed decision on peace than was the case for the two broadly representative parties in the United States.

18. There of course was a tendency on the part of peace enthusiasts to count as many noses as possible. H. Runham Brown, *Cutting Ice* (Enfield, England, 1930), a typical tract put out in the name of the War Resisters' International, lists (pp. 17–18) an impressive array of antiwar resolutions and declarations.

19. See above, pp. 16–17.

II

Foremost among American peace organizations was the Carnegie Endowment for International Peace. Organized in 1910, the Endowment began life with a Carnegie gift of $10,000,000 in five-per-cent first-mortgage bonds of the United States Steel Corporation; and during the first World War these bonds appreciated very considerably in value—offering the somewhat anomalous picture of a peace organization operating on the profits of war. The Endowment in the decade of the twenties eagerly followed the progress of peace in Europe and elsewhere in the world. In its monthly bulletin, *International Conciliation,* which it sold at nominal subscription rates, it printed texts and commentaries on the outstanding international acts of the period. It also sponsored International Relations Clubs among college and high-school students and gave away books for International Mind Alcoves in small libraries throughout the United States. The Carnegie Endowment had many other activities, such as financing smaller peace organizations in the United States and abroad, conducting a Paris Center for European peace, rebuilding the Louvain Library in Belgium, reconstructing the war-devastated French village of Fargniers-sur-Aisne, endowing university chairs of international relations, financing exchange visits of European and American newspapermen and educators, and advancing codification of international law. The Endowment had a liberal budget, and in the fiscal year ending June 30, 1927, for example, spent a total of $613,881.50.[20] Obviously there was no need for niggardliness in paying the salaries of the Endowment's president and directors.[21] Nor were expense accounts to be doled out sparingly. When in the summer of 1927 three trustees attended the Honolulu Conference on Pacific Rela-

20. Carnegie Endowment for International Peace, *Year Book: 1928,* p. 19.
21. According to Carnegie's letter of Dec. 14, 1910, establishing the Endowment, "The President shall be granted such honoraria as the Trustees think proper and as he can be prevaild [*sic*] upon to accept." President Butler is reported to have received $20,000 a year, plus a very generous expense account.

tions, each received $2,000 for expenses, of which they later refunded $110.07.[22] The Endowment's most publicized assets, however, were not its $10,000,000 capital and $613,881.50 annual budget. Rather were they two individuals: the Endowment's president, Dr. Nicholas Murray Butler, and its director of the Division of Economics and History, Professor James Thomson Shotwell.

Of all the people in the United States, no one worked more assiduously for peace during the twenties than did Nicholas Murray Butler, president of Columbia University and president of the Carnegie Endowment for International Peace. A large, well-built man with bristling mustache and searching eyes, Dr. Butler spoke, wrote, and traveled the world over in defense of peace, and his efforts rallied countless individuals to the banner of the League of Nations and the World Court. Butler believed firmly in what his opponents termed the "European system" of force. Peace, he reiterated, must have the backing of an international Big Stick; otherwise peace could exist only on the limited tolerance of some would-be aggressor nation. Dr. Butler was a most redoubtable speaker who almost at the drop of a hat could deliver a polished oration without any notes. Sprinkling his speeches with impressive references to philosophers and events of the past, he had a way of sweeping an audience off its feet in approval of whatever he was at the time advocating. Nicholas Murray Butler in the 1920's, promoting world peace through the League, was a great force wherever he went.[23]

22. *Year Book: 1928*, p. 80; *1929*, p. 254. The trustees in question were Alfred Holman, Henry S. Pritchett, and James T. Shotwell.

23. Touring Europe shortly after the World War, Butler everywhere found himself heralded as "America's unofficial ambassador." Proudly he collated press captions, which read as follows: WAS NICHOLAS MURRAY BUTLER PRESIDENT HARDING'S REPRESENTATIVE IN RECENT TOUR?; UNPRECEDENTED OFFICIAL RECEPTION; MORE DISTINCTIONS THAN WERE GIVEN EITHER TO THEODORE ROOSEVELT OR TO WILSON; APPEARED BEFORE HOUSE OF COMMONS CONFERENCE FOR HOURS IN EXTRAORDINARY SESSION—UTTERLY UNPRECEDENTED; WEEKEND WITH KING OF BELGIUM; AMERICAN TRAVELER WHO WAS GIVEN A UNIQUE LUNCHEON BY THE BENCHERS OF GRAY'S INN; RECEIVED UNHEARD OF HONORS FROM THE ACADEMIE FRANCAISE AND THE SORBONNE IN PARIS; WEEKEND GUEST OF THE PRIME MINISTER OF ENGLAND. Nicholas Murray Butler, *Across the Busy Years* (2 vols., New York, Charles Scribner's Sons, 1939–40), II, 123.

As president of the Endowment, Dr. Butler held the purse strings to millions, a very strategic position indeed. Needy scholars anxious for grants-in-aid, travel in Europe, or money to put their books through the press swarmed to the Endowment's exchequer for help. Impecunious movements for world peace, or looking obliquely in the direction of world peace, importuned the Endowment as a source of life-giving aid. This is in no sense to hint that President Butler used the bulging Carnegie strongbox to advance his own peace schemes and squelch those with which he disagreed. It is true however that the general policy of the Endowment during the twenties was by no means unfavorable to the League of Nations. The Endowment's manifold and influential activities frequently reflected the views of its president.

Professor James Thomson Shotwell was Butler's junior by a dozen years. He otherwise somewhat resembled his chief in appearance. His countenance reflected a shining love of humanity. He was and remains a firm idealist.[23a] At one time interested in ancient Greek culture, Shotwell turned his attention during and after the war to contemporary international problems, and in the twenties he edited for the Endowment a monumental *Economic and Social History of the World War,* some two hundred volumes. Author of innumerable books on international affairs, Professor Shotwell was second only to Dr. Butler himself as a speechmaker. His speeches could and did draw tears of sympathy from strong men of good will. Shotwell, like Butler, advocated American participation in the League of Nations.

Yet the Carnegie Endowment for International Peace did not possess anything approaching monopoly over the organized peace movement in the United States. The World Peace Foundation, with a $1,000,000 endowment from the Boston publisher Edwin Ginn, sought also to educate Americans for peace; the foundation was official distributor in the United States for all League of Nations publications and worked especially for American adherence to the World Court. Then there was the Foreign Policy Association, founded in New York exactly one month after the

23a. See James T. Shotwell, "The Faith of an Historian," *Saturday Review of Literature, 34* (Dec. 29, 1951), 6–7, 24–26.

1918 Armistice,[24] which had several thousand members and, like the World Peace Foundation, carried on the work of education for peace. In the busy vineyard of peace labored also the League of Nations Non-Partisan Association, organized early in 1923 as a reincarnation of the League to Enforce Peace; the Non-Partisan Association strove to make the League a great national, non-partisan issue.[25] Helping with the heavy task was the Woodrow Wilson Foundation, established the same year as the League Non-Partisan Association with nearly a million dollars and the mission of perpetuating Wilsonian ideals; the foundation worked unsteadily, however, drifting from peace award to essay contest to collecting a library, and did not seem to produce much.

In addition to all these secular peace organizations there were two church groups. Andrew Carnegie in 1914 started the Church Peace Union on its way with $2,000,000, and during the World War the union sponsored the World Alliance for International Friendship through the Churches. The World Alliance did its best to advance the cause of the Prince of Peace, a not inconsiderable task even within the disparate confines of Protestant Christianity.[26] It received much help in the United States from the Federal Council of Churches of Christ, whose busy Commission on International Justice and Goodwill was "committed to unremitting activity until a peace system takes the place of competitive armaments and recurring war."[27]

A special sort of peace organization was the American Founda-

24. The association was known as the League of Free Nations Association until Apr. 1921. In 1922 it changed its program to education and research rather than action. It had 9,000 members in 1929.

25. It appears to have had a membership of something under 50,000: the Association's *League of Nations Herald* (a subscription to which was included in each membership fee) reported a subscription list of 35,000 after its first six months.

26. The alliance sought membership of individuals from all religious faiths but appears to have been predominantly a Christian and Protestant organization. Its budget for 1930 was approximately $117,000, of which $65,000 went for American work. *Condensed Outline of the History and Objectives of the Programme of the World Alliance . . .* (New York, 1930).

27. During the postwar years the commission began to take a sizable portion of the federal council's annual budget. By 1928 the commission was spending $121,348.91 (out of the federal council's total budget of $407,216.01)

tion, established to administer the Bok Peace Plan Award. Edward Bok, the well-known publisher, in 1922 sought to bring peace to the world in not more than 5,000 words. He offered $100,000 to the author of a winning peace plan, $50,000 to be paid immediately and $50,000 to be paid when either the plan went into operation or evidenced an adequate degree of popular support. Organizations and individuals could submit plans. Over a quarter of a million American citizens wrote to ask for the conditions of the contest. Among the 22,165 plans actually submitted were plans from William Jennings Bryan, the former secretary of state, and Franklin D. Roosevelt, unsuccessful candidate for the vice-presidency in the election of 1920.[28] The winner of the contest was Charles H. Levermore, the elderly secretary of the New York Peace Society, who gave to his scheme the latitudinarian title of "Progressive Cooperation with the Organized World, Sustained by the Moral Force of Public Opinion and by Developing Law." [29] The American Foundation did not cease to function after Levermore had won the $50,000. The foundation continued in existence and undertook an educational campaign for American adherence to the World Court.[30]

---

in unremitting activity for a peace system. Samuel McCrea Cavert, ed., *Twenty Years of Church Federation* (New York, 1929), pp. 280–281.

28. Roosevelt advocated, in place of the League of Nations, a permanent and continuing International Conference to be known as the Society of Nations. For the plan, see Eleanor Roosevelt, *This I Remember* (New York, Harper, 1949), pp. 353–366. Mrs. Roosevelt helped Miss Esther Everett Lape organize the Bok Award. "In conversations with Esther Lape in later years," she recalls, "Franklin often referred to the peace plan he submitted in the first Bok competition. I think he never forgot the ideas that he set down then. The writing of this peace plan was proposed largely as something to keep alive his interest in outside matters during the first years of adjustment to his illness . . ." *Ibid.*, p. 24.

29. Levermore did not receive the second $50,000, for the Committee of Award decided that his plan had not produced evidence of sufficient popular support. Most of the ballots sent out by the committee returned with favorable marks, but there was much talk about the pro-League attitude of the Committee of Award, and this apparently was taken to mean lack of sufficient popular support.

30. Nor was this the end of essay contests. Edward Filene, the Boston merchant, after watching the Bok contest decided to offer something similar to Europe. Held in 1923 in France, Italy, Britain, and Germany, the Filene contest attracted over 15,000 plans. First prize in each country was $10,000.

Such were the labors of the American Foundation, the Carnegie Endowment for International Peace, the World Peace Foundation, Foreign Policy Association, League of Nations Non-Partisan Association, Woodrow Wilson Foundation, World Alliance for International Friendship through the Churches, and the Commission on International Justice and Goodwill of the Federal Council of Churches of Christ in America. These groups formed what one might call the "conservative" organizations of the American peace movement. All of them championed the World Court—least controversial of American peace issues. All, in more or less enthusiastic manner, advocated American membership in the League of Nations (enthusiasm seems to have waned during the later twenties). Some of these conservative organizations—notably the Carnegie Endowment—took little interest in disarmament, while others, such as the Federal Council of Churches, came to see in disarmament the hope of the world. As for that other American peace issue, militarism, all peace organizations were against it in principle. There was a tendency, however, for educational groups such as the World Peace Foundation, Foreign Policy Association, and Woodrow Wilson Foundation to refrain from discussing militarism. Some of the other groups discussed it but disagreed on definitions: the Carnegie Endowment usually viewed the United States Government's army and navy budgets as primarily for "defense," whereas in the same budgets the Federal Council of Churches frequently espied clear-cut proofs of "militarism."

The work of the conservative peace groups is only part of the history of the organized peace movement in the United States during the 1920's. There also were many "radical" peace groups. These were the evangelists of the peace movement. Like Paul on the road to Damascus each had seen a sign and heard a call.

III

The radical peace groups were crusaders. Small in numbers and limited in finances, they made up for such deficiencies by excess of zeal. This crusading zeal, rather than difference of ultimate objective, distinguished the radicals from the more conservative groups. The radicals, like the conservatives, tended to agree on the World Court, and most of them were somewhat friendly toward the League; but they divided over the extent and nature of disarmament and, although uniting to oppose militarism in general, split apart in disagreement over its particulars. Unlike the conservatives, however, they worked with a sense of urgency, with a feeling that time was of the essence, that a "peace system" must replace the existing "war system" or else civilization would go down to ruin in the holocaust of the Next War.

The conservative peace groups staidly organized against war. The radicals wasted no time and veritably scrambled into the fight. After the 1918 Armistice scores of new peace groups mushroomed into existence. The usual procedure was first to choose an impressive name and to select appropriate stationery (ordinarily a propagandistic, name-studded letterhead). There then began a frenzied round of fund-raising, conventioning, writing to congressmen. It was truly remarkable the amount of activity these crusading peace groups could generate.

Someone, sometime, will make a careful study of all the radical peace groups in the United States during the twenties.[31] Such a

31. Counting the number of peace organizations in the United States, radical and otherwise, is a difficult task, for one encounters the problem of categories. Should one count only those organizations working solely for peace? engaged in part-time work for peace? working on a national level? on a local level? According to *Organizations in the United States That Promote Better International Understanding and World Peace* there were the following radical national peace organizations: American Committee for the Outlawry of War, American Friends Service Committee (100,000 members), American Goodwill Association (5,000), American School Citizenship League, Arbitration Crusade, Association for Peace Education, Association to Abolish War (400), Catholic Association for International Peace, Committee on Militarism in Education, Corda Fratres Association of Cosmopolitan Clubs (1,000), Fellowship for a Christian Social Order (2,500), Fellowship of Reconciliation (4,500), Fellowship of Youth for Peace, Friends General Conference (20,000), Intercollegiate Peace Association, National Committee on the Cause and Cure of War, National Council for Prevention of War, Parliament of Peace and Universal Brotherhood, Peace Association of Friends in America (90,000), Peace Heroes Memorial Society, School World Friendship League, Society to Eliminate Economic Causes of War (150), War Resisters' League (400), War

study would prove greatly rewarding as an analysis of organization techniques and also should reveal many interesting and hitherto obscure exigencies of postwar American diplomacy.[32] In the following pages it is possible only to examine those radical groups which during the late twenties took an especial interest in the renunciation and outlawry of war.

Foremost among the radicals stood the National Council for Prevention of War. The national council did not consider itself a peace group but rather a coordinator of peace groups throughout the country. The council nonetheless had its own program and during the twenties laid down a barrage of peace propaganda the like of which has seldom been seen in the United States.

At the head of this efficient organization was Frederick J. Libby, the council's executive secretary. A pacifist Congregationalist minister who after the World War became a Friend, Libby in 1921 inaugurated the council as an emergency peace organization for the Washington Naval Disarmament Conference. After the conference adjourned he continued the council, working chiefly for disarmament but also fighting any and all aspects of militarism. Libby's group maintained offices in Washington, where a small number of enthusiastic workers tackled the job of peace. The NCPW in 1927 had a budget of $113,040, raised mostly by the indefatigable Mr. Libby.[33] In January of that year the NCPW sent out more than 430,000 pieces of antiwar literature.[34]

A close second to the NCPW in propagandizing for peace was the American Branch of the Women's International League for

---

Resisters' International (United States Committee), Women's International League for Peace and Freedom (6,000), Women's Peace Society (2,000), Women's Peace Union of the Western Hemisphere, World Peace Association, World Peace Mission (58). Doubtless there were other national radical peace groups.

32. The Swarthmore College Peace Collection, with its unrivaled facilities for such research, remains largely unexploited.

33. Receipts of the NCPW: 1923, $51,252; 1924, $56,624; 1925, $60,378; 1926, $77,011. In 1928 there were 12 secretaries and 18 office workers. "Report of the Executive Secretary of the NCPW at its Annual Meeting, October 16, 1928," NCPW files, SCPC.

34. Miss Mary Winder to C. Altschel, Feb. 24, 1927, NCPW files, SCPC.

Peace and Freedom. Jane Addams, as mentioned before, was the guiding light of the International, and Miss Addams kept a close connection with the American branch through her good friend (and president of the branch) Miss Emily Balch.[35] The WILPF-US, because of Jane Addams' influence, tended strongly toward pacifism. It went so far as to issue to its membership small stickers, to be attached to income tax reports and bearing the legend: "That part of this income tax which is levied for preparation for War is paid only under Protest and Duress." [36] But although a certain amount of the activity of the WILPF-US was rather trivial in importance—such as discussing girls' rifle teams in colleges and investigating militaristic tendencies among the Boy Scouts [37]—nevertheless the several thousand members of the WILPF-US battled hard and effectively for their conviction that war should not come again to the United States. They fondly remembered the words of Jeanette Rankin, who during the fateful roll call in the House of Representatives, April 6, 1917, had cried: "I want to stand by my country—but I cannot vote for war!"

As the WILPF-US was dominated by Jane Addams and the NCPW by Frederick J. Libby, so the National Committee on the Cause and Cure of War was the creation of Mrs. Carrie Chapman Catt. A feminist of renown, Mrs. Catt had watched the Eighteenth and Nineteenth [38] Amendments take away the raison d'être of much of her public life. Like many other feminists Mrs. Catt began casting about for a new issue, and in 1921 she found it. In a speech before the League of Women Voters in Cleveland she put aside the text she had planned to use and instead announced a campaign against war. Closing her emotion-filled speech that afternoon, she threw out a challenge to her listeners: "The women in this room can do this thing! The women in this room can do this thing!"

35. Miss Balch in 1946 received the Nobel Peace Prize. Jane Addams, in 1931, had shared the prize with Nicholas Murray Butler.

36. Jane Addams MSS, deposited in SCPC.

37. The WILPF-US national board discussed these matters at its meeting in Philadelphia, June 9, 1927. Minutes of the national board, WILPF-US files, SCPC.

38. "The right of citizens of the United States to vote shall not be denied or abridged by the United States or by any States on account of sex."

For a few years Mrs. Catt sought to do this thing through the already existing organization, the WILPF. Somehow she came into disagreement with Jane Addams. Mrs. Catt then undertook to found her own organization, and there arose the National Committee on the Cause and Cure of War, a grand federation for peace of nine national women's organizations.

With this as her stage the indomitable lady set out on her campaign against war in the same militant manner in which she had fought for women's rights. That she would be in some measure successful was hardly matter for doubt. In the twenties women no longer heard the raucous antisuffrage cry of "Go home and wash the dishes!" The ladies now constituted one half of the electorate. They were saying: "Go out and abolish war!" Legislators in Washington were excessively sensitive to all women's movements purporting to represent the new female vote: it was not yet understood that equal suffrage would make no noticeable difference in the American political balance.

Radical peace work however was by no means confined to ex-suffragists like Mrs. Catt, or to social workers like Jane Addams, or to former ministers like Frederick J. Libby. The radicals had in their very midst a wealthy corporation lawyer, who had dedicated his life to getting rid of war.

Chapter Three: SALMON O. LEVINSON

AND THE OUTLAWRY OF WAR

Salmon O. Levinson of Chicago, Illinois, had in the years before 1914 made a fortune reorganizing decrepit business ventures, but never had given much thought to international affairs until he observed at the beginning of the war that the battles in Europe were affecting the stock market.[1] From this perception of truth he quickly went on to solving problems arising out of the war, and by 1918, after American entry into the European conflict, Levinson had evolved a plan to "outlaw," i.e., to make illegal, all wars. "There was stimulus—indeed, there was a kind of inspiration —in coming in contact with his abounding energy, which surpassed that of any single person I have ever known . . ." later wrote the philosopher John Dewey.[2] A go-getter of the expert sort, the stocky Levinson set to work with the greatest determination. Out of a dinner party in his Chicago home, December 9, 1921, there arose the American Committee for the Outlawry of War.

Having organized his committee, Levinson drew up a formal statement, "A Plan to Outlaw War." This he printed in time to circularize all 1,100 members of the Washington Disarmament Conference, and also sundry other people from the president of the

1. John E. Stoner, *S. O. Levinson and the Pact of Paris: A Study in the Techniques of Influence* (Chicago, University of Chicago Press, 1942), p. 12. Professor Stoner has written a definitive account of Salmon O. Levinson's influence upon the Kellogg pact.

2. John Dewey, foreword to J. Stoner, *Levinson,* p. vii.

United States and his Cabinet down through the hierarchy at Washington, and then out into the grass roots by way of Senator Arthur Capper's mailing list.[3] All types of organizations received copies of the plan: the Anti-Saloon League, for example, obtained parcels of copies for distribution to interested members. Senator Borah of Idaho in January 1922 offered the plan for printing in the *Congressional Record,* and after that Levinson had copies printed by the Government Printing Office.[4]

He enlisted prominent people in his cause, including—in addition to John Dewey—the Reverend John Haynes Holmes, the pacifist minister of New York's Community Church, and Dr. Charles Clayton Morrison, the influential editor of the *Christian Century.* Colonel Raymond Robins, the wartime head of American Red Cross activities in Russia and a stalwart crusader for innumerable reforms, also took outlawry to his heart and made it his special interest.

These men who gathered around Salmon O. Levinson were, each in his own sphere, powerful advocates of outlawry, or as they wrote among themselves, Outlawry. In the pages of the *New Republic* Dewey scattered philosophic essays on outlawing war; if people did not think in terms of war, there might be no war, thought America's most famous philosopher. John Haynes Holmes advocated Outlawry in the pages of his religious weekly, *Unity,* and preached Outlawry to his congregation. Charles Clayton Morrison, editing perhaps the foremost religious magazine in America, never failed to break a lance for outlawing war and in the spring of 1927 was at work on a book which would contain the very essence of Levinson's proposal.

But the greatest power for Outlawry was Colonel Robins, a self-made man who began life as a coal digger in Kentucky but soon migrated to the Yukon where he dug in quantity a more precious mineral. Financially independent, he thereafter employed himself with vast effectiveness at all sorts of reforming and social betterment. His speeches, permeated with Biblical phraseology and mil-

3. Capper, senator from Kansas, was publisher of numerous farm journals. See below, p. 117.

4. J. Stoner, *Levinson,* pp. 72–73.

SALMON O. LEVINSON AND OUTLAWRY 33

lennial aspiration, frequently raised audiences to near-ecstatic
heights. Every time the colonel went out on a circuit for Outlawry
he left a trail of resolutions behind him, and enthusiastic converts
inundated Levinson's private secretary in Chicago with requests
for leaflets and other explanatory material.

A wavering convert to Outlawry was Senator William E. Borah
of Idaho. Borah's relationship to Outlawry was a most interesting
one, perhaps because the leonine Idahoan was himself a most interesting person. William E. Borah had never been outside the
United States, but by seniority he succeeded to the chairmanship of
the Senate Committee on Foreign Relations, vacated in 1924 by
the death of Senator Henry Cabot Lodge. The Idaho senator
was a most attractive public figure, especially in the Senate
chamber. Unlike some of his less engaging confreres, who emptied
seats as soon as they arose to speak, Borah packed the floor and
galleries every time. The mere whisper that "Borah is speaking"
would start crowds of people stampeding toward Capitol Hill. The
lion of Idaho nevertheless always seemed to touch every question
and come to grips with none. He never appeared able to transform
his "attractive provincial insurgency," [5] his so engagingly "progressive" outlook, into any sort of coherent national policy, much
less international concept. Unwilling to promote any peace scheme
which rested ultimately on physical force, the senator began to
be accused of obstructionism, of having no program at all except
being "agin" everything. He became famous for his contrariness.
One day President Coolidge saw Borah clopping along on horse-
back. In his best Vermont twang the president commented to some
intimates sitting on the White House porch: "Well, there is Senator Borah riding on a horse, and they are both going the same
way!" [6] On February 13, 1923, however, after much backing and
filling, Borah introduced a resolution into the Senate proposing
the outlawry of war, codification of international law, and creation
of a world court with "affirmative" jurisdiction.[7]

5. Walter Lippmann, *Men of Destiny* (New York, Macmillan, 1927), p. 144.
6. James E. Watson, *As I Knew Them* (Indianapolis, Bobbs-Merrill, 1936),
p. 237.
7. Apparently Borah introduced his resolution partly to counter President

These three points, Outlawry, Code, and Court, were the complete Levinson program.

The first step was to delegalize war, to make a warring nation an international outlaw. Levinson talked and wrote incessantly about the legal status of war in international law, forgetting that war in international law generally was considered neither legal nor illegal, but rather nonlegal: although nearly half the law of nations dealt with rules of warfare, war itself was not in any way recognized as legal but as a contingency to be provided against, similar to earthquakes and floods in municipal law.[8] Nevertheless, if war was nonlegal it was still possible to declare it illegal, and this was the heart of Levinson's program. But by declaring all wars illegal Levinson did not propose to abolish the right of self-defense. This right he held was a kind of police action, really not war at all. In advocating Outlawry the Chicago lawyer, turned peacemaker, did not often mention his reservation of self-defense;[9] this qualification appeared in his expositions only casually or when opponents pinned him down.

As for codification of international law, Levinson thought an international conference could produce a code in two years, maybe three. The code, he affirmed, should be "comprehensive and the wisdom of the ages should be distilled and all good things that have been developed in international law should be preserved and the evil cast out."[10] Once completed the code would be submitted "to each civilized nation and be by it approved. As each of such nations will participate in the preparation of the code, general

Harding's proposal, made a few days later, that the United States join the World Court.

8. Professor Quincy Wright of the University of Chicago examined the writings of twenty-two authorities on international law and found that nineteen considered war nonlegal. "Changes in the Conception of War," *American Journal of International Law, 18* (1924), 757, n. 15.

9. He never would have called the right of self-defense a reservation. Levinson would have argued that self-defense, not being war but rather a police action, did not have anything to do with Outlawry of war.

10. Levinson to Frances Kellor, Mar. 23, 1923, in J. Stoner, *Levinson*, pp. 100–101.

harmony may be expected." [11] And once the world outlawed war and codified international law a world court—not the World Court, for that was all mixed up with the League—would almost automatically begin supervising the rule of law in international relations.

Most efforts of the American Committee for the Outlawry of War went into preaching the first step, Outlawry, from which the other two would come as day followed night. The Outlawrists sought to inject their program into politics by the Borah Resolution of February 1923 and its subsequent renewals. They also attempted to commit presidential candidates, but with disappointing results. From Harding in 1920 came a master "bloviation," [12] which must be read to be believed: "I have a very clear idea of what I think we can do and should do in working out an international agreement, but as a candidate of a party I do not want to make my plan an issue in a campaign which I am waging upon the theory that international agreements ought to be made a concerted agreement of the executive and the congress." [13] Coolidge in 1924 wrote a letter to Colonel Robins which almost matched that of Harding: "I trust that our country is in theoretical harmony with the position you are striving to reach. It is exceedingly difficult, in fact almost impossible, to get any consideration of international questions in Washington at the present time. It would be especially so just before the Presidential election. Some of the things that you mention I am trying to do, in so far as I can find them practicable." [14] But the Outlawrists persevered.

When the famous English peace leader, Lord Robert Cecil, came to America in the spring of 1923 Levinson cornered him in Chicago and talked Outlawry so hard that he gave Cecil a headache.[15] Other Englishmen likewise began to hear about the program

11. From a commentary on Outlawry by Levinson, printed in Senate Document No. 115, 67th Cong., 2d Sess., quoted by J. Stoner, *Levinson*, p. 200.

12. Adept at coining new words, Harding liked to describe his campaign oratory and statement-making as the art of "bloviation."

13. Harding to Levinson, Sept. 20, 1920, in J. Stoner, *Levinson*, p. 55.

14. Coolidge to Raymond Robins, Nov. 13, 1923, *ibid.*, p. 124.

15. Cecil in the summer of 1923 nevertheless told Judge Florence E. Allen

to outlaw war, men such as Gilbert Murray, the Oxford professor, J. L. Garvin, editor of the London *Observer,* Philip Kerr, Lloyd George's former secretary and later Lord Lothian, and Arthur Ponsonby, a leading Labor M.P.

In America S. O. (Sol) Levinson never failed to buttonhole as many influential people as he could, but he had better success cultivating the grass roots. Outlawry held great attraction for churches and women's clubs. The former were against the "war system" as a matter of principle, the latter, too. The incomparable Colonel Robins, crusader extraordinary, had an unerring eye for the churches and the ladies when he passionately declaimed: "Humanity is not helpless. This is God's world! We can outlaw this war system just as we outlawed slavery and the saloon." [16]

Such were the activities of the American Committee for the Outlawry of War.

Certainly the very heart of Outlawry—that war was a crime— was not a new idea. Andrew Carnegie in 1910, in his letter to the proposed trustees of his Endowment for International Peace, had described war as a crime. Moreover, one of the basic ideas of the wartime League to Enforce Peace was the criminality of war. Levinson's contribution was to take the current idea of criminality and affix to it a new word: Outlawry. The Chicago lawyer personally spent over $15,000 a year to spread the gospel of Outlawry.[17] If the other parts of the gospel—Code and Court—did not enter

---

of Ohio that he intended to get Outlawry into the Pact of Mutual Assistance then being drafted at Geneva (the statement that aggressive war was a crime got into Article 1; there were, incidentally, similar terms in the preamble to the 1924 Geneva Protocol). Allen to Levinson, Sept. 25, 1923, in J. Stoner, *Levinson,* p. 112.

16. Raymond Robins, "The Outlawry of War—The Next Step in Civilization," *Annals of the American Academy of Political and Social Science, 120* (July 1925), 154.

17. Professor John E. Stoner estimates that Levinson paid 95 per cent of the bills of the American Committee for the Outlawry of War. J. Stoner, *Levinson,* p. 70. Professor Stoner once asked Levinson about the costs of Outlawry, but Levinson refused to tell how much he had spent.

the public consciousness, surely the idea of outlawing war became common in American thought.[18]

Thus during the twenties one sees the Western world searching for peace. Private citizens, especially in the United States, enthusiastically sought ways to peace. In the United States various programs—the League of Nations, disarmament, the World Court, Outlawry—all had advocates.

What, meanwhile, were the world's diplomats, the professional peacemakers, themselves doing about the problem of peace? Were they attacking it with vigor and determination? Or were they talking rather than doing?

To the less obvious activities of the diplomats, paralleling the peace campaigning of the citizen advocates, we now must turn.

18. Of the 22,165 plans submitted for the Bok Award, most of them desired to outlaw war, and perhaps one third of the plans used the phrase. Esther Everett Lape, ed., *Ways to Peace* (New York, 1924), p. 30.

Chapter Four: THE SEARCH

FOR PEACE: THE DIPLOMATS

I. At the insistence of President Woodrow Wilson
the victorious Allies after the 1918 Armistice made provision in
the Versailles treaty for a new organization of the nations, "to
promote international cooperation and to achieve international
peace and security." No longer, thought Wilson, should war be
necessary to resolve great differences between nations; instead,
statesmen would assemble at Geneva and amicably talk over and
peacefully settle their differences. Article 19 of the League Covenant made express provision for this: "The [League] Assembly
may from time to time advise the reconsideration by Members of
the League of treaties which have become inapplicable and the
consideration of international conditions whose continuance might
endanger the peace of the world." When statesmen on June 28,
1919, signed the Versailles treaty, which included the League Covenant, it was not then evident that the Covenant's Article 19 would
be neglected in practice, and that the League consequently would
prove incapable of establishing conditions necessary for lasting
peace. In 1919 the future was unknown but hopeful; and few persons would have predicted that twenty-six years later the world
again would meet vainly—this time at San Francisco—hoping to
"save succeeding generations from the scourge of war." [1]

1. The preamble to the United Nations Charter begins: "We the peoples
of the United Nations, determined to save succeeding generations from the

THE SEARCH FOR PEACE: THE DIPLOMATS

In addition to Article 19, providing for "peaceful change," the Covenant contained elaborate provisions for preventing resort to war. There were only two "gaps" permitting war, both of these in Article 15. According to this article nations could fight if the League Council failed to reach a unanimous report over a dispute brought before it, parties to the dispute not permitted to vote in the Council or in the Assembly. War also could result from disputes declared to be matters of domestic jurisdiction. To close these gaps was one of the chief preoccupations of postwar European diplomacy. Their existence, however, offered reassurance to all nations jealous of their sovereignty. As British Foreign Secretary Sir Austen Chamberlain once said, there must needs be openings in every building giving power to breathe, and passages giving power to move.[2]

The League of Nations itself thus was hardly an institution which could abridge American sovereignty. But the League's opponents in the United States soon caricatured it as such. As ex-Senator Albert J. Beveridge wrote to ex-President Theodore Roosevelt, President Wilson had "hoisted the motley flag of internationalism. Thank God that he has. That makes the issue, does it not? Straight Americanism for us."[3] The Republicans' arch-strategist, Senator Henry Cabot Lodge, wrote Beveridge that it would be a mistake to admit that the League was a good thing, but "we should [also] make a mistake if we met the proposition with a flat denial. The purpose of the League—that is, the preservation of world peace—we are all anxious to see, but what we oppose is the method."[4]

---

scourge of war . . ." It is interesting that the word "war," a common word in the Covenant of the League of Nations, occurs only twice in the United Nations Charter—once in the preamble, and once in Article 77 in the phrase "Second World War." The Charter employs euphemisms such as "armed attack" and "breach of the peace."

2. League of Nations, *Records of the Eighth Ordinary Session of the Assembly, Plenary Meetings, Text of the Debates* (Geneva, 1927), p. 99.

3. Beveridge to Roosevelt, July 14, 1918, in Claude G. Bowers, *Beveridge and the Progressive Era* (Boston, Houghton Mifflin, 1932), p. 498.

4. "Now the strength of our position is to show up the impossibility of any of the methods proposed and invite them, when they desire our support,

When the United States Senate failed to advise and consent to the Treaty of Versailles there was great surprise and disappointment among the erstwhile European Associates. The "heart of the world" was broken. It was simply impossible adequately to explain Woodrow Wilson's failure at home to the peoples and governments of Europe. They could not grasp the exigencies of the American political system.

Nor could they understand why the United States Government took a firm stand—after funding the Allied war debts radically down to a capacity to pay—in expecting them eventually to be paid according to agreement. There was of course no real reason why the European governments should have expected to go scot-free from paying the war debts, for a good proportion of the debts [5] consisted of postwar loans—"pump primers," to use a later terminology—for starting the European economies on their way again. There was truth in the statement of Secretary of the Treasury Andrew W. Mellon in a letter of March 15, 1927, to President John Grier Hibben of Princeton, that "these were loans and not contributions and though not in form in actual effect loans from individual American citizens rather than contributions from the Treasury of the United States. . . . What we allowed our associates to do, in effect, was to borrow money in our investment market, but since their credit was not as good as ours, to borrow on the credit of the United States rather than on their own." [6]

The European nations did not see things this way, and only after

---

to produce their terms. They cannot do it. My own judgment is that the whole thing will break up in conference. There may be some vague declarations of the beauties of peace . . ." Lodge to Beveridge, December 3, 1918, in C. Bowers, *Beveridge*, p. 500.

5. $3,273,364,324.70 of a total of $10,350,479,074.70. Americans gave to Europe through the Red Cross $978,512,225. Congress also appropriated $100,000,000 for European relief. Senator S. P. Spencer, in the *Congressional Record*, Mar. 4, 1921, estimated $490,000,000 (one-half of the Red Cross total) was contributed through other channels. See Samuel Flagg Bemis, *A Diplomatic History of the United States*, pp. 704 ff.

6. *Papers Relating to the Foreign Relations of the United States: 1927* (3 vols., Washington, 1942), II, 733–734. This and other volumes of the series hereafter cited as *FR*.

much bad feeling and mutual recrimination did they enter into refunding arrangements reducing greatly the amount of the debts and looking toward ultimate payment and extinction of these obligations. Even then they vowed among themselves that they would pay the United States not a cent more than they extracted from Germany in reparations.[7]

With the advantage of hindsight, one must conclude that it would have been better had the United States canceled and forgotten the debts, but the historian should realize that the 1920's were before the days of Lend-Lease; during the twenties, and for many years before, good international faith (not to mention credit) demanded that a government pay, not repudiate, its debts, and it was under this then-prevailing custom that the United States asked for payment. Nevertheless the cry went up that the United States, by refusing debt cancellation, was refusing to bear its load in the organizing of the peace. "À bas l'oncle Shylock" muttered Frenchmen as the Chamber of Deputies in 1927 was still refusing to ratify the Mellon-Béranger debt-funding agreement. Europeans bitterly accused the United States of intervening in the Great War only after the Germans interdicted American commerce, and then walking out on Europe after the war was over, dumping all the enormous problems of organizing the peace into the laps of Europe's statesmen—and then coolly demanding, from across the Atlantic, that Europe pay back even a part of the cost of the war which made the world safe for American commerce.[8]

If there was one question which poisoned international relations almost as much as did the war debts, it was the question of "Who won the war?" The Americans thought they had won it. The French, having made the greatest human sacrifices, justly felt themselves the real victors. Field Marshal Haig announced that the

7. Only much later did it become evident that the United States, in the postwar era, actually lent Germany more money than the latter paid out in reparations.

8. It is important to note that the United States after the World War was the *only* real creditor nation. Although Great Britain had more wartime credits than debts, the balance was in defaulted loans to Russia. Other European nations were debtors for varying sums. Hence there arose the age-old spectacle of the debtors combining against the creditor.

British had won the war. Soon the question degenerated into a disgraceful argument. In America the Socialist Victor L. Berger declared that all the United States received from the war was the flu and prohibition. Many of his countrymen readily agreed. Rudyard Kipling, once the idol of the American reading public, sneered at the American war effort and compared the United States to the laborer who came at the eleventh hour to the vineyard and demanded a full day's wages. Quite a few Americans soon concluded that the United States had been wasting beneficence on ingrates.[9] The European attitude toward the war debts and toward the indispensable American war effort disillusioned many an American who had at first advocated Woodrow Wilson's League of Nations; it helped reconcile him to the Senate's rejection of the Covenant.

One matter at all events was beyond all debate: the war had been very costly, both in human lives and in physical resources. The physical cost was immense. For years afterward, until the second World War made such older calculations wearisome, publicists impressed upon the popular mind the number of houses or libraries or colleges or hospitals which could have been purchased for the cost of the World War. The human waste was incalculable. The fighting had killed ten million men outright—one life for every ten seconds of the war's duration. No figures could tell the cost in stunted and deformed bodies and in dilapidated minds.[10] Not without some justification, many persons after the war began to believe with Norman Angell that the hope of conspicuous national gain out of war was the Great Illusion.[11]

II

The American people, like their European brothers, wanted peace after the World War, and a very vocal segment of the American people wanted peace through American membership in the League of Nations. The Harding Administration, however, came

9. Preston W. Slosson, *The Great Crusade and After,* p. 295.

10. Merle Curti, *Peace or War: The American Struggle 1636–1936* (New York, 1936), p. 269.

11. Norman Angell, *The Great Illusion* (London, 1910).

into office after a confused electoral campaign [12] and chose to interpret its mandate to mean abstention from the League. But to mollify the powerful bloc of pro-Leaguers within the Republican party the new administration had to do something concrete in the way of perpetuating the peace of the world, and this exigency helped pave the way to the Washington Naval Disarmament Conference of 1921–22.

The conference concerned itself primarily with peace in the Far East, and its basic achievement was to interrupt the naval race then in progress between the United States and Japan. After the World War the American Government had resumed its naval program of 1916, in abeyance during the war in order to permit concentration on destroyers and other weapons against submarines. Between 1918 and 1921 it laid keels for all the capital ships authorized in the Act of 1916. By 1921 the British Government had not actually taken up the challenge, but the Japanese had: the Japanese in that year spent one third of their national budget on their navy. Perhaps if America had continued to build, the Japanese would soon have had to call a halt because of prohibitive costs, but in 1921–22 it seemed better economy to come to an agreement. Unfortunately the 5–5–3 ratio established by the conference gave the Japanese Navy supremacy in the far Pacific—to the world's later mortification.

In so far as concerned the future peace of the world, rather than the immediate peace in the Pacific and the Far East, the Washington conference probably did more harm than good, for—among other reasons—it recognized the Italian Government's claim to naval parity with France. This action deeply wounded the latter state's pride, made impossible the extension of the ratio of 5–5–3–1.7–1.7 to cruisers and auxiliary craft, and especially exacerbated Franco-American relations—for the French maintained that the Americans did not understand France's Mediterranean position.

12. The presidential campaign of 1920 hardly was a "solemn referendum" (as Wilson had proposed) for the League. The Democratic candidate, Governor James M. Cox, advocated the League. The Republican candidate, Senator Harding, came out for "an association of nations"; some of his followers claimed that this meant the League, and some argued that it didn't.

The ruffled pride of France took years to soothe, and it had frequent unfortunate manifestations in later French diplomacy.[13]

After the Washington Disarmament Conference the United States did offer to join the Permanent Court of International Justice, the juridical organ of the League. Here was an immediate goal for American peace advocates, and here was something which the new Republican Administration might do to please them and keep their votes. Shortly after Senator William E. Borah in February 1923 perfunctorily introduced his resolution looking toward the universal Outlawry of war, the Harding Administration came out for adherence to the protocol of the World Court. Because the Court functioned on the basis of a protocol separate from the Versailles treaty, and dealt only with "legal" not "political" questions, it seemed safe to join. Secretary of State Hughes, together with all the proponents of American entry into the League, zealously and sincerely espoused the Court and American participation therein. The World Court probably had enough friends in the Senate to secure American adherence. But the isolationists, as the anti-League forces were coming to be known, managed to seize upon the Court's right, as defined in its protocol, to render advisory opinions to the League Council, and succeeded in placing the following reservation in the Senate's advice and consent of January 27, 1926: ". . . nor shall it [the Court], without the consent of the United States, entertain any request for an advisory opinion touching any dispute or question in which the United States has or claims an interest." American adherence with this reservation proved unacceptable to the forty-eight states signatory to the Court protocol, and at the end of the 1920's the question of the World Court still was frustrated. Even this modest hope of American supporters of the League proved incapable of realization throughout the entire interwar period.

It had taken nearly three years—from 1923 to 1926—for the Senate to receive, debate, and in the end virtually reject the World Court. During this ordeal it was only natural that government officialdom in Washington should become more and more chary

13. See below, p. 68.

of all projects for world peace. Neither the American people nor their representatives in Congress seemed capable of agreeing on any one peace program. That oracle of the politicians, Mr. John Q. Public, wanted peace with all his heart and soul; that was certain. But just how this longing should be translated into a program of action was not evident, and in the face of indecision the Administrations of Presidents Harding and Coolidge therefore paused and waited. During the pausing and waiting proposals for peace received considerate but noncommittal official attention.

Typical of the government's extreme timidity toward projects for international peace was the fear and trembling with which President Coolidge's secretary, C. Bascom Slemp, received on January 7, 1925, a communication from a Mrs. William E. Chamberlain, requesting that the president meet a delegation of women from the forthcoming Conference on the Cause and Cure of War. The general chairman of the conference was to be that indomitable female crusader, Mrs. Carrie Chapman Catt. Mrs. Catt's name appeared at the head of the list of Coolidge's proposed visitors. The president's secretary sent Mrs. Chamberlain's letter posthaste to the State Department for expert opinion. Secretary Hughes replied the same day that it would be difficult for the president to refuse to meet the distinguished delegation, and that it would be all right for Coolidge "to make some general observations with respect to his interest in the prevention of war. This might meet the exigency." Across the top of Hughes' letter to Slemp, recommending that the president receive the ladies, there then was scrawled the presidential decision: "Let 'em call." [14] They called, and that was that.

III

Meanwhile statesmen in the Old World labored, amidst intense national rivalries, to perfect the organization of peace. The task in Europe was enormous. The French Government generally wished to hold the lid on German discontent, whereas the British Government desired rapprochement, by means of concessions, with the

14. Coolidge MSS, in the Library of Congress.

new republican government in Germany.[15] To have nursed along the German Republic, giving sufficient concessions to satisfy without whetting hunger for more—this would have been an exceedingly difficult endeavor. The forces of reaction in Germany always were strong, and concessions to the Republic might only have accrued, by a sudden change of government, to the Republic's enemies. To pursue the French policy of force, however, meant ultimately to push Germany into the arms of the other great revisionist power in Europe, Soviet Russia—and this is what finally happened. The *organisation de la paix* after the first World War was one of the most difficult problems ever to face the world's statesmen—exceeded in difficulty only by the even greater task which has arisen so ominously after the second World War.

For seven years after the Armistice of 1918 the German Government remained an outcast from the society of nations, and only in 1925, with the signing of the Locarno treaties, did Germany receive a welcome back into the fold. Sir Austen Chamberlain in a sense was right when he described Locarno as the real dividing line between the years of war and the years of peace.[16] It was during these years after 1918 and prior to Locarno that there occurred the German currency inflation, followed by the defaulting of reparations payments and French occupation of the Ruhr Valley. Passive German resistance in the Ruhr broke down under the crippling effect of the Ruhr's detachment from the German economy; Chancellor Stresemann had to admit defeat. Yet the consequences to France were also severe, for mounting military costs of occupation brought on a financial crisis, and British displeasure at Premier Poincaré's use of force against Germany nearly brought about a

15. The basic Franco-British difference lay in their respective attitudes toward German power: Britain, farther away from Germany than France, advocated more armament for Germany than France was willing to concede. In attempting to resolve this basic conflict the two allies eventually defeated each other. For a good exposition of these rival policies see Arnold Wolfers, *Britain and France between Two Wars: Conflicting Strategies of Peace since Versailles* (New York, 1940).

16. London *Times,* Oct. 24, 1925. Locarno made no distinction between Germany and France; theoretically, sanctions might have been applied to either.

Franco-British diplomatic rupture. The next year, 1924, the British Government took its revenge by refusing to sign the so-called Geneva Protocol—an ambitious project for prohibiting war in Europe, closing by arbitration and conciliation the two gaps in the League Covenant's Article 15.[17]

The Geneva Protocol remained for long afterward the darling of French diplomacy, the hope of all French statesmen.[18] Neverthe-

17. The main provisions of the protocol were as follows: signatories might resort to war only in case of resistance to acts of aggression, or when acting in agreement with the League Council or Assembly; signatories bound themselves to sign the optional clause of the World Court; all disputes to be settled by judicial decision, arbitral award, or report of the Council; the World Court would decide whether or not disputes were matters of domestic jurisdiction; before or during proceedings for pacific settlement states would not increase their armaments or effectives in any way; "Every State which resorts to war in violation of the undertakings contained in the Covenant or in the present Protocol is an aggressor" (Art. 10); sanctions, if ordered by the Council under the provisions of the protocol, were mandatory only in the degree which a state's "geographical position and its particular situation as regards armaments" allowed; signatories might deposit with the League secretariat, for registration and publication, detailed military plans to go into effect in case of breach of the protocol; signatories undertook to participate in a disarmament conference; the protocol would come into force only when planned measures of disarmament had (1) been accepted and (2) carried out. For a convenient text, see *International Conciliation*, No. 205 (Dec. 1924).

18. It is quite doubtful however if the French demand for security could have been satisfied even with the Geneva Protocol. As Leon Blum once said, "If the Protocol were more than a mere matter of hope and regret, it would not satisfy us any more than all the rest [of the post-1918 treaties and agreements]." For the protocol would have bound a signatory state "to cooperate loyally and effectively in support of the Covenant of the League of Nations, and in resistance to any act of aggression, [only] in the degree to which its geographic position and its particular situation as regards armaments allow." (See above, note 17.) This hardly constituted an airtight promise of assistance. As Eduard Beneš complained, "Many states would require to know what military support they could count on." Austen Chamberlain in 1925 realized that the French would not accept the protocol as adequate solution for the problem of security unless the protocol were reinforced by a supplementary pact of military assistance. Knowing also that the British public would not support any military alliance, Chamberlain therefore suggested the more limited agreement concluded at Locarno. W. M. Jordan, *Great Britain, France, and the German Problem: 1918–1939* (London, 1943), p. 208.

less half a loaf was better than none, and the group of treaties concluded at the little Swiss town of Locarno in the fall of 1925 did apply the rejected protocol's principles at least to the Franco-German and Belgo-German frontiers. The German Government, persuaded by Gustav Stresemann who was now its foreign minister, freely" [19] signed the Locarno treaties, and peace-lovers throughout the world rejoiced at the end of Germany's diplomatic isolation from the West and forthcoming return to the League of Nations.

There quickly arose the "Locarno spirit." "The days after the conclusion of the Treaty of Locarno, and the admission of Germany to the League," Stresemann later wrote to a friend, "were in some sort Sundays in the life of nations." [20] These were the golden days of the League. For years afterward men of peace took pleasure in recalling the manner in which Aristide Briand, the foreign minister of France, presided at an emergency meeting of the League Council in 1925 and by the sheer weight of the League's authority forced the squabbling governments of Greece and Bulgaria to halt a recently broken-out war. The men of peace, mesmerized by this display of the League's authority, did not know that simultaneously Sir Austen Chamberlain called the Greek minister in London on to one of the numerous carpets in the Foreign Office and tendered him some "most urgent advice," of a nature which quickly induced the Greek Government to change its attitude.[21] Nonetheless it was true that during the days after Locarno there existed a profound feeling

19. As opposed to the *Diktat* of Versailles.

20. To Dr. Gebhart-Opladen, Oct. 3, 1928, quoted in Eric Sutton, ed., *Gustav Stresemann: His Diaries, Letters and Papers* (London, Macmillan, 1935–40), III, 401.

21. According to Caclamanos, the Greek minister, Sir Austen gave "most urgent advice" to withdraw the Greek forces. "Greece, Sir Austen added, was surrounded at this time by rivals rather than friends, and her disinterested friends and protectors were too far from the spot to give an effective support." In a dispatch immediately afterward to Athens, Caclamanos called this a "grave warning." The Greek Government backed down immediately, and the Paris proceedings were in fact a mere ratification of Chamberlain's work. See Caclamanos's letter to the London *Times*, Mar. 19, 1937.

of peace in Europe, a Sabbath in the life of nations, brought on by the Locarno spirit.[22]

In reality the Locarno treaties had some very bad effects on the peace of Europe. Firstly, they had the effect of grading frontiers in Europe into those which were guaranteed (the western frontiers of Germany) and those which were not guaranteed (namely, Germany's eastern frontiers). Sir James Headlam-Morley, the historical advisor of the British Foreign Office, put the case sharply when Britain was considering entering into the Locarno treaties. "We can, as is proposed," wrote Sir James, "give a guarantee against German aggression on the Rhine or through Belgium. But in the future the real danger may lie, not here, but rather on the eastern frontiers of Germany—Danzig, Poland, Czechoslovakia—for it is in these districts that the settlement of Paris would be, when the time came, most easily overthrown." [23] The Locarno treaties, with their classification of frontiers in Europe, really opened as many, perhaps more, gaps in the structure of European peace than they closed.

A second untoward result of Locarno was to reopen the disarmament question. It will be recalled that the Allies had justified German disarmament under the Versailles treaty as merely the first step in a general, all-around disarmament of the nations.[24] The members of the League recognized in Article 8 of the Covenant "that the maintenance of peace requires the reduction of national

22. The Locarno spirit, even in the era of its greatest influence, did not convert all the sophisticates in European foreign offices. One day soon after conclusion of the Locarno treaties Sir Hughe Knatchbull-Hugessen, then a member of the British Embassy in Paris, went to the Quai d'Orsay to urge a certain concession to Germany. He was to argue that this would be in keeping with the Locarno spirit. He saw René Massigli, at that time in an important position at the French Foreign Office. Massigli was not sympathetic to Hugessen's approach. "Mon cher Hugessen," he said, "il y a trois choses, le *Locarno spirit*, l'esprit de Locarno, et le *Locarnogeist*." Sir Hughe Knatchbull-Hugessen, *Diplomat in Peace and War* (London, J. Murray, 1949), pp. 52–53.

23. J. W. Headlam-Morley, *Studies in Diplomatic History* (London, Methuen, 1930), p. 156.

24. The preamble to Part V of the Versailles Treaty declared that Germany undertook to disarm "in order to render possible the initiation of a general limitation of the armaments of all nations."

armaments to the lowest point consistent with national safety and
the enforcement by common action of international obligations."
After the Locarno treaties and Germany's entrance into the League
it was agreed that a Preparatory Commission, looking toward a
future disarmament conference, should begin its labors. The commission labored hard. One of its officials, the Spanish publicist-
diplomatist Salvador de Madariaga, later asserted that a subcommittee alone used 3,750,000 sheets of typescript, enough to permit the
League's Polish or Swedish delegations to walk home on a path
made of League paper.[25] The deliberations of the Preparatory
Commission, to which, incidentally, the United States sent a delegation, brought into the open the difficult problem of Allied disarmament vis-à-vis Germany's great industrial potential for war:
Germany desired the erstwhile Allies to disarm, to reduce themselves to a German par from which in some future contingency rearmament might begin again, to German advantage. The problem
of disarmament was further complicated by an Anglo-French ri-
valry: the British wished to disarm the French Army, and the
French countered by requesting the disarmament of the Royal
Navy.

Disarmament, as the French persistently stated, was quite impossible until the nations had solved the question of security (presumably by resuscitating the Geneva Protocol). Without first meeting
the problem of security the disarmament confabulations took on
the color of unreality. The British Government during the twenties
absolutely refused to consider reviving the protocol. Disarmament
discussions might well have then relegated themselves to some
limbo of the League's activities at Geneva had there not been a
vociferous demand for disarmament from taxpayers and peace devo-
tees the world over. As the *Survey of American Foreign Relations*
for 1927 optimistically put it: "We may be confident that decrease
in armaments is an indication of stability and peace; the level of
armaments is a thermometer which all can read; every reduction
means a waning of the war-fever, an approach to the reëstablish-

25. Alfred Zimmern, *The League of Nations and the Rule of Law: 1918–
1935* (London, 1936; 2d ed., 1939), p. 377.

ment of health and peace." [26] And so the European statesmen, plagued by a thousand other difficulties of maintaining the peace, had also to meet a deafening demand for disarmament from millions of their unrealistic fellow-countrymen. Organizing the Preparatory Commission, incident to Germany's signature of Locarno, did not advance the cause of peace. The futile disarmament discussions at Geneva poisoned European international relations. In such an atmosphere of distrust, ally versus ally, and Allies versus Germany, the Locarno spirit soon withered and died.

With this brief appreciation of the peace efforts and problems of governments in Europe and the United States during the period 1918–27, it is now perhaps advisable to observe closely a very special aspect of the diplomatic search for peace—and security. For out of the French Republic's new postwar system of alliances, negotiated to maintain the peace of Europe, there eventually came the Kellogg-Briand Pact.

26. Charles P. Howland, *Survey of American Foreign Relations: 1928* (New Haven, Yale University Press, 1928), p. 499.

Chapter Five: FRANCE AND HER NEW ALLIES

During the years after the first World War the French Government maintained an army of impressive size and strength. This large standing army, Frenchmen avowed, was for their country's security.

There were of course means other than arms, i.e., diplomatic means, for achieving *sécurité*. These the French experimented with, for what they were worth. At times there appeared a possibility of rapprochement with Germany. Then there always was the alternate hope of making the League of Nations in effect an alliance against any resurgence of German power. For a while it seemed that the Geneva Protocol might bring success. But the French never abandoned the army as a means of security. In spite of loud international cries of militarism, and popular pleas for disarmament Frenchmen continued to stick to their guns.

It should be emphasized here—although this has already been remarked in the previous chapter—that Frenchmen had every right thus to seek security for their country. It was one of the greatest tragedies of the interwar period that so many people, especially in Britain and America, statesmen as well as citizens, minimized the French need for security. Not until the terrible days of June 1940 did Britishers and Americans really begin to appreciate France's plight—her perilous situation in living beside a nation not only twice her size but a nation which, historically, was highly proficient in war. The French search for sécurité was in every sense of the term a vital quest. Few people today will blame the French for maintaining a large army during the years after the first World War.

Because a basic means of French security during the twenties and thirties was the army, it followed that the Republic of France should also have as many military allies as possible. Alliances would serve a double purpose. They would impress the neighboring German people with the number and strength of France's friends; and, secondly, if the Next War came the more allies the better. But, peace-lovers asked, and so did others during the twenties from quite different motives, were not alliances out of fashion in the post-1918 world? Had not the terrible World War resulted from the evil competition of Triple Alliance and Triple Entente? Was not the balance of power an evil thing, "forever discredited," in Woodrow Wilson's words? In a sense these questionings were right. But in the postwar world, the balance of power, although discredited, could yet be made to serve French security—if the balance could indeed be arranged against Germany.

This more favorable shift in the balance of power French diplomacy set out to achieve.

I

In many ways it was not an easy matter, after 1918, to create a new system of alliances.

France's old prewar ally, Russia, labored with highly uncertain revolution. France's other principal ally, Britain, soon after the Armistice began to follow her own counsels; although British statesmen occasionally proclaimed the Anglo-French entente of 1904 as still in effect, there were no more military "conversations" between the French and British General Staffs. A French attempt at Versailles to conclude a postwar "guarantee alliance" with the United States (and also Britain) failed to obtain the advice and consent of the American Senate. Although Britain actually exchanged ratifications of her guarantee alliance with France, the

British instrument contained a stipulation that it should not go
into effect until ratification of the American alliance.[1]

As if the defection of Russia, the initial aloofness of Britain, and
the apparent disinterest of the United States were not enough obstacles toward constructing a new system of alliances, the French in
their desire for a postwar series of definite, unequivocal, and automatic defense agreements confronted also—as we have seen—a
hostile public opinion. People in many countries had become convinced that alliances caused wars rather than prevented them; want-
ing no more war, they likewise wanted no more alliances.

People with a fervor almost equaling their ignorance of international relations especially condemned secret diplomacy—an essential adjunct of most alliance-making because of the necessary
secrecy of prearranged military plans. Postwar public opinion considered secret diplomacy undemocratic. The first World War had
been fought, President Woodrow Wilson had said, to make the
world safe for democracy. Wilson had voiced a popular mood in
the very first of his Fourteen Points: [2] "Open covenants of peace
openly arrived at, after which there shall be no private international
understandings of any kind but diplomacy shall proceed always
frankly and in the public view." [3]

1. For the ill-fated guarantee treaties, see J. Paul Selsam, *The Attempts To
Form an Anglo-French Alliance: 1919–1924* (Philadelphia, 1936).

2. Enunciated after the Russian Bolshevik Government's untimely publication of a number of Allied secret World War treaties.

3. Wilson did not mean that all negotiation should be public. ". . . certainly when I pronounced for open diplomacy," he wrote Secretary of State
Robert Lansing, "I meant, not that there should be no private discussion of
delicate matters, but that no secret agreements of any sort should be entered
into, and that all international relations when fixed should be open, above-
board, and explicit." Wilson to Lansing, Mar. 12, 1918, in David Hunter
Miller, *The Drafting of the Covenant* (2 vols., New York, G. P. Putnam's, 1928),
I, 19 n.

It is not generally realized that Colonel House, rather than Wilson himself,
was directly responsible for inclusion of the "open covenants" declaration as
Point 1 of the Fourteen Points. See Charles Seymour, ed., *The Intimate Papers
of Colonel House* (4 vols., Boston and New York, 1926–28), III, 326. The House
diary, presently in the House Collection at Yale and now open to historical
students, indicates moreover that the colonel was a very ardent disciple of

Wilsonian dislike of secret diplomacy found its way into the Covenant of the League of Nations. According to Article 18, "Every treaty or international engagement entered into hereafter by any Member of the League shall be forthwith registered with the Secretariat and shall as soon as possible be published by it. No such treaty or international engagement shall be binding until so registered." If this blunt declaration required any interpretation, it could be found in an official memorandum approved by the Council of the League of Nations during a meeting in Rome, May 19, 1920. Material to be registered in accordance with Article 18, the Council stipulated, "comprises not only every formal Treaty of whatsoever character and every International Convention, but also any other International Engagement or Act." [4]

It would seem perfectly clear—from the first of Wilson's Fourteen Points, from the eighteenth article of the Covenant, and from the memorandum of May 1920—that old-style alliances, with their secret military provisions, no longer were possible among League members. Language itself could not be more explicit.

Nor could language itself scarcely be more foolish. To ask the French nation to abide by such arbitrary and legalistic rules was to ask the impossible: idealists in Britain and the United States—and realists in Germany and Italy—actually were proposing to isolate France, to cut her off from any chance of military alliance. France should not, could not, and of course would not have submitted to such a proposition. Less than four months after the Council so strictly interpreted the registration provisions of Article 18, the governments of France and Belgium signed a secret military alliance.

Here was the first in the new, postwar system of French alliances. Its provisions were never registered with the League of Nations. An exchange of notes between the Belgian and French Governments,

open diplomacy, perhaps more so than the president. This is a point which needs investigation.

4. "The Registration and Publication of Treaties as prescribed under Article 18 of the Covenant of the League of Nations: Memorandum Approved by the Council of the League of Nations, Meeting in Rome, on May 19, 1920." League of Nations, *Treaty Series, 1,* 7–13.

dated September 10 and 15, 1920, merely announced that the object
of the two countries' "understanding" was to reinforce the guarantees of peace and security found in the Covenant.[5] Spokesmen for
the two governments stated that, because of the technical character
of the understanding, it would not be submitted to the Belgian and
French parliaments.[6] Over ten years later, in 1931, Paul Hymans,
then Belgian foreign minister, publicly admitted what everyone
had known all along—that the alliance contained military measures
to be taken "in the event of common action being necessary . . .
against an unprovoked attack by Germany."[7] No further details
were ever revealed.

Negotiation of the secret Franco-Belgian military understanding provoked a storm of indignation from liberals all over the
Continent. Especially of course in Germany. At the League Assembly in the fall of 1920 there was much talk about the terms of the
Covenant's Article 18. A committee of jurists was appointed to look
into the matter. Several months later they diplomatically recom-
mended a formula to the effect that purely technical or administrative instruments, not political in nature, defining or carrying into
effect another instrument already registered, should be excepted
from compulsory registration.[8] While the jurists were formulating
their opinions the French Government, February 19, 1921, signed
a second alliance, this time a "political agreement" with Poland.

The Franco-Polish *accord politique*, the text of which became

5. The letters contained a covert reference to "the eventuality contemplated by the present understanding." League of Nations, *Treaty Series*, 2,
127–130.

6. London *Times*, Sept. 3, 1920.

7. New York *Times*, Mar. 5, 1931. The alliance underwent a change in
1936 when Premier Paul van Zeeland announced in the Belgian parliament
that the military agreement had been reduced to a simple arrangement for
only military staff consultation. *Ibid.*, Mar. 12, 1936.

8. League of Nations, *Records of the Second Assembly*, II, *Meetings of the
Committees*, I (Geneva, 1921), 169–170. Regarding the jurists' report, League
Assembly subcommittee number five of the First Committee "unanimously
concurred in the spirit of this suggestion, which, without affecting in any way
the lofty aim underlying Article 18, is calculated greatly to facilitate its practical application." *Ibid.*, p. 169.

public two and a half years later when it was registered with the
League of Nations, consisted of several articles, some commercial
and some political—the latter calling for nothing more objectionable than consultation if "notwithstanding the sincerely peaceful
views and intentions of the two Contracting States, either or both
of them should be attacked without giving provocation." The two
governments promised to take concerted measures for defense of
their territory and protection of their legitimate interests. All concerted measures were to be "within the limits specified in the
preamble." The preamble was composed of rather uninteresting
verbiage, and vaguely said something about Franco-Polish security
and "common political and economic interests." [9] Probably there
was a secret military annex to this second French treaty, the Franco-
Polish political agreement of 1921. The Polish Army at that time,
we recall, was filled with French military advisors, the chief of
whom, General Maxime Weygand, recently had saved Warsaw from
the invading hordes of Bolshevist Russia.

When the League of Nations assembled in the fall of 1921
there occurred another debate on registering treaties. Viscount
Cecil declared registration was "really a question of very great
importance and one upon which . . . public opinion is very sensitive. . . . we have to consider, not only what we believe will be the
operation of a particular provision, but what the public, looking at
it, will think would be a fair provision." [10] Cecil seemed to be
saying, diplomatically, that the public had to be pleased. Cecil's
colleague, Lord Balfour, agreed that the subject of Article 18 was
one of "very great difficulty and complexity." Balfour mentioned
financial arrangements as coming within the category of treaties
which often could not be published. Then he mentioned "other
treaties, not of a financial character," i.e., the Franco-Belgian treaty
of alliance. To register such a treaty, said Balfour with some irritation, was "impossible, and cannot, and will not, be done." [11] The

9. For the text of this treaty, see League of Nations, *Treaty Series, 18,* 11–13.
10. League of Nations, *Records of the Second Assembly, Plenary Meetings*
(Geneva, 1921), Oct. 5, 1921, p. 844.
11. *Ibid.,* pp. 847–848.

Assembly duly passed a resolution deferring further debate on Article 18 for another year.[12]

So much for Article 18, registration of treaties, in the 1921 Assembly of the League of Nations. The French were safely over that barrier. But there was another obstacle in the Covenant. A difficulty had arisen in connection with the *casus foederis* of the two new French alliances, the military understanding with Belgium, and the political agreement with Poland. Would not resort to war, in accordance with the terms of the alliances, have to await execution of the complicated provisions of the Covenant's Article 15, which required a certain amount of time before quarreling states could maneuver themselves down to the Article's two gaps [13] that tacitly allowed for war? Would not the automatic, immediate nature of the new French alliances be frustrated when, after a breach of the Covenant, the Council in accordance with Article 15 debated and debated over whether or not there had been an act of unwarranted aggression, justifying measures of defense? As if to answer, the League Assembly in 1921 passed a resolution: "It is the duty of

12. There was a curious situation in regard to this resolution. As originally proposed by Balfour, the resolution read as follows: "The Assembly, taking note of the proposal for the amendment of Article 18 contained in the report of Committee No. 1 [namely, for exception from registration of all agreements of a "purely technical or administrative nature"], decides to adjourn further consideration of this amendment until the third Assembly, *it being understood that, in the meantime, Members of the League are at liberty to interpret their obligations under Article 18 in conformity with the proposed amendment.*" Italics inserted. The Assembly, before passing the Balfour resolution, divided it into two sections. The nonitalicized part passed unanimously. The italicized section passed by a vote of 28 for, 5 against. League of Nations, *Records of the Second Assembly, Plenary Meetings*, Oct. 5, 1921, pp. 851–852. Later the same day the vote on the second section was challenged on a point of order, and the president of the Assembly ruled that the second section had *not* passed, because resolutions, to pass, required unanimity. Nonetheless the second section was declared not to have been defeated by the Assembly—for it obviously had received a majority vote. Vittorio Scialoja (Italy) in explaining this complicated situation implied that the Assembly had approved Balfour's second section, although the approval did not take the form of a resolution. *Ibid.*, p. 895.

13. For which, see above, p. 39.

each Member of the League *to decide for itself* whether a breach of the Covenant has been committed." [14]

The prime minister of Great Britain, Lloyd George, early in January 1922 offered France an alliance with Britain in case of "direct and unprovoked aggression against the soil of France by Germany." The French Government endeavored to extend the British offer to include cooperation in eastern Europe—with France's ally Poland. Suddenly, however, as is the wont in French politics, the cabinet fell; and after the change of ministers the Franco-British alliance negotiations languished.[15] In the meantime the new republican government of Germany concluded at Rapallo an economic and political treaty with Soviet Russia which contained military implications.[16]

Of the making of alliances there thus was no end. When the League of Nations assembled again in September 1922 the First Committee reported on the problem of Article 18, registration of treaties. The *rapporteur,* C. T. Zahle of Denmark, informed the Assembly that Article 18 was one of the banners at the very top of the palace of the League of Nations and should not be hauled down, unless absolutely necessary. Zahle did not lower the banner. He asked a resolution again to postpone the question of Article 18. The resolution passed, unanimously.[17] A few days later in a flurry

14. League of Nations, *Records of the Second Assembly, Plenary Meetings,* Sept. 27, 1921, p. 453. Italics inserted.

15. J. P. Selsam, *The Attempts To Form an Anglo-French Alliance.* Lloyd George's proposed treaty had a time limit of ten years. It is interesting that this period approximately equaled the time which, according to rumor, the British General Staff considered as possessing the best prospects of peace—a time during which the General Staff believed there would be no threat to the British position. In other words the British offered a treaty when they didn't think they would be called upon to honor it.

16. The Russian delegation at the Genoa conference promptly denied specifically that there were any unpublished articles, or that the treaty had been accompanied by a secret military convention. Later events were to show however that Rapallo inaugurated a long period of German-Russian military cooperation, lasting unbroken until Hitler in January 1934 concluded a non-aggression pact with Poland.

17. League of Nations, *Records of the Third Assembly, Plenary Meetings* (Geneva, 1922), Sept. 23, 1922, p. 281.

of resolution making the Assembly decided that: "In the present state of the world many Governments would be unable to accept the responsibility for a serious reduction of armaments unless they received in exchange a satisfactory guarantee of the safety of their country. Such a guarantee can be found *in a defensive agreement,* which should be open to all countries, binding them to provide immediate and effective assistance *in accordance with a prearranged plan* in the event of one of them being attacked . . ." [18]

Here, indeed, was something new. States no longer were being silently allowed to make alliances, but were even declared to be in special need of such alliances. The door of League approval, long so apparently shut, now was wide open. But the public of whom Lord Cecil had spoken, that public which was "very sensitive" to secret alliances, undoubtedly never noticed this remarkable League resolution. The resolution appeared within a long series of sixteen resolves. Permission having at long last been granted, the French Government, January 25, 1924, signed an outright "Treaty of Alliance and Friendship" with Czechoslovakia.

According to "official statements," the Czech treaty contained no secret military clauses.[19] But their absence did not exclude an accompanying, although separate, military agreement. There were bitter comments in Germany when, March 18, 1924, the *Berliner*

18. *Ibid.,* Sept. 27, 1922, p. 291. Italics inserted.

19. London *Times,* Jan. 26, 1924. The treaty was duly registered. It contained a preamble and eight articles. The preamble claimed the treaty was for the purpose of "certain mutual guarantees . . . indispensable for security against possible aggression and for the protection of their [the signatories'] common interests." Most of the articles called for consultation under various contingencies. Important were Articles 2 and 6:

"Article 2. The High Contracting Parties shall agree together as to the measures to be adopted to safeguard their common interests in case the latter are threatened."

"Article 6. In conformity with the principles laid down in the Covenant of the League of Nations, the High Contracting Parties agree that if in future any dispute should arise between them which cannot be settled by friendly agreement and through diplomatic channels, they will submit such dispute either to the Permanent Court of International Justice or to such other arbitrator or arbitrators as they may select."

For the complete text, see League of Nations, *Treaty Series, 23,* 163–169.

Tageblatt published its alleged text. Foreign Minister Eduard Beneš of Czechoslovakia is reported to have denounced this revelation as foolish and false and without foundation,[20] which perhaps it was. There was, of course, no available way of making certain.

After the treaty of alliance and friendship with Czechoslovakia France found her energies occupied by what could have been the grandest alliance of all, the Geneva Protocol.[21] The protocol might have turned the League of Nations into an alliance against all revisionist states. As has been seen in the previous chapter, France signed the watered-down Locarno agreements with reluctance. Notable among the several Locarno treaties, however, were two treaties of "mutual guarantee," between France and Poland and between France and Czechoslovakia. The two treaties were, *mutatis mutandis*, identical. In case Poland or France (or Czechoslovakia or France) suffered from a failure to observe the undertakings of the Locarno treaties between them and Germany, and if "such a failure is accompanied by an unprovoked recourse to arms," the casus foederis arose immediately. There were no detailed military provisions.[22]

Thus the years 1920–25 had witnessed some remarkable achievements in France's quest for allies. Bravely, in the teeth of foreign public opinion, she had set up a new system of European alliances to compensate for the loss of her prewar ally, Russia, and the uncertain support of Great Britain and the United States. There was the secret military understanding with Belgium (1920), the political agreement with Poland (1921), the outright treaty of alliance and friendship with Czechoslovakia (1924), and two treaties of mutual guarantee with Czechoslovakia and Poland (1925). All but one of these instruments, it is important to note, bore pleasant, pacific-sounding titles, omitting the ominous word "alliance." Diplomats in the postwar years were adept at such verbal substitutions, which made their diplomacy more palatable to public opinion. To the uninitiated this new verbiage seemed like a basic change in the aims

20. New York *Times,* Mar. 20, 1924.

21. For a summary of the protocol's provisions, see above, p. 47n.

22. For the treaties, see League of Nations, *Treaty Series, 54,* 353–357, 359–363.

and methods of international relations, and came to be known,
rather unappropriately, as the "new diplomacy."

Conclusion of the mutual guarantee treaties of Locarno did
not mark the end of French alliances in the postwar era. Frenchmen, it has often been remarked, suffered from "pactomania."
Observing their restless neighbors across the Rhine, they desired
all the written assurances they could obtain. It therefore was an
enormous piece of good fortune for France when in the spring of
1925 a master of the art of diplomatic agreement, a Frenchman
magnificently skilled in the verbal techniques of the new diplomacy,
assumed control of the Quai d'Orsay. Once the Locarno ceremonies
were out of the way the new French foreign minister, Aristide
Briand, began anew the search for allies.

II

Aristide Briand was a most striking personality.

He was, first and foremost, a consummate politician. For years
he had held portfolios of one sort or another in various French
cabinets. Often—nine times already—he had possessed the premier-
ship itself. Briand could conduct the most difficult of political negotiations with flawless perfection. He achieved, moreover, a great
popular following in his capacity as a superb orator. He could
charm League audiences for hours with the splendid vacuities of
his peace speeches.

There was another, considerably more interesting and much less
public, side to Briand. This was Briand the individual, a grand
character indeed. Paris gossip had it that he was a cynical, fast-living
old bachelor. In appearance Briand stood of medium height, with
broad, stooping shoulders, an untidy shock of graying hair crown-
ing his massive head. "A heavy drooping moustache half hid a
slightly crooked, full-lipped mouth, whose ugliness was redeemed
by an enchanting smile that matched well the bright eyes dancing
with an often slightly malicious wit." Sir Austen Chamberlain
found him "indeed, incorrigibly witty . . . 'Tell me Briand's latest,' was the greeting with which Lord Balfour used to receive me
on my return from my visits to Geneva . . ." [23]

23. Austen Chamberlain, *Down the Years* (London, Cassell, 1935), p. 180.

This, then, was the charming, brilliant, capable, experienced, realistic old gentleman who, as foreign minister of France, took up the French post-Locarno quest for alliances.

Briand noted that all the important countries bordering on German territory (Belgium, Poland, and Czechoslovakia) already were allied with France against the Germans. Obviously, there was little value in making overtures to such military nonentities as Holland, Denmark, Switzerland, and Austria. Briand turned therefore to the Balkans.

The problem was to secure France's southern flank, the French-Italian border along the Riviera, in the event of war with Germany. Ideally it would have been best to have made friends with Italy, but the Mussolini government was not especially to be trusted; it also had designs on French territory: Nice, Corsica, Tunis. There remained enlistment of some of the east European countries so that they, by threat of military action, would tie Italy down, keeping the Italian Army away from the French border in case of war. What nations should be chosen? Czechoslovakia, Rumania, and Yugoslavia, the so-called Little Entente, already united out of fear of Hungarian and Bulgarian revisionism, fearing also Italian ambitions in Albania and elsewhere, naturally tended to gravitate toward friendship with France. Czechoslovakia had already sealed her friendship by reason of her German frontier. There remained the two obvious candidates, Rumania and Yugoslavia.

For purposes of his new Balkan courtship Briand decided that he required a new treaty formula. There was one at hand, offered, of all states, by the Kingdom of Siam, the neighbor of France's eastern colony of Indo-China. The Siamese Government in 1925 had concluded arbitration treaties with several European nations: France, Italy, the Netherlands, Spain, Denmark, and Sweden. Now no one in Europe in 1925 was thinking much about attacking Siam. Probably for that reason the Siamese arbitration treaties, contrary to usual European custom, had no loopholes—no gaps at all. The treaty between Siam and France, for example, contained an unequivocal Article 1: "There shall be constant peace and perpetual friendship between the French Republic and the Kingdom of Siam." Article 2 provided, albeit in several long, involved paragraphs, for settlement of *all* disputes whatsoever by pacific means.

Although the treaty had many other articles they merely filled in the details of the important Articles 1 and 2.[24]

Briand lost little time, after Locarno, in negotiating his Balkan treaties. Rumania and France, June 10, 1926, signed a "treaty of friendship." The treaty's preamble declared for "fresh guarantees of peace, goodwill, and friendship." There were nine articles.[25] Most interesting were Articles 1 and 2, which appeared as if they might have come from Siam:

> Article I. France and Rumania mutually undertake that they will in no case attack or invade each other or resort to war against each other. . . .
>
> Article II. In view of the undertakings entered into in Article I of the present Treaty, France and Rumania undertake to settle by peaceful means and in the manner laid down herein all questions of every kind which may arise between them and which it may not be possible to settle by the normal methods of diplomacy. . . .[26]

Simultaneously with the negotiation of this Franco-Rumanian treaty, Briand had sought a treaty with Yugoslavia. The French foreign minister and Momčilo Ninčić, the foreign minister of Yugoslavia, initialed a new pact in the spring of 1926. Signature could occur at the request of either party; and in the meantime the initialed treaty—although the text itself, as was to be expected, contained no specific military agreements—did not have to be registered with the League of Nations. As eventually signed and published the Yugoslav treaty, in the new Style of Siam, was identical with the Rumanian treaty, mutatis mutandis, except that it was for five years instead of ten and bore the title "Treaty of Friendly Understanding." [27]

24. For the "Treaty of Friendship, Commerce and Navigation" between France and Siam, signed February 14, 1925, see League of Nations, *Treaty Series, 43,* 189–209.

25. Also an annexed protocol in which Rumania disclaimed any intention of attacking Russia.

26. League of Nations, *Treaty Series, 58,* 225–231.

27. For events surrounding signature of the Yugoslav treaty, see below, p. 125. The treaty's text is in *Treaty Series, 68,* 373–379.

Such was the development and status of France's new system of alliances by the spring of 1927. These alliances could never have been made had Frenchmen taken seriously Wilson's declaration for "open covenants . . . openly arrived at." Even when this popularly acclaimed dictum had received legal expression in Article 18 of the League Covenant, which called unequivocally for registration of all international agreements, the French realistically—and rightfully, as we now see—gave little attention to it and soon afterward concluded the first of their postwar alliances, an avowedly secret military understanding with Belgium. Confronted with a fait accompli, statesmen in the Assembly of the League of Nations, alive to the inevitability if not the necessity of French alliance-making, avoided express amendment of Article 18 but instead unobtrusively changed its meaning by passing compromising resolutions. Meanwhile the French Government, skillfully using the unoffensive wording of the new diplomacy, continued to negotiate more political agreements, treaties of friendship, and treaties of friendly understanding.

Precisely in what manner, we may well inquire, were these new French alliances of the 1920's in essence different from those of prewar days? Surely the friends of France virtually surrounded Germany in 1927 as they had in 1914. Russia, of course, was out of the picture, but Poland had taken her place. England appeared disinterested,[28] but then there was the new Czechoslovakia, an armed salient into the very heart of German territory. Although Italy acted noisily unfriendly, she was neutralized by the new Yugoslavia and the enlarged Rumania. Altogether, the alliance situation in the spring of 1927 looked rather favorable for France.

Yet the search for security never ended. No Frenchman could ever be certain that his country had sufficient guarantees.

Aristide Briand, in his capacity as French foreign minister, ever cognizant of the latent menace of a German rearmament, undoubtedly asked himself again and again what more he could do to enhance France's new system of alliances.

28. Locarno, we recall, stipulated British armed support of *either* France or Germany, whichever was victim of aggression.

Chapter Six: RENUNCIATION OF WAR—

BETWEEN FRANCE AND THE UNITED STATES

One day in June 1926 Dr. Nicholas Murray Butler, visiting in Paris, was congratulating Aristide Briand at the Quai d'Orsay on the steady and hopeful progress which he was making in the cause of international peace.

"What could we do next?" Briand suddenly asked Butler.

"My dear Briand," the president of Columbia replied, "I have just been reading a book. . . . Its title is *Vom Kriege,* and its author was Karl von Clausewitz . . . I came upon an extraordinary chapter in its third volume, entitled 'War as an Instrument of Policy.' [1] Why has not the time come for the civilized governments of the world formally to renounce war as an instrument of policy?"

"Would not that be wonderful if it were possible?" responded Briand. "I must read that book."

Briand's reading of Clausewitz's *Vom Kriege,* Butler concluded many years later, was the origin of the Kellogg-Briand Pact. [2]

Just how Dr. Butler arrived at this conclusion is obscure. There is not the least shred of evidence that the French foreign minister read the writings of a nineteenth-century German military theorist to learn how to conduct twentieth-century French diplomacy.

1. Actually, *"Der Krieg ist ein Instrument der Politik"* is Bk. VIII, chap. vi, sec. B.

2. Nicholas Murray Butler, *Across the Busy Years,* II, 202–203.

Briand, moreover, never enjoyed a reputation for bookishness. He preferred to develop his ideas in conversation, or in extemporaneous speechmaking, vis-à-vis, where he could carefully watch his auditors' response. According to a then current quip, Briand's superior, Premier Poincaré, "read everything and understood nothing," whereas the subtle and sensitive foreign minister "read nothing and understood everything."

It is not impossible, however, that Briand, listening courteously to Dr. Butler's suggestion for renouncing war, recalled silently the new French postwar system of alliances. The very month he was conversing with Butler the foreign minister signed a pact of friendship with Rumania, and he had initialed another pact with Yugoslavia. Would it not be wonderful, if it were possible, to make an alliance with the United States?

Briand did not pursue the thought of renouncing war with the United States until several months later, early in 1927, when Professor James Thomson Shotwell arrived in Europe.

I

Professor Shotwell in March 1927 served as Visiting Carnegie Professor of International Relations at the Hochschule für Politik in Berlin.[3] For his inaugural address he chose the challenging topic, "Are We at a Turning Point in the History of the World?" The address received the highest official attention. The German chancellor and his cabinet attended. The chief justice of Germany presided. Also present were members of the War Office staff, appearing—so someone told Professor Shotwell—for the first time after the war in a public assembly with all their wartime decorations. The main thesis of the inaugural address was that, in the complex and interrelated modern world, war no longer profited a nation: consequently the time had arrived when nations should abolish war as a means of policy.[4] It is not recorded precisely what the reaction was

3. The Carnegie Endowment for International Peace had endowed two chairs at the Hochschule, one for a German historian and one for visiting professors.

4. James T. Shotwell, *Lesson of the Last World War: A Brochure* (New York, 1942), p. 12.

to Professor Shotwell's startling thesis, but it would seem that to advocate the abolition of war in front of members of the German War Office staff, wearing all their wartime decorations, was an ambitious performance.

The American professor after his address at the Hochschule believed his thesis might be more welcome elsewhere, perhaps at Paris. He consequently journeyed to the French capital and with the help of his friend Albert Thomas, director of the International Labor Organization at Geneva, obtained an interview with Briand.

Shotwell and Thomas on March 22, 1927, were ushered into the French foreign minister's office at the Quai d'Orsay. Professor Shotwell there stood face to face with Aristide Briand. Shotwell, transparently sincere, eager to promote the cause of international peace, fondly cherishing Andrew Carnegie's ringing injunction to "hasten the abolition of international war, the foulest blot upon our civilization." Briand, one of the wisest French statesmen of his generation, engrossed in the tragic quest for French security, unwearily searching for ways to increase the number of France's faithful allies in the not impossible event of the Next War. Briand probably smiled as he shook hands with his guest, the professor from the United States.

Professor Shotwell found Briand depressed over the misunderstanding in the United States of what Americans called French militarism.[5] France had just refused an American invitation to a disarmament conference. President Coolidge recently had proposed a five-power naval disarmament conference to be held at Geneva in the early summer of 1927 and the French Government, still smarting over its treatment at the Washington conference [6] (where Briand, incidentally, had headed the French delegation), had not seen its way clear to enter another conference. "This naturally," Shotwell wrote later, "carried us over to the question of war renunciation, and I suggested that the best way for M. Briand to meet such suspicion of French militarism would be for him, in the name of France, to propose renunciation of war as an instrument of

5. The following account is from Shotwell's *Lesson of the Last World War*, p. 13.

6. See above, pp. 43-44.

national policy and that a treaty should be made along that line." Briand responded that all his efforts had been to that great end. He affirmed, however, that he was ready to proceed to a more definite statement, and it was agreed that he should address a letter to the American people on April 6, 1927, the tenth anniversary of America's entry into the World War.

Before examining Briand's public message of April 6 we should mention a current irritant of Franco-American relations other than French refusal to attend the Geneva Naval Conference. In the spring of 1927 the war debt question had reached an impasse. Ambassador Myron T. Herrick wrote from Paris to Secretary of State Frank B. Kellogg on January 19, 1927, that as a result of "buck-passing" between Premier Poincaré and the Chamber of Deputies' Commission on Finance, the Chamber had indefinitely shelved ratification of the Mellon-Béranger debt-funding agreement. Herrick, the suave, polished *doyen* of American diplomats abroad, did not believe the Chamber would lift the debt question off the shelf until Poincaré gave the word, and that might not occur until after the French elections in 1928.[7] The American ambassador on March 1 did receive a letter from Poincaré with a signed annex promising to pay ten million dollars on June 15.[8] But simultaneously the French Government was expressing its desire to refund in the United States the eight-per-cent loan issued by France in 1920; the French treasury insisted that a lower interest rate was necessary. This wish to refund the eight-per-cent loan, when coupled with the shelving of the Mellon-Béranger agreement, raised a delicate problem, for the United States Government had placed a ban on all loans to countries failing to refund and to begin payment on their war debts.[9] It is not impossible, there-

7. Herrick to Kellogg, Jan. 19, 1927, 800.51W89 France/460, records of the Department of State now deposited in the National Archives. Hereafter all documentary citations followed by file numbers refer to the records of the Department of State.

8. Herrick to Kellogg, Mar. 1, 1927, 800.51W89 France/477.

9. During the Harding Administration the State Department made a voluntary arrangement with American bankers permitting the Department to scan foreign loans. From this arrangement arose the ban on loans to countries failing to refund and to begin payment on war debts. For a lucid exposition of Ameri-

fore, that when Shotwell found Briand depressed over Franco-American relations not only the matter of the Geneva conference but also the problem of the war debts weighed heavily on Briand's thoughts.[10] (And did not Briand also think of the new system of French alliances, and the desirability, if it were possible, of a pact with the United States?)

As April 6 drew near, France's determination to stay away from the Geneva conference became more evident. Ambassador Herrick on April 3 sent to Secretary Kellogg a *note verbale* of the French Government, dated April 2, in which France deferred sending even an observer to the forthcoming conference.[11] This disappointing news appeared in the New York *Times* of April 5.

II

Salmon O. Levinson and family left Chicago for New York on Wednesday, April 6, 1927, preparatory to sailing the following Saturday on the *Leviathan* for a long-awaited trip to Europe.[12] One can only imagine Levinson's great surprise when, as the train neared Cleveland, he nonchalantly took up a newspaper purchased from a train newsboy and beheld a proposal to outlaw war, made by no less a personage than Aristide Briand, foreign minister of France!

In a message addressed directly to the American people Briand proposed to renounce and outlaw all war between France and the United States. "The discussions over disarmament," he affirmed,

---

can postwar lending policies, see Herbert Feis, *The Diplomacy of the Dollar: First Era 1919–1932* (Baltimore, 1950).

10. But see Professor Shotwell's vigorous denial: "The charges made in a part of the conservative American press that M. Briand was merely playing with the formula of peace in order to secure better terms of debt settlement is not only unworthy but untrue." James T. Shotwell, *War as an Instrument of National Policy: And Its Renunciation in the Pact of Paris* (New York, Harcourt, Brace, 1929), p. 49. Shotwell reasoned that Premier Poincaré had charge of the debt negotiations, not Briand. But did the French Government so utterly compartmentalize its activities?

11. *FR: 1927*, I, 31–32.

12. As early as March 17 Levinson had taken reservations on the *Leviathan* for April 9.

. . . have served at least to make clear, politically, the common inspiration and identity of aims which exist between France and the United States. . . . If there were any need between these two great democracies to testify more convincingly in favor of peace and to present to the peoples a more solemn example, France would be ready publicly to subscribe, with the United States, to any mutual engagement tending, as between those two countries, to 'outlaw war,' to use an American expression. The renunciation of war as an instrument of national policy is a conception already familiar to the signatories of the Covenant of the League of Nations and of the Treaties of Locarno. Any engagement subscribed to in the same spirit by the United States with another nation such as France would greatly contribute in the eyes of the world to broaden and strengthen the foundation upon which the international policy of peace is being raised. Thus two great friendly nations, equally devoted to the cause of peace, would give the world the best illustrations of this truth, that the accomplishment most immediately to be attained is not so much disarmament as the practice of peace.[13]

Here was success! Outlawry, full of promise for world peace, had entered into the calculations of the foreign minister of France! Salmon Levinson, "Captain General" [14] of the Outlawry cohorts, must have been speechless with joy as he read the message from his new supporter. After nearly ten years of ceaseless propagandizing Levinson suddenly had met with success.

More careful readers of Briand's proposition perhaps noticed its preoccupation with France's failure to attend the Geneva Disarmament Conference. Reference to the conference ran like a thread through Briand's entire message. A few readers may have observed, moreover, the extremely clever way in which Briand juxtaposed Outlawry of war (the Levinson program) with renunciation of war as an instrument of national policy (Shotwell's thesis).

13. *FR: 1927*, II, 611–613. This is a translation of a copy received by the Department of State from Paul Claudel, the French ambassador, May 28, 1927.

14. So Colonel Robins frequently addressed him.

But the most astute phrasing of Briand's message was the studied casualness with which he introduced his proposal of friendship: "If there were any need between these two great democracies to testify more convincingly in favor of peace and to present to the peoples a more solemn example . . ."

This message of April 6, 1927, to the American people might well rank as one of Briand's most felicitous compositions—and Briand was famous as a master of the apt phrase. Professor Shotwell, however, in a recent conversation with the writer, declared he wrote the Briand message himself and that the French foreign minister, after insignificant verbal changes, obligingly released it to the press.[15] Shotwell said nothing publicly at that time about the real authorship of the message.[16]

Senator Borah nonetheless learned of it through an American living in Paris, Joseph Agan, who volunteered the news in a letter of May 7, 1927.[17] Briand, Agan wrote, had agreeably repeated on April 6 Shotwell's draft, word for word.[18] Borah promptly replied to his correspondent in Paris that he, Borah, now knew from Agan's letter what Briand had done. In fact, the senator thought so highly of Agan's letter that he instructed his secretary to make a number of copies to send out to friends.[19] Borah the isolationist must have enjoyed knowing that he had learned about the activities of his foe, the League advocate Shotwell.

Agan also told Borah that, concerning Briand's proposition to

15. Conversation of Dec. 6, 1949, in Professor Shotwell's office in New York at the Carnegie Endowment for International Peace. (Having retired from Columbia, Professor Shotwell was then president of the Endowment.)

16. Privately Shotwell told John Dewey that he had written Briand's message. Dewey to Salmon O. Levinson, Feb. 29, 1928, Levinson MSS, deposited in the Library of the University of Chicago.

17. Agan was no ordinary informant. An accomplished scholar, he was the author of *The Diplomatic Relations of the United States and Brazil*, Vol. I, *The Portuguese Court at Rio de Janeiro* (Paris, 1926). His untimely death prevented publication of sequent volumes.

18. Joseph Agan to William E. Borah, May 7, 1927, Borah MSS.

19. There are carbon copies in the Borah MSS. Borah's official biographer, Claudius O. Johnson, in *Borah of Idaho* (New York, Longmans, Green, 1936), pp. 397–398, quotes extensively from the Agan letter and describes it as "exact information."

outlaw war between France and the United States, when Frenchmen did not laugh at the proposal they considered it an offer of alliance, for Frenchmen believed that Americans owed such an offer to France. This, too, Borah accepted as the truth. Indeed, Briand's proposed pact did resemble a negative military alliance: in any future war in which France engaged—say a war with Germany—the United States Government, having adhered to an antiwar treaty with the French Government, would in effect have announced its neutrality in advance; France would hold the assurance that under no circumstances—even if France grossly violated American neutrality, as Britain had done in the World War— would the United States enter the war against France. Furthermore, such a pact would be of inestimable prestige value to France even in times of peace. "Look here," Frenchmen could say to their restless German neighbors, "*We* have a pact with the United States." France already possessed an impressive array of alliances with European countries. To this grand design for her security she could add the most powerful of non-Continental nations, the United States of America. That this was Briand's purpose would seem evident from (1) his announced desire to outlaw war between France and the United States, and (2) the fact that the most recent French alliances themselves actually resembled bilateral Outlawry treaties. According to Article 1 of the Rumanian treaty: "France and Rumania mutually undertake that they will in no case attack or invade each other or resort to war against each other." Professor Shotwell nevertheless—ever since he talked with Briand on March 22, 1927—has reiterated in his books and speeches that Briand had no such scheme in mind. ". . . I owe it to the memory of M. Briand," wrote Shotwell during the 1930's, "to deny categorically the statement that he fathered this proposal with an eye to enticing the United States into a disguised alliance with France. . . . He could not speak for any other nation and therefore limited his offer for the outlawry of war to the United States and France . . ." [20] Recently Professor Shotwell vigorously assured the

20. James T. Shotwell, *On the Rim of the Abyss* (New York, Macmillan, 1936), pp. 132–134. As for the interpretation of a negative military alliance, Professor Shotwell wrote in his earlier *War as an Instrument of National Policy,*

present writer that Briand was by no stretch of the imagination angling for a negative alliance.[21] No one would gainsay Shotwell's veracity on this point, least of all this writer: Shotwell believed Briand, and we believe he believed him; but no experienced diplomatist would do so.

III

The message of April 6, 1927, appeared on page five of the New York *Times,* and on page twelve of the *Herald-Tribune.* A search in some other American newspapers indicates even more indifference to Briand's truly notable proposal.[22] Much more newspaper space went to the now-forgotten Butler-Borah debate on prohibition held April 8 at Boston: Borah wished to outlaw rum rather than war, but Butler maintained that was too difficult.[23]

There followed after Briand's proposal a nineteen-day lull during which Professor Shotwell was sailing across the ocean to New York and Salmon O. Levinson by sheer coincidence was proceeding in the opposite direction to Paris.

---

p. 116: "This argument subsequently gained credence from its constant iteration and ultimately became an accepted part of what may be called the mythical history of the Briand peace proposal." In support of Professor Shotwell's views stands the opinion of David Hunter Miller, who for many years was the treaty expert of the Department of State. In his *Peace Pact of Paris: A Study of the Briand-Kellogg Treaty* (New York, G. P. Putnam's Sons, 1928), p. 16, n. 2, Miller wrote: ". . . the view advanced in some quarters that such a treaty with France would have been in the nature of a 'defensive alliance' is wholly untenable and mistaken."

21. Conversation of Dec. 6, 1949.

22. The Washington *Post* displayed the story on page four. The Chicago *Daily Tribune* and the Los Angeles *Times* ignored it altogether.

23. Butler championed repeal and Borah opposed. Prohibition, said Butler that night, "raises issues more important, as I view it, than any which the American people have been called upon to face since our fathers and our grandfathers had to deal with the issue of slavery and secession." The exciting Butler-Borah contest reminded some spectators of the Lincoln-Douglas debates. Six of the nine "unofficial" judges selected by the Boston *Herald*—four wet, four dry, and one neutral—gave the verdict to Borah. For a good account, see "The Butler-Borah Debate on Prohibition," *Literary Digest, 93* (Apr. 23, 1927), 10.

Suddenly on the morning of April 25, 1927, there appeared in the New York *Times* a letter to the editor from Nicholas Murray Butler. The president of Columbia pointed out that the Briand proposal of April 6 had "every merit of practicability and practicality," and that such a proposition, coming from the foreign minister of France, must have been offered with the consent of the French Cabinet. A pact renouncing war between France and the United States would be "progressive and constructive," Butler wrote. "The adhesion and cooperation of other powers would, of course, be secured later on, but the first thing is to act, and unless the American people are both physically and morally deaf, they will hear and will act quickly." Butler mentioned "those moral forces" which, when aroused, stir and compel governmental action. "M. Briand's mind is thoroughly practical," he reminded the *Times* readers; Briand asked not for American membership in the League, or Locarno, or the World Court; all he asked was a Franco-American renunciation of war. "M. Briand, speaking the voice and expressing the soul of France," Butler concluded, "has called out to us across the ocean. What answer is he to hear?" [24]

Briand had not called out in vain. The New York *Times,* with which President Butler must have had some intimate connections,[25] spoke up for renunciation of war the very day it printed Butler's letter. In an editorial, "Ending Wars One by One," the *Times* noticed how odd it was that Senator Borah had kept silent after Briand's démarche of April 6, for Borah was "a passionate advocate of outlawing war." The *Times* thought that outlawing war universally would be difficult, but outlawing one war at a time—war between France and the United States—would be a step forward.

It is altogether remarkable how President Butler's letter to the New York *Times* awakened interest in Briand's proposal. Before April 25 almost no one gave attention to the April 6 message. But after the 25th there suddenly began a rush for the band wagon, hitherto so empty. Upon reading Butler's letter Senators Norris and

24. New York *Times,* Apr. 25, 1927.

25. The *Times* throughout the campaign which followed the printing of Butler's letter was extremely cooperative, keeping the fires of renunciation of war burning either with editorials or by printing letters to the editor.

Copeland were reported as saying that "We should jump at the chance." Senator Shipstead declared Briand was "entitled to the gratitude of the world." Senator King avowed that "the noble suggestion should be promptly accepted." [26] But Senator Borah maintained stony silence.

Edwin L. James, the New York *Times* astute and exceptionally well-informed Paris correspondent who often voiced opinions of the French Foreign Office,[27] soon reported that not a single Frenchman would oppose a nonaggression pact with the United States. Butler's letter, James wrote, was widely commented upon in parliamentary and diplomatic circles: in Paris some persons even raised the possibility of a three-cornered peace compact, with England as the third partner; for according to Briand's friends the French foreign minister for some time past had been nursing the idea of an Atlantic Locarno. Briand, reported James, had hoped the suggestion might come from Washington, for there was somewhat of a natural timidity among European statesmen about suggesting anything to Washington. It was believed that a private citizen from America, however, had offered a scheme close to that of Briand. The dispatch concluded by alleging that if President Coolidge should inject Briand's offer into the deliberations of the Naval Disarmament Conference the French would be very happy and might even send a delegate to Geneva.[28]

The New York *Times* London correspondent reported British opinion as cool toward Briand's proposal. The British press was virtually ignoring the French foreign minister's new offer. Students of world politics, reported the London correspondent, were reluctant to see France and America join hands perpetually.[29]

Beating the drum in front of the band wagon, the New York

26. New York *Times,* Apr. 26, 1927.

27. William R. Castle, in 1927 assistant secretary of state in charge of western European affairs, recently told the writer that the Quai d'Orsay under Briand consistently "leaked" information through James' Paris dispatches to the New York *Times.* Hence James' dispatches often had a semi-official character.

28. New York *Times,* Apr. 27, 1927.

29. New York *Times,* Apr. 29, 1927.

Times on May 2 again wondered editorially why Borah had not yet "found his voice" regarding Briand's remarkable offer. The *Times* did not know that Borah had found his voice several days before in a private letter to Sherwood Eddy. Confidentially, the senator told Eddy, Briand's idea of Outlawry was so utterly different from his and Eddy's that he could not seriously and conscientiously take any stand on the matter. ". . . I wish I knew," the puzzled Borah mused, "of some way by which to apply Briand's statement as a practical proposition to the Chinese situation [the civil war then raging in China]." [30]

On the evening of May 2 the League of Nations Non-Partisan Association held a dinner in New York, and Professor Shotwell spoke. The association adopted a resolution approving the Briand proposal and sent copies to President Coolidge, Secretary of State Kellogg, and every member of the Senate. In a letter of reply addressed to the association's chairman, Raymond B. Fosdick, Senator Borah finally made his first public statement. Borah trusted that Briand would reduce his suggestions to the form of a draft treaty, so that the United States Government could deal "intelligently" with the subject of Outlawry. [31]

Meanwhile the Coolidge Administration remained officially silent. When Secretary Kellogg on May 12 duly made his reply to Fosdick and the League Non-Partisan Association, he simply took pleasure in conveying "an expression of appreciation of your courtesy" in transmitting the association's resolution. [32] Unlike Senator Borah, the secretary of state—speaking, as he had to, as a representative of the United States Government—did not make even the slightest hint to the association that the French foreign minister should offer, for purposes of negotiation, a draft treaty. Rumor had it that the president and Secretary Kellogg were piqued

30. Borah to Sherwood Eddy, Apr. 29, 1927, Borah MSS. To Professor Jerome Davis of Yale Borah wrote on May 3: "I do not know just how much politics and how much outlawry there is in this [Briand] statement . . ." Borah MSS.

31. Borah to Raymond B. Fosdick, May 4, 1927, in the New York *Times*, May 6, 1927.

32. Kellogg to Fosdick, May 12, 1927, 711.5112 France/2.

because Briand had addressed his message to the American people
instead of through proper diplomatic channels.[33]

President Coolidge indeed was piqued. Dr. Henry S. Pritchett
of the Carnegie Foundation for the Advancement of Teaching
wrote to Coolidge on May 7 soliciting a presidential interview for
Professor Shotwell. Shotwell, Pritchett wrote, had had three weeks
ago a highly informative conference with Briand, and Coolidge
might be interested in it. After consulting the president, Coolidge's
secretary noted at the bottom of Pritchett's letter that "Pres advised no suggestion from French Govt has come to State Dept. Until such suggestion is made by French to Am govt Pres sees no
advantage in conferring with volunteers." [34]

Perhaps Coolidge, speaking of volunteers, remembered a certain famous incident in American diplomatic history. During the
United States' undeclared maritime war with France at the end of
the eighteenth century a well-meaning but naive American Quaker,
one George Logan, had approached the French Minister Talley-
rand with suggestions for amicable adjustment of Franco-American
relations. His volunteer mission led Congress in 1799 to pass the
celebrated Logan Act, stipulating that if any American citizen
"shall, without the permission or authority of the government of
the United States, directly or indirectly, commence, or carry on,
any verbal or written correspondence or intercourse with any for-

33. The State Department truly maintained a studied silence. On May 12
J. Theodore Marriner, chief of the Department's Division of Western European
Affairs, wrote a memorandum to Assistant Secretary William R. Castle proposing that, because of the pressure on the Department to do something about
the Briand proposal, one of the correspondents be primed to ask Kellogg a
question on the proposal at the next press conference, at which time Kellogg
would be primed to mention the Bryan and Root treaties and state that he
thought they sufficed for what Briand had in mind. Castle bucked this proposal
of Marriner's to Michael J. McDermott, the Department's press officer, who
asked Kellogg about it. Kellogg replied that it would be better to let the matter
drop and not to bring it up and bear the responsibility of gracing Briand's proposal—transmitted through the press only—with an official explanation. 711.-
5112 France/45.

34. Coolidge MSS. The secretary then wrote to Dr. Pritchett the president's
thanks and recommendation that Pritchett take up the matter with the secretary of state.

eign government . . . with an intent to influence the measures or
conduct of any foreign government . . . in relation to any disputes or controversies with the United States, or defeat the measures of the government of the United States . . . [he] shall be
punished by a fine not exceeding five thousand dollars, and by
imprisonment during a term not less than six months, nor exceeding three years." [35]

President Coolidge, although he may well have desired to,
probably never would have attempted to invoke the Logan Act
against Professor Shotwell, Dr. Butler, et al. Public opinion would
not have permitted such action—although Shotwell, Butler, and
other peace leaders probably had incriminated themselves. Small
wonder, however, that Coolidge, dictating letters to his stenographer, was irritated at the prospect of American citizens taking
delicate diplomatic negotiations into their own hands, making it
easy for the foreign minister of France to use their inexperience to
advance his own arrangements.[36]

And how did Secretary Kellogg regard this situation?

Physically a small person with gnarled and shaking hands,
white-haired, seventy years of age in 1927, Frank B. Kellogg was
at the end of a long and successful public career. He had risen to

35. *U.S. Statutes at Large,* I, 313.

36. Coolidge's annoyance at the diplomatic activities of Shotwell and Butler
may also have had another basis. Was there not an underlying antagonism between the president of Columbia and the president of the United States, an
antagonism which reflected itself throughout all their relations?

Butler, a prominent Republican, was a perennial dark horse candidate for
the Republican presidential nomination. From examination of the Butler MSS
at Columbia, it appears that Butler at times even cultivated his candidacy, although in carefully sheltered ways—such as modestly encouraging his friends to
activity, or himself making speeches or advocating issues at strategic moments.
Shortly after Coolidge, anent the Briand negotiations, referred to Butler and
Shotwell as volunteers, Butler in the New York *Times* of May 21, 1927, volunteered the opinion that Coolidge would not run for a third term in 1928. It
has always been a controversial question as to whether Coolidge desired the
1928 nomination. Although Coolidge eventually did not choose to run, he
perhaps would have liked to have been drafted. If so, then Butler's volunteer
opinion of May 21, 1927, made the president of Columbia definitely persona
non grata at the White House, if he had not been so before.

the third highest office in the government of the United States. In many ways Kellogg's life was a classic example of the triumph of the "American dream"—the success, in American democracy, of sheer ability. As a boy, Kellogg had migrated with his parents from New York State to Minnesota, just after the Civil War. In a Rochester, Minnesota, law office the future secretary of state received his formal education. Kellogg never attended a grade school or yet a high school. He never went to college.[37] But as a young lawyer he rose rapidly, achieving fame as a trust-buster under President Theodore Roosevelt; he prosecuted the Standard Oil Company. Kellogg then turned corporation lawyer (surrendering himself, according to some critics, to the interests he hitherto had fought). In 1917 he entered the Senate, but at the end of his first term he met electoral defeat at the hands of a Farmer-Laborite opponent, an erstwhile dentist and extraordinarily competent politician, Henrik Shipstead. Soon thereafter Kellogg became American ambassador at the Court of St. James. In 1925 he was translated to the high office of secretary of state.

At the State Department Frank B. Kellogg became noted for his industry and also his explosive and often profane temper. Especially the temper. The secretary of state would arrive at his office at approximately 8:45 A.M. On his desk was a keyboard with buttons which summoned the various officers of the Department. If Kellogg had read something irritating in the morning paper before he reached his office, he would strike the keyboard like a piano concertmaster, all fingers at once, and summon everybody he could think of. As Department officers scurried into the secretary's office he would greet them with a storm of rage.[38] One can thus realize the Kellogg humor on the morning he read Nicholas Murray Butler's letter to the New York *Times*.

Kellogg quickly let Butler know how he felt. The secretary of

37. Occasionally, as secretary of state, Kellogg revealed certain minor gaps in his education. Reading his speeches, the secretary would encounter the phrase "M. Briand," and likely as not would pronounce the "M" as if it were Briand's first initial.

38. Hugh R. Wilson, *Diplomat between Wars* (New York, Longmans, Green, 1941), p. 174. Wilson for a while was Kellogg's press officer.

state sent word through a mutual friend, George Barton French of New York.

French met Kellogg in Washington at the Mayflower, and the secretary immediately started talking about Butler's peace activities. At no time during the conversation did he mention Butler personally, although the implication remained altogether clear. Kellogg angrily asserted that Butler and French were a set of "——— ——— fools" making unworkable suggestions which could have no issue except temporarily to embarrass the State Department and himself. The secretary of state added, by way of emphasis, that if there was one thing in the world he hated, it was the "——— ——— pacifists." In later recalling this incident for the edification of Butler, French remarked on Frank Kellogg's having a doctor's degree in profanity and invectives and being given when excited to raising his voice. Mrs. French, trying to visit with Mrs. Kellogg at the other end of the Mayflower salon, therefore easily heard much of the talk between her husband and the secretary of state. When the Kelloggs departed she advised her husband to telephone Butler at once and tell him that the State Department opposed his peace activities and that Frank Kellogg undoubtedly was going to fight them.[39]

With this heavy note of official disapproval there ended one of the most notable chapters in the history of what later became the Kellogg-Briand multilateral treaty for the renunciation of war. Briand's suggestion for renunciation of war—between France and the United States—manifestly had received a very mixed reception in America. Although peace leaders such as Dr. Butler, Professor Shotwell, and Salmon O. Levinson found Briand's proposal an answer to their fondest hopes, the Coolidge Administration, in the

39. French orally reported this conversation to Butler immediately upon returning to New York. Butler's reply to Kellogg was, "We must let public opinion have something to say about that." Nicholas Murray Butler, *Across the Busy Years*, II, 208. Butler, ever with an eye to posterity, later (Jan. 20, 1930) wrote to French asking "for my personal files, an exact record of the happening when Frank Kellogg called upon you in Washington and made his statement about the principle of what is now become the Pact of Paris." French replied the next day, Jan. 21, 1930. Butler MSS, deposited in the Library of Columbia University. By permission of Columbia University.

words of Secretary of State Kellogg, regarded the enthusiastic peace leaders as a set of "——— ——— fools" making foolish suggestions. "Volunteers," snapped Coolidge to his stenographer. "——— ——— pacifists," Kellogg shouted to French. Surely the peace leaders and the Coolidge Administration disagreed violently over Briand's proposal.

This of course is precisely the type of situation which constantly arises in the diplomacy of a democracy: public opinion imperatively demanding a course of action which, in the considered opinion of the government, is impossible to pursue. In this particular instance the foreign minister of France, Aristide Briand, had gone over the heads of the American Government to send his subtle message to the American people. Garbed in the alluring rhetoric of friendship and peace, the foreign minister's proposal soon attracted the American peace workers. They espied a new highway to peace, untraveled. Down it they rushed joyously. And what could the Coolidge Administration say publicly to these good people who were also voters? Could Secretary Kellogg baldly announce Briand's real objectives? Briand would only, in a very hurt and most sincere manner, deny them. Could the administration coldly reject the French foreign minister's overture? Such rejection would indicate lack of interest in world peace—and just around the political corner waited the Democrats, athirst for public office, eager to find the Republicans inattentive to proposals for world peace.[40] What course of action, then, was politic? Obviously the American Government, confronting Briand's new proposition, confronting also the American electorate, would not be able to speak frankly in public; and, if it had to act, must employ the devious wordings and tactics of the new diplomacy.

Perhaps there was no need for action. President Coolidge and Secretary of State Kellogg had not yet embarked on official negotiations with the French Government. The Briand proposition still was only an unofficial affair between the foreign minister and the American people—to whom, as Dr. Butler put it, Briand had "called out across the ocean." Suppose the American people should forget Briand's call to renunciation and Outlawry? Disillusioned

40. The next year, 1928, was a presidential election year.

by the World War Americans had not exhibited much regard for Frenchmen, and the war debts and forthcoming Geneva Naval Disarmament Conference could be counted upon to keep the kettle of mutual animosity simmering. Perhaps the Coolidge Administration thus would not have to answer Briand's embarrassing proposal.

Unfortunately for the administration, and providentially for Aristide Briand and the peace forces, there now occurred an adventitious event of breath-taking interest to the entire world, an event which tightened remarkably the hitherto loose bonds of Franco-American amity.

On May 21, 1927, Lindbergh landed at Le Bourget.

Chapter Seven: AIRPLANE DIPLOMACY

Over a hundred thousand wildly cheering Frenchmen saw the silvery *Spirit of St. Louis* slip from the evening sky as if by a miracle and land at Le Bourget after a nonstop flight all the way from New York. France joyously and unreservedly took the boyish Lindbergh to her heart. Ambassador Herrick soon was writing Secretary Kellogg that Lindbergh had done more to improve Franco-American relations than years of effort by the professional diplomats.[1] In like manner the American people took vicarious pleasure in their Lindbergh's gracious reception in France, and much of the hard anti-French feeling in America began at last to disappear. Truly, this "airplane diplomacy" was effective.[2]

1. ". . . the arrival of Captain Lindbergh in Paris and the week's visit which he spent here have created an entirely new atmosphere in the relations between the two countries. . . . A small example of the feeling which exists is the fact that the crowds outside the Hotel de Ville, upon the occasion of Lindbergh's reception there, cheered not only for Lindbergh but for the United States." Herrick to Kellogg, June 2, 1927, 800.51W89 France/495 1/2.

An incentive for Lindbergh's flight to Paris was the $25,000 prize offered by Raymond Orteig, a Frenchman. Orteig was filled with a burning desire to increase Franco-American amity. See John Lardner, "The Lindbergh Legends," in Isabel Leighton, ed., *The Aspirin Age,* pp. 198–199.

2. A few days before Lindbergh successfully flew the Atlantic the French aviators Nungessor and Coli left Paris for New York. As the hours passed and no news came from the two gallant Frenchmen there began a frantic search of the Atlantic for telltale wreckage. President Lebrun of France exchanged

There was another, almost intangible but yet exceedingly important, result of Lindbergh's magnificent flight to Paris. Lindbergh had valorously shown that the "impossible" was possible. Idealists everywhere began to take heart. Workers for world peace received new courage. People all over the world felt like doing, rather than talking—a spirit which the following little dialect verse so well catches:

> Vile udder folks talkin'
>   An' vunderin' how,
> An' ban gettin' ready
>   Purty soon but not now,
> By yiminy, Lindbergh,
>   He yumped up an' vaded
> Right out in the air
>   An', by yingo, he made it. [3]

I

Briand gave a lunch for Lindbergh on May 26, and the French foreign minister seized the occasion to inform Herrick that he wished to talk with him in a few days about the suggested pact between France and the United States. Briand said that the reception of the idea was so favorable that it ought to be studied, but that he did not desire to move unless he was in entire agreement with President Coolidge.[4] This seemingly casual conversation with Herrick marked the first time Briand had mentioned his proposal to an American diplomat.

The next development did not come from the professionals like Briand and Herrick, but rather from those two irrepressible volunteer diplomats, Nicholas Murray Butler and James T. Shotwell.

Shortly after his letter appeared in the New York Times Dr.

---

messages with President Coolidge, and the tragedy already was bringing together the peoples of France and the United States when Lindbergh flew out of New York toward Paris.

3. From a poem by James W. Foley, "How Lindbergh Did It," in the New York Times, May 31, 1927.

4. Herrick to Kellogg, May 27, 1927, FR: 1927, II, 613.

Butler went to Washington to attend the annual meeting of the trustees of the Carnegie Endowment for International Peace. While in the capital he visited the State Department and saw Undersecretary Robert E. Olds, who was himself a trustee of the Endowment. Butler inquired what action the Department intended to take in reference to Briand's proposal. "To my astonishment," wrote Butler later, "the answer of Mr. Olds was that they did not propose to do anything. I criticized this attitude most sharply, pointing out its impoliteness and its lack of vision." After such sharp reproof Colonel Olds asked Butler what *he* thought the Department should do. Butler replied that since they had neglected to act promptly they should draft a treaty and offer it for discussion with Briand. "What sort of a treaty?" countered Colonel Olds. "Why do you not yourself outline what you have in mind?" So Butler journeyed back to New York and summoned his colleagues, Professors Shotwell and Joseph P. Chamberlain, the latter a professor of law at Columbia. The two professors set to work on a draft treaty.[5]

When a draft was ready Shotwell showed it to Olds at the State Department. According to Shotwell the undersecretary approved it and desired it to be put up as a trial balloon.[6] Shotwell sent Colonel Olds a copy of the final draft of the proposed treaty on May 25 with the news that he was releasing the draft to the American and European press on the following Tuesday. He told Olds he sincerely hoped "the test of public opinion which should come from the publication of this treaty will help you."[7]

Professor Shotwell presented his draft during Memorial Day exercises at Columbia University, May 30, 1927. Both he and Dr. Butler made speeches. The next day the text of "An American Locarno" appeared in the press.[8]

Briefly, the draft treaty had three parts: Renunciation of War, Arbitration and Conciliation, and Ratification. Specifically ex-

5. Nicholas Murray Butler, *Across the Busy Years*, II, 207.
6. James T. Shotwell to Nicholas Murray Butler, May 18, 1927, Butler MSS.
7. Shotwell to Robert E. Olds, May 25, 1927, 711.5112 France/7.
8. For the text of the Shotwell-Chamberlain draft, see Shotwell's *War as an Instrument of National Policy*, pp. 271–278.

cepted from Part I were self-defense and the Monroe Doctrine. In case of a breach of the treaty the parties recovered full liberty of action. Part II reserved from arbitration or conciliation all matters of domestic jurisdiction. Reserved from arbitration also were questions of vital interest, independence, or national honor, or disputes involving third parties. Each case to be arbitrated required— as did the Root treaties—advice and consent of the United States Senate. Indeed, the Shotwell-Chamberlain draft was only a composite of the Bryan [9] and Root treaties. The Foreign Policy Association announced after studying the new draft treaty that it showed few innovations when compared to the existing treaties with France. But the draft treaty's proposal for the renunciation of war, the association believed, "introduces a new feature never applied previously in the case of an American treaty." [10]

Professor Shotwell in his history of the negotiation of the Kellogg-Briand Pact has written that his draft treaty became "an item of national and even international news," copied from paper to paper and greatly commented upon.[11] He may be right, although it is doubtful if a long and complicated draft treaty drew much attention from the man in the street. The Shotwell-Chamberlain draft probably appealed only to a few conscientious newspaper readers and to students of various sorts. It may have had an influence in another respect, however, which shall be noted later.[12]

9. The "cooling-off" conciliation treaties negotiated by Woodrow Wilson's secretary of state. These treaties forbade during a cooling-off period any outbreak of hostilities between signatories. In the meantime a conciliation commission would investigate and bring in a report.

10. New York *Times,* May 31, 1927.

11. James T. Shotwell, *War as an Instrument of National Policy,* p. 54.

12. Below, pp. 96–97, 162. There were at least two competitors to the Shotwell-Chamberlain draft treaty. The Women's International League for Peace and Freedom and the American Arbitration Crusade made public on June 2, 1927, a draft treaty by Dr. Francis E. Sayre, professor of law at Harvard and Woodrow Wilson's son-in-law. Sayre proposed to turn over all justiciable questions (as defined in Article 36 of the World Court protocol) to the World Court; a Permanent Conciliation Commission would deal with all remaining questions—that is, with political questions—of vital interests, independence, or national honor. New York *Times,* June 3, 1927.

The American Foundation made public a draft treaty on May 28. Article 1

Memorial Day is the traditional occasion in the United States for innumerable sermons and speeches on war and peace, and so it was fitting that Ambassador Herrick on May 30, 1927, should deliver a Memorial Day oration at the American military cemetery at Suresnes, France. There were high hopes he would discuss the Outlawry of war. Salmon O. Levinson had arrived on the Continent a week or so after Briand's message of April 6, and among other activities—of which more later—he importuned Herrick to speak about Outlawry on Memorial Day. At Herrick's request Levinson prepared for him a paper setting forth the full Outlawry program. When the day finally came the ambassador, to the disgust of Levinson, devoted himself instead to the Red Peril and the "scourge of Bolshevism." He mentioned Briand's démarche of April 6, but only as evidence of the world's quest to get to the bottom of war.[13]

President Coolidge in his Memorial Day address spoke before more than three thousand people in the marble amphitheater at Arlington. Hundreds more stood outside the enclosure and about the tomb of the unknown soldier, where they heard his speech through amplifiers. The president spoke into a microphone which carried his address to distant points by radio in a national network. The United States Government, he declared, desired to discard the element of force and compulsion in international agreements and conduct, relying rather on reason and law. This vision, the president added, would not of course be realized immediately, yet "little by little, step by step, in every practical way," Americans

provided for conciliation, arbitration, or judicial settlement of disputes between states (these three provisions in general terms only), reserving the right of self-defense; Article 2 allowed for settlement by other peaceful means; Article 3 dealt with appointment of members to conciliation commissions and also with the commissions' procedure; Article 4 provided for arbitration through the Hague Court or otherwise, each case requiring a *compromis* advised and consented to by the United States Senate; Article 5 provided for judicial settlement by the World Court, each case also requiring a compromis as in Article 4; Article 6 concerned formation and procedure of special arbitral tribunals, a compromis again being necessary in each case; Article 7 dealt with ratification. New York *Times,* May 29, 1927.

13. New York *Times,* May 31, 1927.

should show their determination. The president said that the United States never had gone to war for aggression, and that in all its history had resorted to war always for a "justifiable cause." He pictured the United States in possession of great wealth and high place, with nearly every civilized nation its debtor.[14]

Memorial Day was a Monday, and the following Thursday afternoon Briand informed Ambassador Herrick that that morning he had received authorization to inquire whether the United States would enter into diplomatic conversations looking toward a pact renouncing war between France and America. Briand believed that discussions should begin before outsiders created complications. He nevertheless would make no move without the approval of Coolidge.[15]

The very day Briand talked with Herrick the New York *Times* carried a dispatch from Paris reporting that if ever Briand received the least hint that the United States would accept his proposal, or was willing to discuss it, then Briand would use the occasion to develop his idea and make every possible effort to conclude a definite treaty. According to the *Times* Paris correspondent Briand had in mind something less complicated than the Shotwell-Chamberlain draft treaty. Although it was entirely open to the American Government to apply any Atlantic peace compact to nations other than France, Briand was for the present solely for conclusion of such an accord between France and the United States. Even a three-cornered arrangement, adding Britain, although favored by the French Government was not its immediate concern. Briand, wrote the *Times* correspondent, thought that the more public discussion devoted to the Outlawry proposal the easier it would be for the governments concerned to act.[16]

But did not Briand speak differently to Herrick, saying that discussions should begin before outsiders created complications? The State Department had reason to suspect that the French foreign minister was playing a double game, informing the Department that the peace enthusiasts were forcing his hand, all the

14. New York *Times*, May 31, 1927.
15. Herrick to Kellogg, June 2, 1927, *FR: 1927*, II, 613–614.
16. New York *Times*, June 2, 1927.

while urging the peace advocates to force the Department's hand.

Even among the peace workers themselves, Briand did not allow the right hand to know what the left was about. On the one hand he encouraged Butler and Shotwell, helping them to feel that they were in the midst of great events and playing an important role therein. Briand gave the impression that the rival Levinson Outlawry group annoyed him. Shotwell received from Dr. Earl B. Babcock, the Carnegie Endowment's Paris representative, the following cable on May 13: LONG TALK LEGER [Alexis Léger, Briand's confidant and *chef de cabinet*] DISTURBED BECAUSE LEVINSON GROUP SEIZED OUTLAW WAR PHRASE [17] AS ENDORSEMENT THEIR PEACE IDEAS READY WITH FURTHER DECLARATION BUT WISHES APPEAL TO AMERICAN PUBLIC OPINION OF ALL GROUPS NOT ONE CAN BUTLER SUBJECT NEW FORMULAE FOR STATEMENT HERE. Shotwell cabled back immediately: REASSURE LEGER PHRASE OUTLAWRY WAR UNIMPORTANT LEVINSON'S GROUP SUBMERGED IN GENERAL APPROVAL. Shotwell cabled Babcock again on May 18, having learned of Levinson's presence in Paris: TAKE GREAT PAINS TO DISASSOCIATE BRIAND PROPOSAL FROM LEVINSON.[18] Clearly, the Butler-Shotwell group believed that they alone were Briand's intimates and that the Levinson group were on the outside.

Little did Shotwell and Butler suspect that Léger had a different story for Salmon O. Levinson in Paris. In a diary of his European trip Levinson recorded on May 23, 1927, that Léger "told us he had spent [a] two-day week end with M. Briand at the latter's country place and that M. Briand was in full accord with every thing we were doing in developing and offering to America an Outlawry Treaty by France." And later, on June 4, Levinson wrote that "we met Léger at his office at 11 o'clock. He told us that he and Briand had been very much disturbed by the outside interference of Shotwell and others at Columbia University prematurely and

17. In Briand's Apr. 6 message.
18. Shotwell to Robert E. Olds, May 25, 1927, 711.5112 France/7. Professor Shotwell did not send these cables from animus against Levinson personally, but rather from fear that Levinson's arduous activity in Europe would influence the Quai d'Orsay against renunciation of war. Professor Shotwell to the writer, Sept. 20, 1951.

without warrant offering a form of Outlawry Treaty burdened with many complicated promises, etc. Léger spoke with a great deal of feeling and quite at length." [19]

Levinson, unaware of the thin ice of French intrigue over which he skated, made a remarkable performance of his several weeks' stay in Europe. What a coincidence that the founder of the Outlawry movement planned a trip to Europe during the very period when Aristide Briand began to talk about Outlawry! Levinson dedicated his vacation to the cause. Drew Pearson and Constantine Brown later wrote in their *American Diplomatic Game* [20] that Levinson pursued his mission with "all the irrepressible fervor of a howling dervish." Paris, London, and Berlin soon echoed to the arguments of the Chicago lawyer. In his numerous conversations with influential people Levinson refused to receive no for an answer. His life motto was "to turn liabilities into assets." [21] No amount of lukewarmness toward Outlawry could affect his enthusiasm. Only once did he feel personally hurt. That was when Harrison Brown, an enterprising young Englishman who for several years had done odd jobs in Europe for Levinson's Outlawry committee, sought an interview for his employer at the British Foreign Office, only to be told curtly that "the outlawry of war is all buncombe." [22]

The Captain General of Outlawry nonetheless fought on. In England he saw Arthur Ponsonby, J. L. Garvin, and Norman Angell. The Independent Labor party called a special meeting for

19. J. Stoner, *Levinson,* pp. 221, 229–230. It might seem at second glance that Léger and Briand became aroused at Shotwell and Butler only after the Shotwell-Chamberlain draft appeared. Léger, however, told Levinson that Shotwell had given him a copy of the draft treaty early in May (J. Stoner, *Levinson,* p. 232), that is, considerably before Memorial Day when Shotwell published it. Hence if Léger really had wanted to stop Shotwell's drafting activities he easily could have done so. Levinson, it is true, might have discerned this himself, but he appears to have been so elated at Léger's ingenuous pique toward the Shotwell-Butler group that he did not notice the incongruity of Léger's statements.

20. (New York, Doubleday, Doran, 1935), p. 20.

21. J. Stoner, *Levinson, passim.*

22. Levinson to Commander Kenworthy, June 5, 1928, *ibid.,* p. 216.

him. In Paris he talked to editors such as Stephen Lauzanne, who appeared to reconsider a previously skeptical attitude toward Outlawry of war. Motoring to Geneva with Senator Walsh of Montana he there talked with Norman Davis, Arthur Sweetser, and others. He arrived on May 25 in Berlin where he saw officials of the German Foreign Office and also conversed with Jacob Schurman, the American ambassador. While in Berlin Levinson had in mind the coupling of an Outlawry treaty with a deletion of Article 231 [23] from the Treaty of Versailles, together with a comprehensive settlement of all war debts and reparations. Finally, before sailing back to America he again visited Léger. During the leavetaking Briand's chef de cabinet put his arm on Levinson's shoulder and said: "I don't know what we would have done without you in this critical situation. You have been of splendid service to us. I hope we will be able to continue our mutual relations." [24]

II

In the early days of June 1927 as sentiment—impelled by the French Foreign Office, by the volunteer diplomatists, and by airplane diplomacy—was rising in the United States for conclusion of a pact of friendship with France, the State Department, perhaps in imitation of the Quai d'Orsay, began issuing backdoor comments to the press. The New York *Times* Washington correspondent reported on June 7 a belief in governmental circles that a renewal of the expiring [25] Root arbitration treaty with France would be all that was necessary in answer to Briand's proposal of April 6. On June 8 the Department announced—this time by the front door —that Secretary Kellogg would be very glad to discuss anything that looked toward preservation of international peace. The same day the *Times* Washington correspondent obtained the impression "somewhere" that the Briand proposal amounted to a negative military alliance. The thought was current, he reported, that all the

23. The "war guilt" article.
24. J. Stoner, *Levinson*, p. 230.
25. In the spring of 1928.

great powers would have to sign an Outlawry proposal to make it acceptable to the American Government.[26]

But on Friday, June 10, Nicholas Murray Butler debarked at Le Havre. In Paris he brushed aside impatiently the arguments against a proposed Franco-American treaty, arguments such as the need for a debt settlement, the superfluity of a new treaty because of existence of the Bryan and Root treaties, and the difficulty of American neutrality after conclusion of an Outlawry treaty in case France should go to war. "We'll never get anywhere if we are going to talk about the possibility of war whenever we meet with differences of opinion," he sputtered wrathfully. "As to America's interests in the event of a European war, her position would remain juridically exactly the same, regardless of the peace pact, and her recourse would be through juridical channels." [27]

Aristide Briand himself denied the talk about negative alliances. The same day Dr. Butler gave his juridical explanation Briand was reported in the press as saying that his proposed treaty for the renunciation of war should not be regarded as a treaty of alliance or even as a defensive entente. Such a compact as he had in mind would be only a consecration of the hitherto unbroken peace between France and America. According to Briand the proposed treaty should be as simple as possible, containing only a solemn declaration not to resort to war, but to keep the peace always. Such a compact he regarded as infinitely preferable for the moment to any other more grandiose scheme.[28]

On the Friday that Butler arrived in Paris Secretary Kellogg in Washington read in his New York *Times* that Briand, a week before, had given Ambassador Herrick a note proposing how the treaty renouncing war should be framed. The *Times* also declared that Herrick had sent the note off to Washington.[29] Apparently the Quai d'Orsay was putting up another trial balloon. Kellogg cast down his New York *Times* in disgust and irritation and cabled Herrick;

26. New York *Times*, June 9, 1927.
27. *Ibid.*, June 11.
28. New York *Times*, June 10, 1927.
29. *Ibid.*

the ambassador cabled back the next day that he had received no note and had given no information to the press.[30]

While Herrick was cabling back to Kellogg, the secretary of state was sending still another cable to his ambassador in Paris, this time paying back with interest the Quai d'Orsay's latest maneuver. Kellogg instructed Herrick to inform Briand orally that the American Government would be pleased to enter into diplomatic conversations with respect to Briand's proposal. Herrick then was to add that these conversations at first ought to be of an informal nature and that they should be carried on through the French ambassador in Washington when he returned to America (he then was in France).[31] By this skillful counterstroke Secretary Kellogg in effect proposed to stall for weeks the unwanted negotiations for a bilateral antiwar treaty.

But Kellogg could not stop the irresistible march of public opinion. On Thursday, June 16, having been in France not quite a week, Dr. Butler made a speech before the American Club in Paris. Butler now proposed an agreement between France and the United States which would be short and plain, a proposal in marked contrast to the involved provisions of the Shotwell-Chamberlain draft. There should be only three paragraphs declaring: (1) that France and the United States renounced war as an instrument of their policy in dealing with each other; (2) that both accepted the Locarno definition of an aggressor;[32] (3) that each agreed not to aid an aggressor in case of war. The club members and their guests, who filled Langer's restaurant on the Champs Élysées and overflowed onto the terrace, received the speech enthusiastically. "That's all—," said Dr. Butler, "three short paragraphs, each of which can be learned by children in school."[33]

Interesting in the light of Butler's new advocacy was the report

30. Kellogg to Herrick, June 10, 1927; Herrick to Kellogg, June 11, 1927, *FR: 1927*, II, 614.

31. Kellogg to Herrick, June 11, 1927, *ibid.*, 614.

32. According to Locarno the aggressor was that state which went to war in violation of its pledge to submit disputes to peaceful settlement.

33. New York *Times*, June 17, 1927. Probably no one will ever know exactly what Dr. Butler had in mind. He apparently never elaborated—on paper or otherwise—his new, simplified proposition.

of an interview with Léger which Harrison Brown, Levinson's European lieutenant, sent to his chief in Chicago. "I mentioned Butler," Brown wrote, "and Léger said that Briand had not intended to see him but that he (Léger) had insisted. Butler was talking a lot of bunk about his mile long effusion. Briand had him up and changed his whole tone so that after the interview Butler was stressing the need for simplicity, and saying that only two articles were necessary!" [34]

For the remainder of the week after the Thursday on which Butler spoke to the American Club, there were no noteworthy developments in respect to the proposed Franco-American treaty. Dr. Albrecht Mendelssohn-Bartholdy, professor of international law at the University of Hamburg and one of the editors of the notable publication, *Die Grosse Politik der Europäischen Kabinette,* arrived in New York the day of Butler's Paris speech and told the press that Germany hoped for a treaty with the United States to outlaw war. He declined to elaborate.[35] That same day the Danish minister, going to Bar Harbor for the summer, called at the State Department and asked Secretary Kellogg about the propositions of France for outlawing war. The secretary said he had no information other than what already had appeared in the press.[36] Little did the secretary and the Danish minister know that there soon would be much more information.

III

Philippe Berthelot, secretary general of the French Ministry of Foreign Affairs, sent for Sheldon Whitehouse, the American chargé d'affaires in Paris, on the evening of June 21. He informed Whitehouse that Secretary Kellogg's suggestions as to conversations on the proposed antiwar pact were very pleasing to his chief, Aristide Briand. But as the French ambassador to the United States would

34. Harrison Brown to Levinson, July 15, 1927, in J. Stoner, *Levinson,* p. 233.

35. New York *Times,* June 17, 1927.

36. Memorandum by Kellogg of a conversation with the Danish minister, June 16, 1927, 124.93/122.

not reach Washington until the end of August Briand thought that was too long a time to delay doing anything about the proposed pact. Briand had, therefore, drafted a suggested text.[37] Clearly Briand had outmaneuvered Secretary Kellogg, who had believed he had stalled off the unwelcome French negotiations.

There was nothing to do except for Ambassador Herrick to take the French text back with him to the United States (Herrick was about to return to America). Chargé Whitehouse meanwhile cabled a translation to Washington. Next day the Quai d'Orsay obligingly informed the press that the French Government had offered a draft treaty to the United States, that the treaty was quite simple, a compact between two countries only, and would not be enlarged to include any other country.[38]

Briand's draft, dated June 20 (the very day the Coolidge Naval Disarmament Conference opened in Geneva), bore the official title of "Pact of Perpetual Friendship." It contained two substantive articles and a third article of ratification.

Article 1 provided that "The high contracting powers solemnly declare in the name of the French people and the people of the United States of America that they condemn recourse to war and renounce it, respectively, as an instrument of their national policy towards each other."

Article 2 avowed that "The settlement or the solution of all disputes or conflicts of whatever nature or of whatever origin they may be which may arise between France and the United States of America shall never be sought by either side except by pacific means." [39]

There were thus two short paragraphs, each of which might be learned by children in school.

The draft treaty was short and simple, as Briand had been advocating ever since he had seen the long, complicated Shotwell-Chamberlain draft. But if one peered more closely at Briand's draft treaty one detected the skeleton of the Shotwell-Chamberlain draft. For the latter, underneath all its words, had had three parts:

37. Whitehouse to Kellogg, June 22, 1927, *FR: 1927*, II, 615–616.
38. New York *Times*, June 24, 1927.
39. The Whitehouse translation, printed in *FR: 1927*, II, 616.

Renunciation of War, Arbitration and Conciliation, and Ratification. So also did Briand's draft have three similar parts. Perhaps the French foreign minister had borrowed his idea from Messrs. Shotwell and Chamberlain.

The similarity between Briand's proposed treaty and the Shotwell draft was more apparent than real. Actually, Briand's proposed Pact of Perpetual Friendship bore a marked resemblance to the Rumanian and Yugoslav alliances—the treaties of friendship and of friendly understanding—negotiated by France in the spring of 1926. Those treaties, it will be recalled, in their first and second articles had borrowed the formula of the Siamese treaties of arbitration: Article 1 renounced all war; Article 2 promised to settle all disputes by peaceful means. Briand's new draft pact with the United States hence had a striking similarity to the latest of France's Continental alliances.

It is not recorded what Secretary Kellogg did or said when he first saw Briand's proposed text. Certain it is that Briand had placed Kellogg in an embarrassing diplomatic position. Should Kellogg give in to the rising popular demand in the United States for a treaty with France? And if not, what other course of action lay open?

Chapter Eight: ACTION AND INACTION

Colonel Raymond Robins lunched with President Coolidge in the early summer of 1927, and during the mealtime conversation the colonel asked the president about Outlawry of war.

"Mr. President," said Robins, "you have immortality lying all around you in this proposal to outlaw war and you are doing nothing about it."

"Well," responded Coolidge, "the people are not interested in that proposition: they probably think it is impractical."

"They ought to be interested," replied Robins, "and it is practical . . ." [1]

I

American peace leaders enthusiastically approved of Briand's proposed bilateral Outlawry pact. This in spite of the marked hesitancy toward Outlawry which continued to flourish in high governmental circles. In fact it soon was evident that Aristide Briand's new proposition had united the American peace movement as it never had been united before. All varieties of peace leaders began to campaign for Franco-American perpetual friendship. This is not to say that sweetness and light now reigned between such confirmed

1. Claudius O. Johnson, *Borah of Idaho*, p. 399. Robins himself told Professor Johnson this story when the latter met the colonel during the summer of 1935 at the Carleton Hotel in Washington.

rivals as the Butler-Shotwell group—which always had advocated the League of Nations—and the Levinson group which definitely was anti-League. There was still many a thrust and jab between them. The fact remained that Briand, by proposing his Pact of Perpetual Friendship, had succeeded in engineering an unprecedented coalition of the peace forces in the United States—thus to place popular pressure on the State Department to accept a treaty that would be an American bulwark to France's system of alliances in Europe.

Nicholas Murray Butler touched off the campaign to arouse public opinion. His first addresses he delivered in Denver, one before the chamber of commerce and the second to a crowded audience in the huge auditorium where William Jennings Bryan once had received nomination for the presidency. Bryan had refused to crucify mankind on a cross of gold. Butler sought to save his fellow men from the cross of war. The president of Columbia later reminisced: "From Colorado I came east through Kansas, Nebraska and Missouri, speaking at various points, and then into Illinois, Indiana and Ohio. After one or two speeches in Pennsylvania and three or four in New England, I closed my campaign . . . at Augusta, Georgia." [2]

Salmon O. Levinson, arrived back in Chicago after his whirlwind tour of Europe, immediately threw himself into the great American battle for Outlawry. The Chicago lawyer's partner, Benjamin V. Becker, was a director of the Chicago *Daily News* and personal counsel of Walter A. Strong who controlled the paper. The *Daily News* came out for Outlawry. Through the *News* European service, subscribed to by over a hundred papers in the Midwest, Levinson's campaign soon received excellent coverage. The two Mowrer brothers, Paul Scott and Edgar Ansel, wrote columns of stories on Outlawry's European progress, and these articles appeared almost automatically in papers in Ohio, Indiana, Illinois, Michigan, and neighboring states.

Levinson on June 16 had a forty-five-minute conference with Secretary Kellogg. "We had a splendid talk," Levinson later informed Harrison Brown, "although I found him quite unac-

2. Nicholas Murray Butler, *Across the Busy Years,* II, 208.

quainted with the theory of Outlawry and considerably in the dark as to what M. Briand really wanted. . . . he was convinced that the adjustment of the debt had nothing to do with Briand's proposal." [3] Kellogg asked Levinson to prepare a draft treaty based on his experiences and contact with the French Foreign Office, and Levinson duly made up a draft and forwarded it to the secretary of state on June 24.[4]

Then on Sunday afternoon, June 26, Bill Borah arrived in Chicago. Sol Levinson spent two hours that day with him and saw the senator the next morning before he departed for Denver. The two Outlawrists held a most pleasing discussion. Among other things, Borah informed Levinson that Kellogg had sent for him, and while he thought it concerned another matter it was only to discuss the Briand proposal and an Outlawry pact. This private interview, according to the senator, offered opportunity to expound to Kellogg the gist of Outlawry.[5]

In those June days when the army of Outlawry was marching so irresistibly onward there occurred a disturbance in the ranks. The Reverend Dr. Charles Clayton Morrison was placing the finishing touches to his volume on Outlawry of war and had added a section on the Briand proposal. Now it happened that Dr. Morrison held his own opinions on outlawing war, although he belonged to the inner circle of Levinson's group. Late in June the captain of the Outlawry cohorts viewed the work of his lieutenant. Levinson threw up his hands in horror: Morrison's last section was "perfectly insulting to France." [6] Not only would the book, if printed as written, have a harmful effect on public opinion; Levinson feared even more that Morrison, whom Borah greatly respected, would convert the senator to his heresy. After much effort Levinson persuaded Morrison to hold out the objectionable addendum on

3. Levinson to Brown, June 28, 1927, J. Stoner, *Levinson*, p. 236.

4. Levinson's draft contained six articles, Article 2 excepting from the treaty any question concerning the Monroe Doctrine, and Article 4 reserving the right of self-defense. J. Stoner, *Levinson*, p. 225.

5. Levinson to Harrison Brown, June 28, 1927, in J. Stoner, *Levinson*, p. 238.

6. Levinson to Raymond Robins, June 30, 1927, J. Stoner, *Levinson*, p. 242.

France until Colonel Robins could get to Chicago for a conference; and when the colonel arrived he sided with Levinson and outvoted Morrison. The latter, at last reduced to submission, removed his addendum and substituted a new one favorable to the Briand proposal. Levinson must have sighed with relief after quelling this incipient mutiny.[7]

Meanwhile Senator Borah had written to Morrison, advising that he omit in his book any addendum touching in any way the Briand proposal. Borah vowed he did not desire Morrison to compromise his book's dignity and force by discussing "Briand's gesture." The senator preferred to wait and "see what that thing is he [Briand] is talking about." [8] To Levinson Borah soon wrote that he had not heard anything from Secretary Kellogg in regard to the Briand proposal. "In my opinion," Borah added, "we will never hear anything from Briand's proposal that amounts to anything. The more I study the Briand proposal, the more I think it a piece of dynamite for outlawry." The senator, moreover, had just read Morrison's revised addendum and could not agree with it: "My opinion is that a two-power treaty is not an aid to outlawry but a distinct hindrance and embarrassment." [9]

Borah's pronouncement on Briand's Outlawry proposal momentarily stunned Levinson. The Chicago lawyer recently had toured Europe. Now his champion, Senator Borah, seemed to be deserting the cause. From an asset Borah suddenly had become a liability. "I am beginning to feel a sense of helplessness . . ." Levinson confided to Colonel Robins.[10] But soon he recovered and sent a cheerful letter to the senator affirming that the publicity and general interest in Outlawry caused by the Briand proposal and

7. It appears that Morrison was not against the bilateral Briand proposal because it might be a negative military alliance, but simply because he thought a bilateral pact would be of limited value. Morrison thus as a matter of principle, rather than politics, preferred a multilateral pact. See Charles Clayton Morrison, *The Outlawry of War: A Constructive Policy for World Peace* (Chicago, Willett, Clark and Colby, 1927), pp. 283–300.

8. Borah to Morrison, July 8, 1927, Levinson MSS.

9. Borah to Levinson, July 12, 1927, in J. Stoner, *Levinson,* p. 243.

10. Levinson to Raymond Robins, July 15, 1927, *ibid.,* p. 243.

subsequent developments could not have been had for $5,000,000 worth of advertising.[11]

The scene in the campaign for Outlawry now shifts to Honolulu. Professor Shotwell was attending the second conference of the Institute of Pacific Relations.[12] The conference lasted from July 15 to July 28, 1927, with delegates in attendance from China, Japan, Great Britain, Australia, Canada, and New Zealand. The day before the conference ended Shotwell in a general forum presented a draft of a proposed treaty for permanent peace in the Pacific regions between the United States and an unnamed power. He then admitted that he had drawn the treaty with Japan in mind and declared such a compact would be "peace insurance" for the Pacific area.[13] The Japanese delegates to the conference viewed Shotwell's proposal with favor but explained politely that their public had not as yet given much thought to such an international undertaking. They queried whether Japan's regional policies should not receive the same consideration as the Monroe Doctrine, and they doubted the wisdom of entirely excluding from the field of international conciliation, as Professor Shotwell's draft suggested, all issues regarded as domestic.[14]

In spite of this chilly Japanese welcome to Shotwell's draft treaty for Pacific peace insurance, his proposal did result in a Japanese study group which met once a fortnight during the autumn and part of the winter of 1927–28, its sessions attended by an official of the Japanese Foreign Office. This study group opened its meetings to the public and was quite active in preparing and disseminating essays and newspaper articles.[15]

During the summer of 1927 there remained some recalcitrant

11. Levinson to Borah, July 21, 1927, *ibid.*, p. 244.

12. The Carnegie Endowment paid all of Shotwell's expenses to Honolulu and back. For details, see above, pp. 21–22.

13. New York *Times,* July 28, 1927.

14. An oblique reference to oriental immigration.

15. Arnold J. Toynbee, *Survey of International Affairs: 1928* (London, 1929), pp. 22–23. For an account of the conference, see George H. Blakeslee, "Results of Honolulu Conference on Problems of the Pacific," *Current History,* 27 (Oct. 1927), 73. The conference published its proceedings in J .B. Condliffe, ed., *Problems of the Pacific* (Chicago, 1928).

individuals in the United States whom the peace forces could not convert. Dr. David Jayne Hill, an expert international lawyer,[16] wrote an article in the *Saturday Evening Post* [17] asserting that to outlaw war was contrary to the Constitution of the United States. Soon Professor Albert Bushnell Hart of Harvard lashed out at a certain amateur diplomat who, he warned, threatened to compromise American national interests. There were, Hart wrote, some questions which the United States would never arbitrate: did Shotwell wish to arbitrate the Monroe Doctrine, or the question of oriental immigration, or war debts? [18] Professor Shotwell, in Hawaii, was not able immediately to reply to Professor Hart, but when Shotwell's answer finally came it was spirited indeed. "It is not often," he declared, "that one is privileged to read an article which contains a 100 per cent. misstatement of the subject with which it deals. Yet Professor Albert Bushnell Hart succeeded in achieving this remarkable feat . . ." [19] Professor Shotwell was not going to permit his fellow academician at Harvard to take any potshots during the fight for renunciation of war.

While sentiment in the United States during the summer months unmistakably was rising in favor of a treaty with France, Salmon O. Levinson was paying thousands of dollars to spread the gospel of Outlawry in Europe. In return for a liberal salary and expense account Harrison Brown buttonholed statesmen and their secretaries in London, Paris, Berlin, and Geneva, sent them Outlawry literature, wrote them letters, and gave copies of Dr. Morrison's book, *The Outlawry of War: A Constructive Policy for World Peace,* to all who promised to read it. As for Morrison's book, however, Brown after a while began to harbor doubts of its effectiveness in Europe: the independent-minded Morrison spelled "League of Nations" as "league of nations" all the way through the book; and the entire work contained a we-Americans-are-better-than-

16. And a trustee of the Carnegie Endowment for International Peace.

17. David Jayne Hill, "Briand's Proposal of Perpetual Peace," *Saturday Evening Post,* 200 (July 30, 1927), 27, 112.

18. Albert Bushnell Hart, "Amateur Diplomacy," *Current History,* 26 (July 1927), 623–624.

19. James T. Shotwell, "The Movement to Renounce War as a Diplomatic Weapon," *Current History,* 27 (Oct. 1927), 62–64.

you-Europeans flavor most unpalatable to sensitive European readers.[20] To add to Brown's trouble with Morrison's book the Commonwealth of Massachusetts chose the summer of 1927 to electrocute two aliens convicted of murder, Nicola Sacco and Bartolomeo Vanzetti. For a short time there was an ugly feeling on the Continent, and Brown and his wife, visiting in Amsterdam, found themselves among murmurs and even leaflets.[21] Brown wrote to Levinson that he met much difficulty talking law in Europe during the Sacco-Vanzetti affair.[22] He nonetheless continued his work. His labors probably won some converts to the Levinson program but were more efficacious in creating in Europe a feeling that Americans, if unpredictable in many matters, were at least exceedingly anxious to outlaw war.

While the great battle for renunciation of war raged in the United States, the New York *Times* in the East and the Chicago *Daily News* in the Midwest almost every day broke lances for the cause. Outlawrists and League supporters, joined in coalition, marched steadily forward. They loosed salvos of speeches, articles, and resolutions, bringing consternation into the emptying camp of the foe.

Busy with the battle, the hitherto rival peace groups of Butler and Shotwell and of Levinson had little time for berating each other as of old. Yet there were occasional discordant sounds in the peace forces' all but unanimous battle song. John Dewey learned that President Butler in London had made a long speech in the

20. Reviewing Dr. Morrison's book the British historian Professor Charles K. Webster wrote: "It is difficult to read it without some amusement and impatience . . . Dr. Morrison is quite ignorant of international politics, but he knows and shares the emotions of a large portion of his countrymen and can generally appeal to their mixture of idealism and nationalism with as sure a touch as Senator Borah himself." Morrison's advocacy of codifying international law, wrote Webster, was "a simple task, in his [Morrison's] opinion, if the lawyers do not interfere too much. Nothing is more delightful in the book than Dr. Morrison's treatment of this question, which must be read to be believed." *Journal of the Royal Institute of International Affairs,* 7 (1928), 339.

21. Harrison Brown to Levinson, Aug. 25, 1927, enclosing a leaflet, Levinson MSS.

22. Brown to Levinson, Aug. 11, 1927, Levinson MSS.

course of which he remarked "those admirable and amiable persons who would outlaw war—admirable and amiable but quite hopeless." Butler had concluded that it would be as easy to outlaw war as to pass a resolution to outlaw pride, vainglory, and hypocrisy. Dewey wrote to Levinson that Butler's pronouncement was only to be expected, for Butler had been born with a reserved seat on the band wagon.[23]

Leaving the band wagon of Outlawry to roll down the road to peace, let us note the activities of Secretary of State Kellogg in Washington during that hot summer of 1927.

II

The *Ile de France* sailed up New York harbor on June 28, 1927, bringing to the United States many notable persons, among them Myron T. Herrick, American ambassador to France. Asked by reporters about the proposed Briand treaty, Herrick sagely replied that it would be both impolitic and indelicate for him to comment. The State Department, he said, would give out information in due course.[24]

While Herrick still was on the high seas Briand had asked Secretary Kellogg through the American chargé in Paris, Sheldon White-house, if it were all right to make a statement about the proposed pact on July 4.[25] For Briand the anniversary of American independence obviously was a strategic occasion; the French foreign minister on July 4, 1927, could say to the American people that France and the United States, once allied in the great cause of American independence, should again join hands—this time for the equally great cause of peace. "No," Kellogg cabled Chargé Whitehouse. The secretary of state added that Briand should discuss his treaty through regular diplomatic channels, in an orderly manner; public statements by no one would stampede the American Government.[26]

By the time Herrick landed in New York the State Department

23. Dewey to Levinson, Sept. 1, 1927, Levinson MSS.
24. New York *Times*, June 29, 1927.
25. Whitehouse to Kellogg, June 26, 1927, *FR: 1927*, II, 618.
26. Kellogg to Whitehouse, June 27, 1927, *ibid.*, 618–619.

had made up its mind about Briand's proposal. J. Theodore Marriner, chief of the Department's Division of Western European Affairs, by June 24 had prepared an official memorandum. This document is so plain spoken, so utterly undisguised by diplomatic euphemisms, that it deserves almost full quotation:

> The text of Mr. Briand's proposals for a Treaty . . . should be carefully considered from every point of view.
>
> Mr. Briand's insistence that negotiations should begin at once without awaiting the arrival in this country of M. Claudel [the French ambassador] would seem to indicate that he was most anxious to keep this topic in the public eye most prominently during the meeting of the Naval Conference at Geneva in order to draw attention away from the fact that France is not there represented in a constructive step towards World Peace.
>
> The vague wording and lack of precision in the draft seems also intended to give the effect of a kind of perpetual alliance between the United States and France, which would certainly serve to disturb the other great European Powers,—England, Germany and Italy. This would be particularly true as it would make the neutral position of the United States during any European war in which France might be engaged extremely difficult, since France might deem it necessary to infringe upon our rights as a neutral under this guaranty of non-aggression. A further point which Mr. Briand has not touched on is the question of France's obligations under the Covenant of the League of Nations to aid the League in the punishment of an aggressor state. It might likewise be used internally in France to postpone the ratification of the Debt Settlement and to create a feeling that payment was unnecessary.
>
> In order to avoid this interpretation, it would be incumbent on the United States at once to offer a treaty in the same terms to England and Japan, more especially as we are negotiating with them at the present moment [at the Geneva Naval Conference] and could hardly wish them to feel that we were entering into an alliance at the same time with another Power.
>
> Certainly a single treaty of this nature, and, according to press despatches, France desires that it be an absolutely unique

instrument, would raise the question of an alliance with a country outside the American hemisphere. A series of such agreements, unless it were absolutely world wide, would raise the same objections. All this tends to indicate that it would be best to keep the subject in abeyance at least until the conclusion of some agreement in Geneva. However, when the time comes actually to negotiate, it would seem that the only answer to the French proposition would be that, as far as our relations with France were concerned, adequate guarantees were contained in the Bryan Treaty, and that if any step further than this were required, it should be in the form of a universal undertaking not to resort to war, to which the United States would at any time be most happy to become a party. Before such a time, treaties of the nature which France suggests become practically negative military alliances.[27]

Secretary Kellogg immediately wrote to President Coolidge, then on vacation in the Dakotas. His letter indicated he had completely digested Marriner's memorandum. Kellogg stated he was satisfied, from Briand's desire to make a speech on July 4 and from the fact that he was giving out to the press the substance of every communication he made to the State Department, that all he was doing was seeking to create a public sentiment during the session of the Geneva Disarmament Conference. ". . . I do not think," Kellogg wrote, "we ought to play into his hands in that way. . . . Of course, the public can see no reason why the United States should not agree with Great Britain and Japan or any other country not to make war. . . . I shall make no answer to France at this time . . ."[28]

From the Dakotas the president sent his approval of Kellogg's conclusions in two sentences and twenty-two words: "Thank you for your letter of the 27th, which I have read with care. I approve of the conclusions you have reached."[29]

Secretary Kellogg received the Japanese ambassador and informed him the United States would not make any new arrange-

27. *FR: 1927*, II, 617–618.
28. Kellogg to Coolidge, June 27, 1927, *FR: 1927*, II, 619–621.
29. Coolidge to Kellogg, June 29, 1927, *ibid.*, 621.

ment with France which it would not be willing to make with
Japan. The ambassador expressed gratification at the secretary's
statement, adding that the Japanese delegates at the Geneva conference had denied in the press that they had instructions to ask
for an antiwar pact (there had been rumors that they had such instructions).[30] The ambassador said it was gratifying to know that
the United States contemplated no special alliance.[31]

The New York *Times* a few days later carried a Paris dispatch
that the French Government viewed the proposed peace pact as
peculiarly proper between the French and American peoples; if
it were extended to other nations the pact would lose much of its
sentimental value.[32]

Sir Esme Howard, the British ambassador in Washington, called
at the State Department on July 6 and received Secretary Kellogg's
assurance that the United States Government would make no treaty
with France which it would not be willing to make with any other
country. Kellogg asked Howard if the British Government would
be willing to discuss the renewal of its soon expiring Root treaty.
Howard then asked Kellogg if that was at the same time the United
States discussed the renewal of the similarly expiring Root treaty
with France, and Kellogg said yes.[33] The secretary of state further
said, concerning Briand's proposal, that he would be glad to support such a treaty if it were of a general nature, but that he could
not favor signing such a pact with one country only because that
would be in his opinion tantamount to an indirect alliance, depriv-
ing the United States of its liberty of action in case of that country
being at war with a third party.[34]

30. The chairman of the American delegation to the Geneva Naval Disarmament Conference, Hugh Gibson, to Kellogg, June 24, 1927, 500.A15A1/323.
The ambassador in Japan, MacVeagh, to Kellogg, June 30, 1927, 500.A15A1/-
353.

31. Memorandum by Marriner of a conversation between the Japanese
ambassador, Tsuneo Matsudaira, and Kellogg, June 30, 1927, 711.5112
France/39.

32. New York *Times*, July 3, 1927.

33. Kellogg to the American ambassador in London, Alanson B. Houghton,
July 15, 1927, *FR: 1927*, II, 624.

34. Sir Esme Howard, *Theatre of Life* (Boston, 1935–36), II, 522. Kellogg

The day before Sir Esme talked with Secretary Kellogg, the American ambassador in London, Alanson B. Houghton, had an informal conversation with Sir Austen Chamberlain concerning renewal of the Root treaty. Sir Austen said the British Government favored renewal but thought something else might be desired. Houghton replied that it was true Briand had made some proposals toward a new treaty but all the ambassador wished to ascertain was Chamberlain's attitude toward renewal of the Root treaty; he would discuss the Briand proposals later. But after having so craftily broached the subject of the Briand proposals Sir Austen refused to let Houghton entice him away. Chamberlain said that Briand undoubtedly put forth his proposals in good faith, but that he, Chamberlain, had discovered from his own experience that Briand did not always work out his propositions beforehand in practical form, and hence, as after Thoiry,[35] he sometimes found that his ideas led into unanticipated difficulties.[36] Sir Austen did not go on to mention the difficulties which Briand would have to face on this new occasion, but presumably one difficulty was the British Government's determination that France alone should not reap the benefits of an antiwar treaty with the United States.[37]

----

apparently made no memorandum of this conversation with Howard. What he said must be reconstructed from Kellogg's later July 15 cable to Houghton and from the account in Howard's memoirs.

35. The famous Briand-Stresemann Thoiry conversations, wherein the two foreign ministers sketched an ambitious program of Franco-German rapprochement. Briand shied away from the Thoiry propositions after he discovered French opinion was not backing him.

36. Houghton to Kellogg, July 6, 1927, 711.4112/175.

37. The British foreign secretary faced a demand for an Anglo-American antiwar treaty during a House of Commons debate of July 11. Arthur Ponsonby and Commander Kenworthy, two Opposition M.P.'s, interrogated Chamberlain. 208 H.C. Deb., 5 s., cc. 1764, 1793. Chamberlain cagily replied that Franco-American negotiations were about to take place; he wished them well, but it would be an impertinence, and worse than an impertinence, if he were to indicate any opinion as to the lines on which such conversations should proceed. "For ourselves," he concluded, "I hope between the United States and this country war is already outlawed, not on paper but in the heart and soul of every citizen." (c. 1777) George Trevelyan, another Opposition M.P., later got the floor and angrily snapped back at Chamberlain: "We have abolished war in

Back in America, Ambassador Herrick and Secretary Kellogg conferred over the Briand draft treaty. Both men afterward declined comment. Someone in the State Department intimated, however, that because of the time Department experts would require for examining the Briand proposal it would not be necessary for Herrick to see the president on the subject for some time.[38] So while the experts leisurely examined the draft treaty Herrick departed for Cleveland, underwent a serious operation, and easily had several months remaining in which to recuperate.

Three weeks before Herrick and Kellogg conferred over the Briand draft—in fact, on the very day Briand had finished preparing his proposed text (June 20)—the Coolidge Naval Disarmament Conference had opened in Geneva. "It was a distressing conference," wrote one of the American delegates, Hugh Wilson.[39] Wilson believed that Rear Admiral Hilary Jones, another of the American delegates, was much at fault for the conference's failure.[40] Admiral Jones during the session disagreed with his British opposite, Walter Bridgeman of the Admiralty. Actually the problem was not one of personalities but of cruisers: should cruisers be above or below 8,000 tons' displacement, and have 6-inch or 8-inch guns? The Americans desired large cruisers and the British insisted on small cruisers. Although the British Government conceded there should be parity between the British and American fleets, the British in reality desired superiority and artfully disguised their desire by stipulating for small cruisers—which Britain could employ to great advantage because of her many naval bases all over the world, and which the United States could use to small advantage because of lack of naval bases. With the Japanese looking

---

our hearts. Well, then, why cannot we abolish it in the terms of Treaty?" (c. 1877).

38. New York *Times,* July 8, 1927.

39. Hugh R. Wilson, *Diplomat between Wars,* p. 218.

40. "He was a man of simplicity and of an honesty so limpid that a glance at his clear eyes convinced you of his character. He was one of the most lovable men that I have encountered and every member of the delegation felt deep affection for him. His idea of debate, however, might be said to lack variety. He made an affirmation, he listened politely to the other man, he restated his affirmation." *Ibid.,* p. 218.

politely on, the British and Americans came gradually to deadlock. The conference adjourned, very much a miserable failure, on August 4, 1927.

This failure paved the way for the largest American naval bill since the World War. ". . . I think there is a pretty strong feeling that we should extend our building program," Secretary Kellogg wrote to Coolidge.[41] The navy's General Board promptly began to prepare plans for an ambitious program of naval construction, so that members of the Senate Committee on Naval Affairs might place it before the forthcoming session of Congress.

It is impossible to measure precisely the repercussions on the Briand proposal of the ill-fated Geneva Naval Conference. The conference's failure disgusted the Coolidge Administration. It was humiliating to have European diplomats whispering to each other that the conference failed because of "lack of preparation"—in other words, Coolidge's and Kellogg's ignorance of European affairs. Surely the dismal end of the conference left Secretary Kellogg irritated at France for not attending, and at Britain for failing to cooperate. If the conference achieved anything it convinced Secretary Kellogg that the farther he kept away from European vicissitudes the better. In effect, the conference's failure threw Kellogg into the arms of isolationists such as Senator Borah. If peace advocates in the United States supposed that Secretary Kellogg was beginning to favor a scheme with France looking toward the peace of the world, they were utterly mistaken.

The State Department on August 19 announced that Ambassador Herrick, recuperating from his operation in Cleveland, was too weak to travel to Washington to confer with Secretary Kellogg on Briand's peace proposal.[42] Herrick was still recuperating on September 14 when Kellogg conversed with the newly returned French ambassador, Paul Claudel. And not only had he been unable to speak with Herrick, Kellogg said, but he had had no opportunity to talk with Coolidge; since the president returned from the Dakotas Kellogg had been busy with matters "exceedingly

41. Kellogg to Coolidge, Aug. 10, 1927, *FR: 1927*, I, 157–159.

42. New York *Times,* Aug. 20, 1927. Presumably Kellogg was also unable to travel to Cleveland.

pressing." Furthermore, the secretary of state told Claudel, he would be unable to discuss the Briand proposal with the president until about the first of October, after returning from his forthcoming trip to St. Paul, Minnesota.[43]

What did Paul Claudel think of Secretary Kellogg's elaborate explanations?

Paul Louis Charles Claudel had had a long and illustrious career in the French foreign service. He had spent twenty years in the Orient. Devoting his leisure there to writing poetry and philosophy, he had achieved considerable success and acclaim in literary circles. Indeed, he distinguished himself as one of the foremost French writers of his generation. The fame of Paul Claudel, mystic poet and Catholic philosopher, already in 1927 was beginning to transcend even the fame of Paul Claudel, professional diplomat. Claudel, personally, was a somewhat difficult individual to know. As French ambassador to the United States, he gained a reputation as the most silent, the most depressing dinner companion in Washington, always appearing as if he were longing for a houseboat at Foochow, or the pale pearl of the tropic sea where, as he once dreamily wrote, "Vénus, telle qu'une lune toute trempée de plus purs rayons, faisait un grand reflet sur les eaux. Et un cocotier, se penchant sur la mer et l'étoile, comme un être accablé d'amour, faisait le geste d'approcher son coeur du feu céleste." [44] But if Claudel appeared absent-minded to casual Washington observers, at the State Department he quickly won another reputation—as, easily, the most astute member of the Washington ambassadorial corps. It required little insight for a man of his experience to see that Kellogg was not in much of a hurry to further negotiations on the Briand treaty.

43. Memorandum by Kellogg of a conversation with Claudel, Sept. 14, 1927, *FR: 1927*, II, 626.

44. Paul Claudel, *Connaissance de l'Est* (Paris, Mercure, 1913), p. 9.

Chapter Nine: AMERICAN ENTHUSIASM AND EUROPEAN REALITIES

Harrison Brown, English publicity agent for Outlawry employed by S. O. Levinson, called on the Honorable John Bassett Moore one day in the late fall of 1927 at the Hague Peace Palace. For more than an hour young Mr. Brown and the elderly American justice of the World Court talked over the outlawing of war. Pondering the conversation afterward, Brown remembered that "old Moore" had made his life work the history of arbitration. In 1898 Moore had written eight volumes, in 1908 another six volumes or so; and now he was seeking to publish some thirty more concerning the history of arbitration in ancient and modern times.

Brown had difficulty talking to the elderly scholar. He believed that he had taken Justice Moore a long way, but it required much persistence and quick slipping in, for Moore wandered off constantly into reminiscences of long past congresses and conferences and details of past conventions in which proceedings had been nullified by reservations inserted after the convention and before ratification by individual states.

Brown asked Moore if perhaps making rules for war was a hopeless job.

No, no, rejoined Moore. Not if you could persuade everyone to sign them.

Brown went into some details, mentioned the World War, and asked if it did not seem that the time had come for a radical

attack upon the whole war system; the problem threatened civilization's very existence.

Moore replied that Brown would be up against human nature
which does not change.

It did change, countered Brown. He offered Moore some examples.

No! No!

Brown expounded with fervor his idea about the contribution
of America to the world, her faculty for tackling old problems in
new ways and freed from old traditions.

Old Moore merely lay back in his chair and smiled at young
Mr. Brown.[1]

I

The month of October came and passed. Ambassador Paul
Claudel still awaited the convenience of Secretary Kellogg.

The peace forces could not understand such dalliance. As the
National Council for Prevention of War complained bitterly in
one of its October News Bulletins, "Why is the State Department
silent on this truly great [antiwar] proposal? . . . Does anyone
doubt that it would be a popular measure?"[2] Paul Scott Mowrer of
the Chicago *Daily News* sought to explain Outlawry of war to the
sophisticated J. Theodore Marriner of the State Department.
Mowrer employed Levinson's analogy of the extinction of dueling
and the extinction of war. The skeptical Marriner asked if any
armaments would be necessary after war had become an inter-

1. Harrison Brown to Levinson, Nov. 9, 1927, Levinson MSS.

2. NCPW, *News Bulletin, 6* (Oct. 1, 1927), 2. Dr. Charles Clayton Morrison's
recently published book clearly had pointed up the inevitable conclusion to
be drawn if diplomats refused to advocate Outlawry: "Could there be any more
vivid lighting up of the hypocrisies of peace diplomacy, of the deceptions which
lie hidden in all the peace rhetoric of our international statesmen, of the thrall-
dom by which the nations are chained to the war system?" "The high-flown
peace talk of the diplomats," Morrison had concluded, "would then be known
for the mere froth that it would thereby be proved to be." C. C. Morrison,
Outlawry of War, pp. 55–56.

national crime. Yes, Mowrer replied blandly, just as swords and pistols had survived the outlawry of dueling, to ward off illegal attacks.[3]

The Outlawrists were especially busy during these days. The Reverend John Haynes Holmes saw Borah early in November, and the two men had a delightful time discussing Mexico, Russia, Prohibition, and Outlawry. Holmes felt immeasurably pleased to observe Borah so emphatic in his arguments, for the senator now had a different attitude toward the Briand proposal. Borah desired a series of bilateral agreements, which he regarded as steps toward the ultimate goal of Outlawry, Code, and Court.[4]

Until this time Borah, as Senate spokesman on foreign policy, could have been glad that his fellow senators refrained from parading in front of the Band Wagon of Peace. Aside from a few pronouncements after Butler's letter to the New York *Times,* the senators had left foreign policy to the chairman of the foreign relations committee. But Senator Arthur Capper of Kansas now stepped out in front by giving to the press the text of a resolution which he announced he shortly would introduce into the Senate.[5] The Capper resolution stated that the United States should (1) conclude renunciation of war treaties with France and other likeminded nations; (2) accept the Locarno definition of an aggressor; (3) by treaty with France and other like-minded nations declare that nationals of the contracting governments should not, in giving aid and comfort to an aggressor nation, receive the protection of their governments.

Capper had previously written Nicholas Murray Butler and offered his services in proposing an antiwar resolution.[6] Butler promptly sent the text of "a very carefully drawn Joint Resolution." Capper, "delighted," promised to introduce it.[7] The presi-

3. Memorandum by Marriner of a conversation with Mowrer, Oct. 6, 1927, 711.5112 France/60.

4. Holmes to Levinson, Nov. 9, 1927, Levinson MSS.

5. He introduced it Dec. 8.

6. Letter of Sept. 26, 1927, Butler MSS.

7. Butler to Capper, Oct. 20, 1927; Capper to Butler, Oct. 25, Butler MSS.

dent of Columbia, also delighted, offered use of the Carnegie Endowment's news service to spread knowledge of the resolution abroad.[8]

Capper tactfully also had sought Levinson's advice before presenting his antiwar resolution. Levinson had given advice (take out the "European" aggressor clause), only to discover that Capper rejected it. Levinson then hurried to Washington, but arrived after Capper had given the text of his proposed resolution to the press.

In the course of corresponding with Senator Capper, Levinson was unable to resist intriguing against his pro-League rival, the president of Columbia University. He warned Capper against the machinations of Butler's peace group and of the dangerous fellowship in which Capper would involve himself by following Butler. Capper forwarded the letter to a stately address on Morningside Heights.[9] The fat was in the fire. Dr. Butler was at the moment touring the West, but when he returned he advised Senator Capper as follows:

> I am back this morning from a notable trip as far as Denver, where I have advocated your [sic] joint resolution before great meetings in Colorado, in Missouri and in Indiana . . . On returning I have your correspondence with Mr. Levinson. He and his group are, in my judgment, absolutely wrong-headed on this subject, and will always prove an obstacle to any practical step forward. His proposal is wholly visionary and is so considered by every one who has any knowledge on the subject. A recent book on the outlawry of war by the editor of a religious journal published in Chicago contains more misstatements of historical and legal fact and exhibits more ignorance of the whole subject than one would think it possible to get between two covers.[10]

8. Butler to Capper, Nov. 7, 1927, Butler MSS.

9. Levinson to Capper, Dec. 5, 1927; Capper to Butler, Dec. 9, Butler MSS.

10. Butler to Capper, Dec. 17, 1927, Butler MSS. But there were other opinions of Morrison's book. A certain "C.W.R." had reviewed the *Outlawry of War* in the Nov. 10, 1927, issue of the *Christian Register*. Concluded C.W.R.: "The fact is that no person is now competent to speak or write on the subject of peace and war unless he has read this book—and read it on bended knees."

The real significance of the Capper resolution lay, however, not in its piquant "secret history" but rather in the fact that it indicated the West awakening to the peace campaign. Senator Capper verily was a farmer of the farmers. He was publisher-proprietor of the Topeka *Daily Capital, Capper's Weekly, Farmers' Mail and Breeze, Household Magazine, Capper's Farmer, Missouri Ruralist, Ohio Farmer, Pennsylvania Farmer,* and *Michigan Farmer.* He also was president of the Board of Regents of Kansas Agricultural College and director of the Farmers National Bank of Topeka. Like no one else, Capper knew the temper of his constituents; an extremely astute politician, people said he kept his ear so close to the ground that the grasshoppers often bit it. The administration had to take notice of the Capper resolution.

And the administration took notice. A White House spokesman on November 25 stated that President Coolidge believed that there was no short cut to peace any more than to any other form of salvation. Outlawing war was something to be approached with fear and trembling. The president held that the chief obstacle to the plan of outlawing war was the provision of the Constitution which gave to Congress the sole power to make war. In the presidential mind the United States had demonstrated in many ways its love of peace and international understanding: its small army, its small navy in comparison with the length of coastline it had to defend, and its general distaste for interferences in the affairs of other nations all testified to America's love of peace.[11]

But when Dr. Charles Clayton Morrison read the newspaper accounts of how Coolidge had poured cold water on Briand's proposal he hurriedly sent the president a telegram. Friends of peace in Chicago, Morrison affirmed, wished to know if it was true that Coolidge considered Outlawry unconstitutional. The president's secretary coolly wrote an acknowledgment, stating that Coolidge assumed no responsibility whatever for newspaper interpretations of his views; whenever the president had definite statements to make he made them either in public addresses or messages to Congress.[12]

11. New York *Times,* Nov. 26, 1927.
12. Telegram and acknowledgment both dated Nov. 26, 1928, Coolidge MSS.

It was nonetheless obvious that Coolidge *had* said Outlawry was unconstitutional. Reporters, following the custom of never quoting the president directly, merely had transferred his remarks into indirect discourse and attributed them to that mythical personage known as the "White House spokesman." According to the official verbatim transcript of Coolidge's press conference of November 25, 1927 (transcripts of all his press conferences are now available at The Forbes Library, Northampton, Massachusetts), the president had said: "I have given some thought to the suggestion for the outlawry of war. Any treaties made on that subject are somewhat difficult under our Constitution. Those difficulties were quite clearly set out some months ago by Dr. David Jayne Hill in an article that was, I think, in the *Saturday Evening Post*. I don't know that they are insuperable, but they are certainly very great . . . There isn't any short cut to peace. There is no short cut to any other salvation. I think we are advised it has to be worked out with fear and trembling."

The afternoon that Coolidge made this unofficial pronouncement on Outlawry Senator Borah informed reporters that because of its crowded schedule of domestic measures he doubted if the Congress would have sufficient time to focus attention on any permanent peace or antiwar plan.[13] But the senator reconsidered, for the next day he was saying that the plan to outlaw war did not take away the constitutional power of Congress to declare war; it merely created a condition where it never would be necessary to exercise that power. "It was gathered from what Mr. Borah said," wrote the New York *Times* Washington correspondent, "that he believed there was an opportunity for some one to come forward with a declaration that war was a crime and lead a crusade. He mentioned no names." [14]

In Chicago on November 27 Rabbi Stephen S. Wise, the famous leader of American Jewry, spoke at the Downtown Forum and dis-

13. New York *Times,* Nov. 26, 1927.

14. Once, said Borah, slavery was legal, but William Lloyd Garrison fought against it, declaring it a crime; thirty years later it was made a crime. New York *Times,* Nov. 27, 1927. Borah was exceedingly sensitive to public opinion, and he knew full well that Outlawry had public support.

cussed the "Best and Worst in America." Under the Best he included Outlawry of war and mentioned Levinson's name two or three times. Wise's advocacy augured well for Outlawry. Only recently the Capper episode had shown that the Levinson Outlawrists and Butler renunciationists cherished a deep mutual dislike which lay only beneath the surface. Rabbi Wise, however, well known as a proponent of the League of Nations, was a leading worker in Butler's camp. And now Wise had declared Outlawry among the Best in America.

Representative Hamilton Fish Jr. introduced a resolution into the House of Representatives on December 7, 1927, requesting the secretary of state to furnish the House with a copy of the French proposition for an antiwar treaty. Fish pointed out that the proper way to approve an antiwar covenant was by joint resolution, for an Outlawry proposal involved the constitutional powers of the House.[15] This effort came to nothing, for Secretary of State Kellogg replied privately to Fish in a letter of December 13 that it would not be in the public interest to reveal the terms of Briand's proposal to the United States.[16]

The peace forces marched on. President Coolidge on December 10 had to assure Jane Addams, president of the Women's International League for Peace and Freedom who headed a delegation calling at the White House, that strong efforts would take place to obtain the adoption of a treaty between the United States and France outlawing war between the two nations. Coolidge, according to Miss Addams, said that upon the return of Ambassador Herrick to France conversations would take place with the French Government relative to Briand's proposal.[17] Miss Addams presented the president with a petition containing 30,000 signatures urging him to take the initiative. (Miss Addams may also have told the president that the Chicago Branch of the WILPF-US had written to Aristide Briand, informing the French foreign minister about the petition and enclosing a copy. In due course Briand had

15. New York *Times*, Dec. 8, 1927.

16. 711.5112 France/68.

17. Such was Miss Addams' report after the interview. New York *Times*, Dec. 11, 1927.

replied, thanking the ladies for their efforts and expressing his interest.) [18]

Thus American peace leaders by December 1927 were excited over the Briand proposal. Nonetheless, whatever move the Coolidge Administration made it would have to be done in the light of certain realities of the European political scene. Those realities the peace enthusiasts tended to overlook or underestimate.

Let us therefore examine closely the proceedings of the Eighth Assembly of the League of Nations, which in the fall of 1927 convened at Geneva. There could be no better way to bring ourselves back into touch with the great international problems and policies of Europe, or to observe the artful way that a proposal for the renunciation of war could affect, and be affected by, those problems and policies. We shall have reason to remember the activities of the Eighth Assembly later in our narrative, when we see how the original Briand proposal for a Pact of Perpetual Friendship between France and the United States took on more ambitious proportions.

II

The second day after the League Assembly opened, namely on Tuesday, September 6, 1927, the Dutch Foreign Minister Beelaerts van Blokland made a speech. "We must realise," he said, "that public opinion in different countries is moving . . . [toward a strong organization of the peace], and that, particularly in overseas countries, there is a growing current of opinion which has adopted as its watchword 'the outlawry of war.' Has not the moment come, I ask, to resume our efforts to bridge the gap in Article 15 of the Covenant by excluding legitimate warfare in the future and by stigmatising a war of aggression as an international crime?" [19] Blokland then proceeded to reintroduce the Geneva Protocol.

18. WILPF, British Section, *Monthly News Sheet* (Dec. 1927).

19. League of Nations, *Records of the Eighth Ordinary Session of the Assembly, Plenary Meetings, Text of the Debates* (Geneva, 1927), p. 40. How did Blokland learn of Outlawry? Perhaps through Harrison Brown, who had contacted Blokland's governmental colleague, Loudon. One of Brown's ac-

He of course suggested to the Assembly only a reconsideration of the "general principles" which underlay the protocol—not reconsideration of the protocol itself. Yet one could not discuss the protocol's general principles without reference to the protocol. Blokland's purpose was clear to everyone.

The next development in the Assembly occurred the following Friday when M. Sokal of Poland proposed a resolution:

The Assembly

Recognising the solidarity which unites the community of nations;

Being inspired by a firm desire for the maintenance of general peace;

Being convinced that a war of aggression can never serve as a means of settling international disputes and is, in consequence, an international crime;

Considering that a solemn renunciation of all wars of aggression would tend to create an atmosphere of general confidence calculated to facilitate the progress of the work undertaken with a view to disarmament;

Declares:

(1) That all wars of aggression are, and shall always be, prohibited;
(2) That every pacific means must be employed to settle disputes, of every description, which may arise between States.

The Assembly declares that the States Members of the League are under an obligation to conform to these principles.[20]

Here was astonishing similarity to Briand's proposed Pact of Perpetual Friendship with the United States. Not to mention that proposal's illustrious forebears, the Rumanian and Yugoslav alli-

---

quaintances, a Mrs. Kluyver of the Dutch delegation at Geneva, also had spoken to Loudon and had persuaded him to read some of the Outlawry literature. J. Stoner, *Levinson,* pp. 254–255.

20. L. of N., *Debates of the Eighth Assembly,* p. 84.

ances. Why did the Polish delegate, Sokal, who represented a nation allied with France, propose such a resolution?

That is not a difficult question, although it necessitates an involved answer.

After Sokal's speech and resolution, Vittorio Scialoja (Italy) remarked that the Assembly must not seek to escape its responsibilities by means of phrases. The public, he thought, should not be led to believe that the Assembly was finding immediate solutions for problems of an immense gravity. Consideration for the credit of the League of Nations should prevent the Assembly from making useless demonstrations.[21]

The next day Briand in the morning made one of his famous speeches. Beyond physical tribunals and established codes, he said, there were moral rules, and there was a tribunal constituted by the universal conscience. Its judgments had weight. After a solemn engagement not to resort to war no country, Briand believed, could let war loose upon the world without preparing for itself an impossible future, even though it should gain what was called a victory. Who could say after the last war in what a victory consisted? The country which committed aggressive war, Briand concluded, would receive the brand of Cain.[22]

Sir Austen Chamberlain that afternoon welcomed the motion of the honorable delegate from Poland, not because it said anything new, but because once again it invited all to join in the solemn resolution to pursue the ways of peace and to eschew the path of war. With this perfunctory introduction Chamberlain turned to the Dutch proposal. Great Britain, he said, was being asked to take for every country and for every frontier the guarantee which she had taken for one frontier only by the Treaty of Locarno. To ask that was to ask the impossible. Concerning the talk about gaps in the Covenant, he reminded the Assembly that there were openings in every building giving power to breathe, and passages giving power to move.[23]

21. *Ibid.*, p. 86.
22. *Ibid.*, p. 93.
23. *Ibid.*, pp. 95–99.

After this unenthusiastic speech the Assembly sent the Dutch and Polish resolutions to the Third Committee.

What now occurred is not very clear. Nothing happened in the Third Committee—its debates were dull and uninformative—but there must have been an attempt in an unofficial way to line up support for a combination of the two resolutions. Apparently the new resolution would have contained the rhetoric of the Polish resolution backed by sanctions resembling the Geneva Protocol. Chamberlain, however, seems to have blocked this scheme by refusing to accept the protocol in any form.[24] In the end there was left only the Polish resolution, which—bereft of sanctions and having only the force of a recommendation—no one considered worth very much.

On September 24 Sokal as rapporteur for the Third Committee informed the Assembly that its committee had taken the view that in the present circumstances a resolution, voted solemnly by the Assembly, declaring that wars of aggression must never be resorted to as a means of settling disputes between states, and branding them as an international crime, would exercise a salutary influence on public opinion and would contribute to the future development of the work of the League in respect of security and disarmament. While agreeing that the draft resolution did not in itself constitute a definite legal instrument, self-sufficing or increasing security in any practical manner, the Third Committee had unanimously agreed as to its great moral and educational value. Sokal then

24. Wrote Stresemann from Geneva to Chancellor Marx, Sept. 21, 1927: ". . . we could only nullify the Polish project—which would have developed into an Eastern Locarno—by the aid of England and France . . . In this business our personal relations with Chamberlain and Briand stood the test admirably. Chamberlain told me in advance that he would not admit any proposal that placed him and myself in opposing camps, and that to him the collaboration of the Locarno Powers was of more value than all the resolutions of the League. . . . The proposal of the Poles for an Eastern Locarno is rejected." Eric Sutton, ed., *Gustav Stresemann: His Diaries, Letters, and Papers,* III, 209. Probably Briand, observing Chamberlain's displeasure with the Polish project, sought to give the appearance of unity with Chamberlain and Stresemann.

offered his resolution against aggressive war. The Assembly, in accord with the dignity of the resolution, voted by roll call, and the president announced that the resolution had passed unanimously.[25]

III

Although a resolution mutually to renounce aggressive war actually held little attraction for European nations, it was possible to discover and offer other, more fetching, propositions. The famous former editor of the London *Times,* H. Wickham Steed, while visiting in the United States in the autumn of 1927, advocated an interesting scheme.

Sensing the rising American feeling against war, Steed proposed that the United States Government issue a unilateral pronouncement, similar to the Monroe Doctrine, that "the United States abhors aggressive war, and that it will never weaken the hands of other nations which may band themselves together for the purpose of deterring an aggressor or of compelling him to desist from aggression." [26] Here was generalization to all nations of part of the benefits France might have expected from the Pact of Perpetual Friendship: the United States would pledge that American neutrality would not follow automatically upon every outbreak in Europe. Furthermore, the Steed proposal would have helped the League administer sanctions; it would condition the United States to aid with the "quarantine." But although Steed engaged in a brief tour of the United States, explaining his plan in public and semi-public addresses, and although he even enjoyed an interview with President Coolidge, his proposal sounded "European" to Americans, and it did not seem to come off.

Another proposal, current in Great Britain in the autumn of 1927, was an "all-in" arbitration treaty between Britain and the United States. After the failure of the Geneva Naval Disarmament Conference, Viscount Cecil resigned from the British Cabinet and launched a great campaign for such an all-in treaty. As Cecil told

25. L. of N., *Debates of the Eighth Assembly,* pp. 155–156.
26. H. Wickham Steed, "A Proposal for an American Doctrine of World Peace," *Current History,* 27 (Dec. 1927), 347–349.

Harrison Brown, he was not opposed to Outlawry of war but he believed it would require many years. The problem of stopping war could not be delayed, said Cecil, and he hoped he could obtain all-in arbitration in time to prevent another large European war. Cecil saw little likelihood of the Conservative government's proposing a Briand pact to the United States, but believed that if the United States Government offered one public opinion in Britain would force its acceptance.[27]

Actually, an all-in arbitration treaty was a pact of perpetual friendship with a different name. The British League of Nations Union candidly advised in its "Notes for Speakers" that, if deemed advisable, speakers could press either for an all-in treaty or a simple antiwar pact. The difference, of course, was only verbal.[28]

The Republic of France on Armistice Day 1927 did finally sign its alliance, hitherto only initialed, with Yugoslavia. Signature in Paris of the Treaty of Friendly Understanding provided occasion for much ceremony. There were many banquets for the Yugoslavs and a considerable distribution of crosses of the Legion of Honor. The Yugoslav Foreign Minister Ninčić announced reassuringly that the treaty was "a compact of peace. If otherwise, neither of the two Governments would sign it." [29] In a speech delivered immediately after the signing Briand himself protested that the treaty contained no spear point directed against any third party whatsoever. It was, he said, oriented entirely toward peace.[30] In Rome, however, this so apparently peaceful Treaty of Friendly Understanding—aimed at no third party whatsoever, oriented entirely toward peace—created a surprising amount of unfriendly misunderstanding. Eleven days later Italy signed a defensive alliance with Albania. Premier Mussolini declared simultaneously that the Italo-Albanian treaty had no connection whatsoever with the Franco-Yugoslav treaty.

27. Brown to Levinson, Nov. 17, 1927, Levinson MSS.
28. The Union first had championed only an all-in treaty. When Arnold Forster told Harrison Brown that he had also included advocacy of a simple antiwar pact in the "Notes for Speakers" Brown joyfully envisioned a new advance for Outlawry. Brown to Levinson, Nov. 22, 1927, Levinson MSS.
29. New York *Times*, Nov. 10, 1927.
30. London *Times*, Nov. 12, 1927.

In Europe in the fall of 1927 there were available, as we have seen, several schemes for organizing the peace. Bilateral treaties of friendly understanding appeared to have a certain efficacy—at least bilaterally. As for all-in arbitration treaties, simple antiwar pacts, and a New Monroe Doctrine—such projects offered perhaps feasible ways to bring the United States into some sort of participation in European affairs. But mere resolutions to renounce aggressive war seemed to Europeans hardly worth serious consideration (unless the resolutions disguised something akin to the Geneva Protocol).[31]

The Search for Peace was no simple matter. Attempting to explain its complexity Aristide Briand, from his office in the Quai d'Orsay, sent a 1927 "Christmas message to the American people." The French foreign minister, as was his custom, did not send the missive to Secretary Kellogg for proper transmission; it seemed that Briand preferred the method of direct approach, perhaps because he was not unmindful of his numerous supporters among the American peace movement. In his message Briand remarked that during the past year Europe had been close to grave dangers. On several occasions it was obvious, he said, that the European situation had not acquired a stability and balance which would permit statesmen to suspend their efforts and watchfulness. "It is an immense task," the foreign minister added, "and a long-range one, really to reestablish peace on a continent which has been so shaken." He described the then current Polish-Lithuanian dispute and said that "In the east of Europe, where some frontiers are not recognized by the countries concerned . . . it is entirely likely, as has often been the case in the Balkan Peninsula, that war, once started, would spread." Briand stressed the value of frequent international meetings at Geneva. "There is no need," he continued, "of my

31. The governments of Europe paid no attention to a proposal advanced on Nov. 30, 1927, by the Soviet Russian Government. The Russian delegate to the Preparatory Commission for Disarmament proposed the immediate and total abolition of all armies, navies, and air forces, the sinking of all warships, the scrapping of all war material, and the demolition of all arms factories! A few weeks later the French Chamber of Deputies voted instead 150,000,000 francs for construction of one 10,000-ton cruiser, six destroyers, five first-class submarines, one mine-sowing submarine, and two dispatch boats.

saying that it would be precious help if the United States of America would join this work of concord and peace." [32]

Europe, Briand had said, needed the help of the United States. The French foreign minister was not thinking of mere international resolutions to renounce aggressive war. The *organisation de la paix* was a sophisticated undertaking; as was evident at the proceedings of the League of Nations' Eighth Assembly, diplomats cared little for gestures. Briand, searching anxiously for ways to peace on the Continent, beholding simultaneously in the United States an immense amount of naive peace enthusiasm, obviously desired to attach that enthusiasm firmly to European realities.

32. New York *Times,* Dec. 25, 1927.

Chapter Ten: DENOUEMENT

As the summer of 1927 turned into fall and then into early winter the foliage around the White House changed from green to brown-and-tan, and then dropped to the ground. There it drifted until men came with baskets and rakes and gathered it up. Each day the president, a thin, wizened figure in tightly fitting business suit and starched collar, took his early morning walk about the grounds and environs. Calvin Coolidge scuffed along among the dead leaves. Occasionally he would kick at them impatiently or step on them heavily. Perhaps at such times he was thinking about Aristide Briand's proposed Pact of Perpetual Friendship between France and the United States.

Across the way from the White House stood the old post-Civil War pile known as the State, War and Navy Building. Each morning Secretary of State Frank B. Kellogg hurried nervously along Seventeenth Street to the side entrance, through the doors, up the elevator to his office. Some days he was quiet and kindly, in excellent humor, at peace with himself and with the world. On other days with flushed face and angry, snapping eyes the secretary pounded his desk, pounced with both hands on his row of buzzers, and swore at everyone unfortunate enough to open his office door. Perhaps at such times he was thinking of the "——— ——— pacifists" with their Outlawry of war, and of Aristide Briand making use of them to open the door of American foreign policy to France's system of European alliances.

The secretary of state and the president were in perfect agree-

ment regarding Briand's proposal for a bilateral pact of friendship. They knew what it in reality meant. To them such a pact was
impossible because of its inherent nature as a negative military alliance. At the same time Coolidge and Kellogg were beginning to see
that the United States Government would have to do something to
mollify the American peace movement, which Briand was astutely
exploiting to bring more and more pressure upon the administration. Briand's proposal of bilateral friendship made necessary a
substitute gesture of some sort toward the cause of peace.

This was the background for the crucial diplomatic negotiations
of November and December 1927. Let us now follow the denouement of Briand's proposal as the Coolidge Administration cautiously searched for the right course of action, and as the Quai
d'Orsay ingeniously maneuvered for bilateral renunciation of war
as an instrument of national policy. Sometimes the French Foreign
Office moved with great energy. At other times it appeared willing
to make startling compromises. Always it sought to extract the very
utmost from the diplomatic situation of the moment.

I

The White House announced on November 4, 1927, that the
president believed the time would soon be ripe for further discussion of Briand's draft treaty. Just what this meant was unclear,
for Coolidge a few days later, according to "guarded comment,"
took the position that the government's chief desire should be so to
conduct its foreign relations as to avoid participation in controversies affecting other governments.[1]

Meanwhile Senator Borah was planning a public pronounce-

1. New York *Times*, Nov. 5, 9, 1927. Coolidge on Nov. 8 had told his press
conference: "I had a short talk with Mr. Steed, Wickham Steed, the editor of the
London *Review of Reviews* when he was here. I didn't have a chance to go into
much of the development of the suggestion that he is making relative to some
position that should be announced by the United States as to what it might do
in certain contingencies, so I have never come to any definite conclusion about
it. I told him I thought it could be assumed that our main desire was to keep
out of controversies that affected other nations." Transcripts of press conferences, deposited in The Forbes Library, Northampton, Mass.

ment for a multipower Outlawry pact in a speech at the Hotel Astor in New York, November 10. When Mrs. Borah became ill the senator sent a telegram to the Reverend Sidney Gulick, secretary of the Federal Council of Churches and chairman of the meeting, canceling his engagement. But he managed to incorporate in his message the gist of his planned proposal: "M. Briand has suggested the first step. Let us suggest the second and include Great Britain, Japan, Germany, and Italy. That would furnish a real foundation for Outlawing War sincerely." [2] One wonders what Ambassador Claudel in Washington thought when he read this public utterance by the chairman of the Senate Committee on Foreign Relations.

Claudel made two speeches in the next few days, models of diplomacy, a different proposal in each speech. At a banquet in Washington, November 14, he said the United States was the arbiter of war or peace in the world. "If she vetoes war, there can be no war, and . . . all by herself, she can do more for the cause of peace, only by opening or by closing her doors, than any continent and than any league of nations." [3] This sounded like Wickham Steed's proposition. The next night at the Sherry-Netherland in New York Claudel told a meeting of the Foreign Press Association that France hated war. "A new word has been coined in America 'to outlaw the war.' It is a splendid word and a good idea. France is as ready to try it as any other [idea?] . . ." [4] This sounded like Briand's proposal.

While the French ambassador maneuvered so astutely, and while Senator Borah pointed the way to the future, the Coolidge Administration made one last effort to tip over the careening Peace Wagon. Using the same argument he had offered "unofficially" in answer to Senator Capper's resolution, President Coolidge now pushed hard in his Annual Message to Congress on the State of the Union, December 6, 1927. "In general," said the president,

2. New York *Times,* Nov. 11, 1927. Levinson took Borah's place at the meeting.

3. New York *Times,* Nov. 15, 1927.

4. *Ibid.,* Nov. 16.

our relations with other countries can be said to have improved within the year. . . . we can afford to be liberal toward others. Our example has become of great importance in the world. It is recognized that we are independent, detached, and can and do take a disinterested position in relation to international affairs. Our charity embraces the earth. . . . Our financial favors are widespread. . . . Proposals for promoting the peace of the world will have careful consideration. But we are not a people who are always seeking for a sign. We know that peace comes from honesty and fair dealing, from moderation, and a generous regard for the rights of others. The heart of the Nation is more important than treaties. . . . We should continue to promote peace by our example, and fortify it by such international covenants against war *as we are permitted under our Constitution to make.*[5]

Coolidge's thrust had no effect. Few people noticed it. The peace movement busily continued its campaign for perpetual peace between France and the United States.

II

William R. Castle, assistant secretary of state for western European affairs, had an office adjoining that of Secretary Kellogg. It was to Castle's office rather than to the secretary's that many of the Washington ambassadors and ministers liked to come to talk over their troubles. Scion of an illustrious Hawaiian family, the assistant secretary of state was a handsome, genial man, who once had been an English professor at Harvard. Bill Castle had a way of disarming people. When he fixed his friendly eyes upon a minister or ambassador the envoy often would completely forget diplomacy and pour out his heart. But behind the friendly eyes lurked a razor-

5. *FR: 1927,* I, xxiv–xxv. Italics inserted. The quoted passages are all from the section on "Foreign Relations." In making up the Annual Message on the State of the Union, it is customary for the Department of State to prepare this section, which then must obtain presidential approval.

sharp mind which soon afterward mercilessly recorded all confessions in official State Department memoranda. Not without reason did the French journalist Pertinax characterize the American assistant secretary of state as the "subtil Mons. Castle."

Now whenever the equally *subtil* Paul Claudel came to confess there was bound to be interesting conversation. Claudel came on December 10, 1927. The conversation was interesting and even startling for Claudel sought to scuttle the antiwar negotiations. He proposed to combine all the recent peace formulas into a renewal of the Franco-American treaty of arbitration.

He began by saying that the French Government thought it very important, since the Franco-American Root treaty was soon to expire, that France and the United States either renew this treaty or sign a more comprehensive treaty.

I asked him in this connection [said Castle] whether he was referring to the draft of a treaty outlawing war submitted through Mr. Herrick by M. Briand. He said that this, of course, was to be taken into consideration. He said that M. Briand was much impressed with the phrase invented in this country "outlawry of war" and felt that the phrase was exceedingly popular in the United States, that to embody the idea in a treaty might be very valuable. The Ambassador went on to say, however, that he thought the world was obviously not yet sufficiently advanced to make a treaty of this nature acceptable. I told him that it seemed to me that, although such a treaty would do no harm and might be of some use in its appeal to sentiment, it could easily be of very real harm if it were a treaty concluded between two countries only, and that I could not see any particular harm in a treaty of this nature if it could be concluded between a great number of countries, but that even so in the present stage of world sentiment, these treaties would hardly be more than words.

The Ambassador said he entirely agreed, but that after all I should not minimize the importance of words, that I probably remembered the phrase "In the beginning was the word" and said that, if the word was the foundation of the world, it must also be considered sometimes as the basis of facts. He then said that next February will be the 150th anniversary of the first treaty between France and the United States, that he thought we ought to produce a document which would appeal to sentiment, as well as insure the arbitration of all questions which can appropriately be arbitrated. He said that he knew the Senate would never agree to a treaty of general arbitration and that, after all, if we could have a really strong preamble we should have done what we could with words and satisfied public sentiment and that it would then do no harm to have what some people would call a "weak treaty."

I told the Ambassador that this seemed to me an admirable suggestion and asked him what he would think of putting into the preamble. His words as I remember were about as follows: "The United States of America and France, looking confidently to the time when arbitration, conciliation and respect for international law shall eliminate the possibility of war, have agreed," etc. He pointed out that the actual treaty might well be substantially the present arbitration treaty. He said that this would be entirely satisfactory to his Government and he supposed would be satisfactory to the Government of the United States. I told him it would be, but I felt there should be some changes in the treaty in order not to make the whole thing an obvious trick.

I told the Ambassador that I should be very glad immediately to take the matter up with the Secretary and to report progress.[6]

What, then, is to be concluded from this document? One may conclude that at least by December 10, 1927, Claudel felt uncertain about his chances of extracting a Pact of Perpetual Friendship from the American Government. That Castle and Claudel knew the meaninglessness of a multilateral treaty renouncing war. That hence the two diplomatists planned to appease public opinion by changing slightly, "in order not to make the whole thing an

6. Memorandum by Castle of a conversation with Claudel, Dec. 10, 1927, 711.5112 U.S./1.

obvious trick," the forthcoming new Franco-American arbitration treaty; among the changes, they proposed to renounce war in the treaty's nonbinding [7] preamble.

Here, incidentally, lies the very origin of what later came to be known as the "Kellogg arbitration treaties," as distinct from the Root arbitration treaties. The new Kellogg treaties, in addition to renouncing war as an instrument of national policy in their preambles, changed ("in order not to make the whole thing an obvious trick") the formula of the Root treaties: [8] the Kellogg treaties excepted from arbitration all disputes (1) within the domestic jurisdiction of the signatories; (2) affecting third parties; (3) involving the Monroe Doctrine; (4) involving the League Covenant. The loophole of the Kellogg formula was the reservation of all questions of "domestic jurisdiction," and this loophole made American arbitration treaties continue to be of questionable value. In the *American Journal of International Law* Professor Manley O. Hudson of Harvard, one of the country's leading experts on international law, wrote disgustedly anent the new Kellogg domestic jurisdiction

7. Is a preamble binding? It is a popular view, and one held even by the State Department during negotiation of the Kellogg-Briand Pact, that a treaty's preamble legally is not binding. It would be more accurate, however, to say "not as binding as the treaty's substantive text." Whenever there are ambiguities in the text itself judges or other inquirers must look elsewhere for the sense of the treaty, and a good place to look is, of course, the preamble. One also would consult statements, written or oral, made contemporaneously during negotiation of the treaty. In case ambiguity remained one would search for the sense of the treaty in other, more remote, declarations. In other words, for interpretative material one would begin with that nearest the instrument itself, and then work gradually into more peripheral matter.

Diplomatists from time immemorial nevertheless have used preambles as verbal dumping grounds, filling them full of discarded ideas and saccharine international flattery. Perhaps we may conclude that, in a narrowly legal sense, a treaty's preamble has weight; but because of time-honored international custom the preamble usually has as much weight as, say, the platforms of the Democratic and Republican parties.

Part of the preamble to the Kellogg-Briand Pact, however, was binding in a special manner, for many of the pact's interpretive notes referred to the preamble clause denying the benefits of the treaty to a transgressor.

8. Vital interests, independence, or national honor, or disputes affecting third parties. See above, p. 6.

formula that "It is a common process in human affairs to throw away an expression which has acquired an unpleasant 'psychic fringe,' and to substitute a new expression of similar content." [9] But the authoritative interpretation of the dropping of the Anglo-French formula was Secretary Kellogg's own judgment in a letter to Elihu Root: "Strictly speaking," Kellogg wrote, "I do not know that the dropping out of this proviso has much practical importance." [10] When the time arrived for signing the new Franco-American arbitration treaty Secretary Kellogg discovered that he had planned a trip to Canada, and so Ambassador Claudel on February 6, 1928—the one-hundred-fiftieth anniversary of the signature of the Franco-American alliance of 1778—signed the new treaty at Washington with Undersecretary of State Robert E. Olds. As if Kellogg's indifference were not sufficiently evident, the French Government later learned that the secretary of state had so carelessly drafted the treaty that an exchange of notes was necessary to clarify its terms.[11]

This excursion into the origin of the Kellogg arbitration treaties has taken us somewhat ahead in time and away from our chief interest, the impending denouement of the negotiations for Briand's Pact of Perpetual Friendship.

Unaware of Assistant Secretary Castle's exceedingly frank conversation with Claudel, Sir Esme Howard called on Secretary Kellogg a few days later and asked about the negotiations with France. Kellogg truthfully said there was nothing definite yet [12]—although

9. Manley O. Hudson, "The New Arbitration Treaty with France," *Am. J. of Int. L.*, 22 (1928), 371.

10. Letter of Dec. 23, 1927, Elihu Root MSS, deposited in the Library of Congress.

The American peace forces in the summer and fall were campaigning against the Franco-British formula. Wrote Frederick J. Libby to Esther Everett Lape, July 2, 1927: "I am very glad that you are campaigning against the phrase 'vital interests and national honor.' I believe that phrase to be the necessary crux in our campaign next fall." NCPW files.

11. As originally drawn, the treaty seemed to abrogate the Bryan treaty with France.

12. Howard saw Kellogg on Dec. 15. The secretary seems to have made no memorandum of the conversation but recalled it later in a cable to Chargé Atherton in London, Dec. 28, 1927, *FR: 1927*, II, 628.

from another point of view the secretary could have said that very much was definite.

The same day that Howard was visiting Secretary Kellogg, Claudel was again chatting with Assistant Secretary Castle.

The French Ambassador came to see me [Castle wrote afterward] about his conversation with the Secretary [of which there is no record] on the subject of a new treaty of arbitration. He said that he was delighted with the suggestions made by the Secretary [whatever they were] as to the form of the treaty. The ambassador then said that, as this treaty would be possibly the first step to be taken toward the outlawry of war, an idea which seemed to be exceedingly popular in the United States, the signature would appear to be the occasion for the blowing of a certain number of trumpets. He said that he thought M. Briand would be very glad to come to America to sign the treaty, but that he did not want to make this suggestion officially because he certainly did not wish to appear to be pushing the whole situation too hard. He said that he would be very grateful for an expression of my reaction to this suggestion.

I told him that I should like to think it over, but that off hand it struck me as a probably unnecessary formality, that it was quite clear that whatever treaty we finally signed would obviously not be a treaty outlawing war and that it would be a poor habit to get started to have ministers of foreign affairs running around the world signing arbitration treaties. I said, however, that I should be very glad to think the matter over and let him know later.

The Ambassador said in any case he hoped the treaty might be signed on February 6th.

A few minutes before the Ambassador came Mr. Herrick talked with me about the Briand treaty suggestion. He said that when Briand gave him the draft it was perfectly obvious to him from what Briand said and from what he did not say that his main purpose in making the suggestion was for the political value it would be to him personally. It is quite clear to me that the suggestion that Briand should come over to America has precisely the same basis. He has the halo of Locarno still over

his head and if he could add the halo of negotiating and signing a treaty looking toward the outlawry of war between France
and the United States, his political position would certainly be
greatly strengthened.[13]

This document scarcely requires comment.

Two days later the State Department told the press that Secretary Kellogg would adapt Briand's plan in part in renegotiation of
the Root treaty with France. The new arbitration treaty would
serve as a model for similar treaties with other nations. Briand's
proposal to outlaw war between France and the United States, the
New York *Times* reported, had raised difficulties, for it might
have proved a "left-handed alliance" which would give France
a free hand in Europe under assurance that she never would have
to face restraint from the United States. The *Times* heard rumors
that the new arbitration treaty with France would contain a statement in the preamble giving voice to Briand's antiwar proposal.[14]

For the next few days things were fairly quiet in the State
Department. So wrote the "subtil Mons. Castle" in his diary.[15] The
assistant secretary did have a long talk with Claudel and again explained the impossibility of a bilateral Outlawry-of-war treaty, how
it would take away the right of Congress to declare war, and how it
would be "playing into the hands of the pacifists." [16] Although

13. Memorandum by Castle of a conversation with Claudel, Dec. 15, 1927,
711.5112 U.S./2.

14. New York *Times,* Dec. 18, 1927.

15. Castle diary, Dec. 21, 1927.

16. "He [Claudel] said that he had just received the first official telegram on
the subject [the new arbitration treaty] from Briand himself, that Briand said
he had made himself the sponsor of the phrase 'outlawry of war' and asked
whether I personally thought it impossible in the treaty to use that phrase; in
other words, impossible to say that France and the United States hereby and
forever outlaw war. . . . I said, furthermore, that, in my opinion [Claudel had
asked for Castle's "totally unofficial reaction"], it would be unfortunate and
might cause very serious criticism to put through such a treaty with France
alone, that this might well cause very serious international comment and would
give the appearance of protecting France, so far as America was concerned, in
any warlike adventure against other countries on which it might decide to
embark. . . . I thought, for example, that he himself would be sorry if, before
the World War, we had had a treaty with Germany which would have made it

Castle told the French ambassador he was only speaking unofficially Claudel evidently cabled his remarks to the French Foreign
Office, for the next day when Castle picked up his New York *Times*
he saw them reflected in a dispatch from the *Times* well-connected
Paris correspondent, Edwin L. James.[17]

Such was the status of the Briand Pact of Perpetual Friendship
when the Senate Committee on Foreign Relations held a closed
meeting on December 22, 1927.

III

Drew Pearson and Constantine Brown, in their surprisingly
accurate *American Diplomatic Game,* have drawn an arresting
picture of this meeting.[18] Secretary Kellogg, appearing before the

impossible for us to enter the War even though we felt our vital interests were
concerned. I said there was a third reason which was purely a matter of internal
concern, which made me personally rather shy away from the phrase 'outlawry
of war.' This reason was that the people who made up the organization in
favor of the outlawry of war were, to a very large extent, pacifists of the most
rabid kind, many of them people who had been bitterly opposed to the entrance
of the United States into the World War and many of them people who had
done everything in their power to prevent participation by the United States.
I said that it seemed to me that the adoption of this phrase might well look at
the moment like capitulation to the pacifists. The Ambassador said he fully
understood the soundness of this reasoning and that he entirely sympathized
with it."

Claudel, however, was concerned with the appearance of the new arbitration treaty. He thought it might be top-heavy. "He said that to add a few paragraphs to the treaty might be very useful." He then proposed a paragraph
declaring for codification of international law. Castle thought that a good (and
harmless?) idea. Memorandum by Castle of a conversation with Claudel, Dec.
19, 1927, 711.5112 France/112.

17. ". . . to whom the French Foreign Office always leaks." Castle diary,
Dec. 21, 1927.

18. The entire Pearson and Brown account reflects much inside information. Apparently it came from Borah: the senator knew what happened at the
Dec. 22 meeting of the foreign relations committee and also knew the details of
Levinson's Outlawry campaign; Borah, moreover, never enjoyed a reputation
for being reticent with the press. The present writer wrote to Pearson about
the sources used in the *American Diplomatic Game,* but received no answer.

Duff Gilfond, *The Rise of Saint Calvin: Merry Sidelights on the Career of*

committee, explained his new arbitration treaty. The committee
members showed no very great interest in it, and Borah as chairman said that he assumed their silence meant consent. "But, Mr.
Secretary," he added, "all this does not dispose of the proposal
to outlaw war." Kellogg, shifting nervously, replied that such a
treaty as Briand proposed meant nothing less than an alliance between the two countries. Then Borah allegedly advocated a counterproposal of extending the treaty to include all the nations of the
world. Borah began to poll the leading members of the committee.
Senator George H. Moses of New Hampshire, famous for his icono-
clastic wit, opined that Borah's suggestion was the best way "to get
rid of the damn thing" (the Briand proposal).[19] The other members
were affirmative or noncommittal. "I think, Mr. Secretary, you may
consider it the sense of this committee," Borah concluded, "that
you go ahead with the negotiation of a pact to include all countries." [20]

Mr. Coolidge (New York, Vanguard, 1932), pp. 262–266, contains an account of
the December 22 foreign relations committee meeting which is substantially
the same as the Pearson and Brown account. Gilfond adds a later private conversation between Kellogg and Borah. It hardly seems possible that Kellogg
would have retold this conversation, for it was not flattering to the secretary.
Borah therefore must have been the source at least for Gilfond.

19. According to Duff Gilfond, *The Rise of Saint Calvin*, Senator Moses
said: "Put the baby on their [France's] doorstep. A multilateral proposal is a
good idea. It will include Germany, and France will never include Germany
in an outlawry-of-war treaty."

20. Drew Pearson and Constantine Brown, *American Diplomatic Game*,
pp. 27–28. Secretary Kellogg told Assistant Secretary Castle about the committee
meeting, and Castle recorded the conversation as follows: "The Secretary had
a successful talk with the Foreign Relations Committee yesterday on the subject of the new French arbitration treaty. It was successful in that the Committee was pleased that he talked with them and especially in that they seemed
to think that it would not be necessary to put matters of 'vital interest and
national honor' as among those which could not be arbitrated, it being of
course understood that matters of purely internal concern were clearly specified. . . . The Committee also agreed with the Secretary that a treaty outlawing war, as suggested by Briand, could not possibly be made with a single nation.
The Secretary thinks it might be a good idea to write the French that we cannot
stand for such a treaty with France alone, but that the United States is quite
willing to sign such a treaty with all the principal nations if they will do the
same between each other." Castle diary, Dec. 22, 1927. Italics inserted.

It may however be incorrect to give to Senator Borah so much credit for extending Briand's proposal. Secretary Kellogg himself has disputed such an interpretation. "The suggestion [of extending Briand's proposal]," Kellogg wrote several years later, "came to me as I pondered on the confused condition of the world, and the relation to it of United States policy. I did not discuss it with any one until I had fully satisfied myself that the idea was sound . . ." [21]

Perhaps neither Kellogg nor Borah should be credited with sole responsibility for the idea of extension. It had a more complex origin.

Soon after Briand's original message to the American people rumors began to appear in the press that the Coolidge Administration could only consider Outlawry in a multilateral form. It is possible but doubtful that Kellogg—or Borah—inspired these rumors. Kellogg's assistants at the State Department must have had a hand in the matter. Assistant Secretary Castle wrote in his diary as early as May 11, 1927: "If we made similar [bilateral] pacts with other nations France would lose interest immediately because it [the proposed Franco-American pact] would give no particular advantage." The succinct Marriner memorandum of June 24, 1927, which so devastatingly analyzed Briand's draft Pact of Perpetual Friendship, had suggested that the United States might perhaps be able to renounce war in a multilateral instrument. Only after the Marriner memorandum does there appear the first definite sign that Kellogg

21. ". . . and until I was prepared to make it public at the opportune moment. It seemed to me the only way to attempt to break the deadlock which international negotiations had reached." From a memorandum by Kellogg, in David Bryn-Jones, *Frank B. Kellogg: A Biography* (New York, G. P. Putnam's Sons, 1937), p. 230.

But see J. Stoner, *Levinson*, p. 268 n: "One story from a most trustworthy source has it that Kellogg went one evening late in the fall to the Borah home and knocked persistently until the Senator, who was alone, finally opened the door. The Secretary related how he had mulled over what to do with the Briand proposal until the answer came to him in a flash in the middle of the night, 'Why not make it a multilateral agreement?' The astonished Borah was shocked into silence that the Secretary should claim to him the authorship of an idea that Borah himself had been advocating for months." The writer asked Professor Stoner about this story, and Stoner replied that Levinson was his source of information.

himself had thought of a multilateral treaty: Kellogg told Sir Esme Howard July 6 that he would support an antiwar treaty if it were of a general nature. The multilateral idea did not, moreover, confine itself to sophisticated diplomatic circles. During the summer of 1927 many of the peace leaders envisioned Outlawry spread over the world, either in a series of bilateral pacts or in one grand all-embracing treaty. When Borah finally counseled multilateral renunciation to the Reverend Sidney Gulick, November 10, 1927, the idea of extension was no longer new.

Who first thought of the idea? May we not conclude that, although it had early currency among Secretary Kellogg's assistants at the State Department, the idea of extension came at different times to many other people, for various reasons.

Once Secretary Kellogg, for his own good reason, had decided upon a multilateral treaty proposal he promptly informed America's distinguished elder statesman, Elihu Root. Regarding the proposed arbitration treaty with France, Kellogg admitted to Root that the preamble was "a little elaborate," but such, he wrote, was the desire of the French ambassador, Claudel. The thing that most interested Briand, Kellogg wrote, was the French foreign minister's proposition for the United States and France to renounce war as a means of settlement of international disputes. But from several conversations with Senator Borah and after a long consultation with the full foreign relations committee, Kellogg was quite sure the Senate would not ratify a treaty such as Briand had proposed. "But the suggestion was made that I propose to France a renewal of the Root Treaty and also by note to France propose that the United States would be willing to sign a treaty along the lines of the Briand proposal if all the leading Powers would join in it." Kellogg had drafted a proposed note to Briand and enclosed a copy for Root's examination. "You know, of course," concluded the secretary of state, "that there is a tremendous demand in this country and probably in foreign countries for the so-called outlawry of war. Nobody knows just what that means. . . . I think this would answer . . ." [22]

22. Kellogg to Root, Dec. 23, 1927, Root MSS. Kellogg added that Undersecretary Olds, who was fully informed as to the antiwar negotiations and

The "so-called outlawry of war" had sorely tried the patience of the secretary of state. For months peace workers had been importuning the Department, pestering, beseeching, indeed demanding that the United States stand for the cause of peace. Kellogg fully understood that behind the men of peace—encouraging them, spurring them on for his own purposes—was Aristide Briand. Kellogg knew that Briand, offering his bilateral Franco-American Pact of Perpetual Friendship, actually was proposing a negative military alliance with the United States to fit into France's design for her own security in Europe. The secretary of state had been maneuvering for months to avoid this clever proposition.

After long and thorough examination Kellogg finally had hit upon a most promising new maneuver. Perhaps an acute observer during those last days of December 1927, watching the white-haired Minnesotan each morning hurry along Seventeenth Street to the side entrance of the State, War and Navy Building, would have remarked a new confidence and buoyancy in the secretary's brisk gait. Kellogg, within the sanctity of his private office, might have leaned back in his chair and rubbed his sturdy hands in quiet contemplation. He was again at peace with himself—and with the world. He had prepared a masterly note to Briand.

For transmitting it, he was awaiting a suitable occasion. But he had to act more quickly than he intended.

IV

From his office in the French Embassy in Washington, Ambassador Paul Claudel on December 28, 1927, rang up the State Department and said he had received a most important note from

problems, was going to New York Saturday morning (Dec. 24) and would be glad to come to Root's house any time Sunday or Monday. Olds would communicate with Root on Sunday morning. Consequently, Root did not have to reply in writing to Kellogg.

Hunter Miller's *Peace Pact of Paris,* p. 134, states that contemporary press reports indicated Kellogg had consulted both Elihu Root and Charles Evans Hughes. The Hughes MSS in the Library of Congress at present are not available for historical research.

Briand which his Embassy was then decoding. He would bring it down to Secretary of State Kellogg's office at four o'clock that afternoon. Secretary Kellogg immediately took the note he had ready for Briand and called on the president of the United States.[23]

Kellogg informed Coolidge he would like to send the note to France at once. The president read the note with care.

"We can do that, can we not?" he asked.

"Yes," responded Kellogg. ". . . I wish to send this to France immediately and send a copy to the French Ambassador before four o'clock."

Coolidge asked his secretary of state what the hurry was, and Kellogg explained that he expected to receive a note from Briand at four o'clock and desired the French Government and the French ambassador to have his note before that time.

"All right," said the president. "Go ahead."

Secretary of State Frank B. Kellogg promptly cabled the American note to France, and sent a copy to Claudel.

He never received the French note, whatever it was. The secretary of state had beat Briand to the draw, for peace.

23. This and the following is from Kellogg's memorandum in D. Bryn-Jones, *Kellogg*, p. 232.

Chapter Eleven: BRIAND'S DILEMMA

The idea of a treaty outlawing war, once wrote Sir Austen Chamberlain, "was first broached by that great Frenchman and friend of peace, Aristide Briand, but it is not, I think, too much to say that the French were surprised and even alarmed when they saw their bantling presented to them in its American clothes." [1]

It is of course true that Briand probably knew several weeks and perhaps months before the denouement the afternoon of December 28, 1927, that the American Government would not accept a bilateral treaty with France. From what Ambassador Claudel was saying during November and December 1927 it appears almost certain that the French Government was backing down on its proposal of perpetual friendship. Claudel and Assistant Secretary Castle had even put their heads together on the new Franco-American arbitration treaty and embodied (should we say embalmed?) Outlawry in its preamble.

Just what Briand had in mind in his uncommunicated note of December 28 probably will not be known until the Quai d'Orsay opens its archives. [2] Perhaps in this withheld note Briand merely was proposing another way to scuttle Outlawry, instead of via the arbitration treaty. But Kellogg thought Briand was about to outmaneuver him. Hence the Kellogg counterthrust of December 28.

Kellogg's proposal was bland in its professions. ". . . it has oc-

1. Austen Chamberlain, *Down the Years,* p. 234.
2. The French Foreign Office archives at present are open only to 1877.

curred to me," wrote the American Secretary of State, "that the two Governments, instead of contenting themselves with a bilateral declaration of the nature suggested by M. Briand, might make a more signal contribution to world peace by joining in an effort to obtain the adherence of all of the principal Powers of the world to a declaration renouncing war as an instrument of national policy." [3]

Aristide Briand did not welcome so signal a contribution. A multilateral pact renouncing war without reservations—for Kellogg had not mentioned reservations—would have disarranged the entire picture of power and politics in Europe and elsewhere: it would have shattered the French alliance treaties with Belgium, Poland, Czechoslovakia, Rumania, and Yugoslavia; transformed the Locarno treaties; put a new and negative aspect on the League of Nations. For the postulate behind all these arrangements so vital to French security was, in certain contingencies, war. It had been to strengthen these treaties, by making sure that the United States would never make war on France should she have to go to war by the terms of her European defensive alliances, that Briand had taken advantage of the peace movement in the United States to propose his bilateral treaty for renunciation of war between the United States and France, a negative military alliance. France could not strengthen her position in Europe by signing a *multilateral* treaty renouncing all war as an instrument of national policy.

Had there been no other complication than the above, Briand could have abruptly turned down Kellogg's multilateral proposal. There was another complication. Very much at stake was Briand's renowned reputation as a man of peace—a "Locarno prophet," [4] holder of the Nobel Peace Prize. How could the French foreign minister maintain his prestige in the world and publicly spurn a great offer for all the nations to renounce war as an instrument of national policy?

3. Kellogg to Claudel, Dec. 28, 1927, *FR: 1927*, II, 627. Kellogg's note differed only slightly from the draft he had sent to Elihu Root on Dec. 23.

4. Ambassador Myron T. Herrick's phrase. Herrick to Kellogg, Feb. 27, 1928, Herrick MSS, deposited in the Library of the Western Reserve Historical Society, Cleveland, Ohio.

Briand could neither accept nor refuse Kellogg's offer. The French foreign minister was nicely caught between his conflicting duties as a great Frenchman and friend of world peace. All because of his proposal of perpetual friendship, now so unbecomingly dressed in its American clothes. Ambassador Claudel consequently called on Secretary Kellogg, December 30, and began what proved to be three months of diplomatic maneuvering.

I

Claudel, undoubtedly under instruction from his superior in Paris, declared that France wanted a bilateral treaty, that he doubted if Briand would consider a multilateral treaty unless Kellogg could explain clearly why the United States could not conclude a bilateral treaty. Kellogg candidly replied that he had always favored a multilateral treaty; the United States, he was sure, could not conclude a bilateral treaty with Germany without arousing French public opinion. American opinion, Kellogg said, would view a two-power treaty unfavorably because it looked too much like an alliance and too short a step toward universal peace.[5] A multilateral treaty, he thought, would have a profound and world-wide influence in promoting the cause of peace.[6]

Although Secretary Kellogg thus was rather frank with Claudel, Assistant Secretary Castle was even more so. As Castle afterward wrote in his diary, the French ambassador came into the assistant secretary's office and said "that Briand had been 'ruffled' because of the frank talks he had had with me on the subject of a possible treaty and that he was sure Briand was not yet ready to accept the idea of a multilateral treaty. He asked me why a bilateral treaty would not be acceptable. I told him . . . that such a treaty would inevitably have more the appearance of a treaty of alliance than a treaty to advance the cause of world peace. . . . He asked why and I countered by asking him what effect he thought a treaty be-

5. But on June 27, 1927, Kellogg had written to Coolidge that "the public can see no reason why the United States should not agree with Great Britain and Japan or any other country not to make war." See above, p. 107.

6. Kellogg to Whitehouse, Dec. 30, 1927, *FR: 1927*, II, 629.

tween the United States and Germany outlawing war would have in France. He admitted that it would have a very exciting effect . . ." In his diary Castle concluded that it was "more and more evident" that Briand had made his bilateral suggestion "for political reasons solely and that he has now got a bad case of cold feet. They will be positively frozen when we drive him into the open and make him do something, or refuse to do something . . ." [7]

Sheldon Whitehouse, the American chargé in Paris, saw Briand and reported to Kellogg, December 31, that the French foreign minister objected to the word "treaty." Briand said he did not intend the proposed pact to take such a form. If America and France should solemnly declare their condemnation of recourse to war on the occasion of renewal of the Root arbitration treaty, it would promote the cause of peace. If at the same time Kellogg desired to draft a "protocol" outlawing war, for signature by all the nations, Briand would be agreeable. He hoped, however, that Kellogg would not make public the note of December 28 to Ambassador Claudel without a previous understanding between the American and French Governments as to what should be given to the press. [8] Whitehouse concluded from his conversation that Briand now understood the situation and was ready to accept what Kellogg could offer him. [9]

But while Briand through Sheldon Whitehouse was pleading for no press releases until after prior confabulation between Washington and Paris, someone in the French capital gave out the substance of Kellogg's counterproposal. As usual with such press leaks, the Quai d'Orsay garbled the presentation, giving an erroneous idea of the State Department's position. This left Kellogg no alter-

7. Castle diary, Jan. 1, 1928.

8. In a speech several months later (Nov. 11, 1928) Kellogg said it was doubtful if the then concluded antiwar treaty "could have been negotiated between the ministers of the different governments in secret. I did not attempt it. Neither did Monsieur Briand." Frank B. Kellogg, *The Settlement of International Controversies by Pacific Means* (Washington, Government Printing Office, 1928), p. 3.

9. Whitehouse to Kellogg, Dec. 31, 1927, *FR: 1927*, II, 630. A friend at the Foreign Office privately told Whitehouse that Briand was much disappointed at the nature of the Dec. 28 note, as he had hoped for a bilateral convention.

native but to give to the press the entire text of his proposal to the French Government.[10]

Kellogg's move had an immediate effect. James, the Paris correspondent of the New York *Times,* noted that spokesmen for the French Foreign Office had dropped their daily criticisms of a multilateral compact outlawing war and announced flatly that the French Government was in favor of the American plan "now and forevermore." [11] The serious French press swung glibly into line with the newly assumed attitude of the Foreign Office. *Le Temps,* for example, which only the day before thought Kellogg was seeking to torpedo the League of Nations, discovered the next day that, after all, such an interpretation was wrong.[12]

Short-lived contrition! Almost as if to counter the publication of Kellogg's famous note of December 28 Briand prepared an immediate answer.[13] Although he began his missive by a show of affability, expressing his government's great approval of Kellogg's new multilateral Outlawry idea, the French foreign minister

10. Kellogg decided for publication on Wednesday morning, Jan. 4. Kellogg to Herrick, Jan. 3, 1928, 711.5112 France/82. When apprised by Whitehouse of the note's forthcoming release, Léger appeared perturbed and surprised. The Foreign Office, he said, had presumed there would be no release until after further discussion between the two governments concerning such release. Whitehouse to Kellogg, Jan. 5, 1928, 711.5112 France/85.

Kellogg also had stated to Herrick, Jan. 3, that he would make an announcement on Jan. 4 that he had proposed a new arbitration treaty to France and that identic treaties were being submitted to other countries which had expiring Root treaties. (On Dec. 29, 1927, Kellogg had addressed a note to the British ambassador proposing a treaty, mutatis mutandis identical with that proposed the day before to France, except for inclusion of certain reservations in Article 2 relative to the Empire.)

11. Dispatch from Paris, Jan. 4, 1928, in New York *Times,* Jan. 5. Initial press reaction to Kellogg's release of the Dec. 28 note had been unfavorable. Although almost every morning paper had published the note, Whitehouse reported to Kellogg on Jan. 5 that its reception was cool indeed. The prevailing thought, wrote the American chargé, was that the note had "distorted" Briand's original suggestion. 711.5112 France/84.

12. Dispatch from Paris, Jan. 5, 1928, in New York *Times,* Jan. 6.

13. Dated Jan. 5, 1928, and transmitted by Claudel to Kellogg, Jan. 6, 1928, *FR: 1928,* I, 1–2.

quickly got to the point—which was sharp indeed. Briand thought it would be "advantageous" for France and the United States to sign the proposed multilateral treaty first and immediately. He dropped the Shotwellian phrase, "renunciation of war as an instrument of national policy," and declared instead for renouncing "all wars of aggression." Why these changes? Undoubtedly the sign-first suggestion would have been highly advantageous for French diplomatic prestige; [14] and the new word "aggression" subtly pointed the way to accepting the Locarno definition of an aggressor, which in turn opened the whole wide—and to the security-conscious French, most pleasurable—vista of the Geneva Protocol!

Washington's reaction to this performance was instantaneous. State Department officials may have wished to applaud Briand's cleverness, but they had nothing but objection to the content of his note. Claudel already on January 4—two days before he delivered the French note—had in Briand's name asked Assistant Secretary Castle whether the United States would object to signing the anti-war treaty first with France, and Castle had replied that Claudel must "well understand" why the United States Government could do no such thing.[15] But either Claudel had not relayed this information to Briand, or Briand had chosen to ignore it, or perhaps it came too late. Anyway, the French ambassador now had to bear the brunt of the State Department's displeasure. Claudel, announced the New York *Times*, was told plainly, "as he has been from the first," that the United States would enter into no bilateral arrangement smack-

14. Also, if the United States and France signed first and if by chance no other nations signed afterward, then Briand would have achieved his negative military alliance.

Hunter Miller in his *Peace Pact of Paris*, p. 20, finds it "very difficult" to understand why the French note of Jan. 5 suggested France and the United States sign first. "If a multilateral treaty were to come into force, it was certainly in the interest of France that the discussions regarding its terms should be participated in at least by the other Great Powers." From a legal viewpoint, yes; from a political, no.

15. "I said . . . he could well understand that we would not want to sign with France unless we knew that the others were going to sign also." Memorandum by Castle of a conversation with Claudel, Jan. 4, 1928, 711.5112 U.S./9.

ing of a negative military alliance. As for Briand's new word aggression, it was a source of "amazement" to Washington officials.[16] ("I had an informal press conference . . . and talked pretty freely," wrote Assistant Secretary Castle in his diary, January 7, 1928. "The result is that we have a good press on the whole this morning.") [17]

16. Dispatch from Washington, Jan. 6 in New York *Times,* Jan. 7, 1928.

17. ". . . there was Briand's answer to our note about outlawing war. The French Government said it was delighted with our note, etc. and that it would be glad to sign a treaty immediately with us, renouncing resort to 'aggressive' war, which treaty could later be signed with other nations. Of course we cannot accept any such thing. It is a new proposition. We shall not sign anything with France unless we know very well that the other nations will sign it also and we shall not be willing to include the phrase 'aggressive war' because that immediately links the thing up with the League of Nations and makes a definition of aggression necessary." Castle diary, Jan. 7, 1928.

It is interesting to recall that President Coolidge, Dec. 3, 1924, in his Annual Message to Congress came out for outlawing aggressive war: "Much interest has of late been manifested in this country in the discussion of various proposals to outlaw aggressive war. I look with great sympathy upon the examination of this subject. It is in harmony with the traditional policy of our country, which is against aggressive war . . ." *FR: 1924,* I, xxi–xxii. Ever since Coolidge had become President, the Outlawrists had been importuning him to outlaw war. The formula he used in his Annual Message, however, was "to outlaw aggressive war." The Levinson group never used this word "aggression," for it was "European." It is quite probable that Coolidge took his idea of outlawing aggressive war from a certain Samuel Colcord of New York. As head of the Committee for Educational Publicity, which listed a number of impressive names on its letterhead, Colcord prior to the 1924 November election fairly peppered Coolidge with letters and telegrams asking for outlawry of aggressive war. On Oct. 20, 1924, for example, Colcord reported to Coolidge that he had given much thought as to how to bring back into the Republican fold those erring brothers who departed in 1922 because the Republicans had done nothing about the League. The answer, declared Colcord, was to outlaw aggressive war. Coolidge MSS. Although the president's secretary, C. Bascom Slemp, was rather cautious in replying to these Colcord letters, one must conclude that Coolidge took notice; for he mentioned outlawry of aggressive war, first in his acceptance speech before the Republican convention, then (in a letter to Colonel James A. Drain, printed in the New York *Times,* Nov. 3, 1924) in connection with Armistice Day, 1924, and finally in his Annual Message to Congress on the State of the Union. Had Aristide Briand, in 1928 himself advocating outlawry of aggressive war, known of Coolidge's prior commitments, he could have cited them with embarrassing effect.

Claudel appears to have been somewhat ashamed of delivering the "amazing" French note. He consequently called on Castle for a confidential tête-à-tête.[18] The ambassador said he felt perhaps everyone had put the wrong emphasis on the antiwar negotiations in that all the discussion centered about war and the Outlawry of war. Agreeing that everybody hoped to see war outlawed, he nonetheless believed that the phrase, as used by "the sentimentalists," might bear within itself great dangers. If the different governments should sign a pact outlawing *all* war, he feared it would be the greatest stimulus to "bolshevists and socialists and cranks of all varieties." He could not escape the feeling that in some cases war was not only not immoral but was absolutely moral and necessary—for example, what the United States then was doing in Nicaragua.[19] Claudel then proposed, strictly as his own idea, a joint declaration of principles, which Castle at the time agilely managed to memorize almost word for word and afterward put down in a Department memorandum. Claudel evidently hoped to see this innocuous declaration [20] substituted for the proposed antiwar treaty. Castle received the ambas-

18. The following account is from Castle's official memorandum of the conversation, Jan. 7, 1928, 711.5112 France/111.

19. American marines were policing the strife-ridden republic.

20. Although Castle afterward wrote down the main points of Claudel's proposal, the French ambassador over two months later (Mar. 24) presented Undersecretary Olds with a copy. 711.5112 France/225, which follows, is the official State Department translation:

"The Signatory States declare that in their reciprocal relations they undertake to be guided by the following principles.

(1) Justice and law, which is the expression of it, must be the sole rule of conduct between the States as between individuals.

(2) In case of conflict of interests, juridical means only are permissible for settlement of differences.

(3) States which shall have recognized these principles are entitled to count upon the council [sic] and upon the support of the other Signatory States in order to help them regulate these differences *by means other than violence* in conformity with justice and law.

(4) Each of the Signatory States retains the right of legitimate defense.

(5) Any State having recourse to war in order to obtain a settlement of its differences with the other Signatories shall ipso facto place itself beyond the pale of the present Treaty."

sador's suggestion courteously, but nothing ever came of it. That
Briand had a hand in Claudel's proposition is virtually certain, for
Claudel two months later proposed his declaration to Undersecretary Olds.[21] It is of course a regular diplomatic practice for ambassadors, under instructions, to offer suggestions as "strictly personal" ideas.

In spite of Claudel's new and professedly personal idea, the
State Department outwardly continued to wear a look of amazement
toward the French replique; and here, with astonishment written
on the faces of high Washington officials, we may momentarily leave
the Franco-American negotiations. Aristide Briand in his note had
startlingly demonstrated the strange vagaries of what many Americans often described as the "European mind." Having acquainted
ourselves with the French aspects of that mind we may now profit-
ably probe the European mind, British model.

II

Officially, Britain had not yet entered into the antiwar discussions, but Outlawry already was a word to conjure with in the British Isles. The Foreign Office, while perhaps still believing Outlawry
of war was buncombe, never again would make such an admission
openly. Harrison Brown therefore had little trouble in obtaining
an interview for Wednesday, January 4, 1928, with Lord Cushendun, Sir Austen Chamberlain's principal assistant at the Foreign
Office.[22]

Brown found Cushendun sitting before a fire, flicking cigarette
ash into it from the depths of a deep chair. He struggled up to welcome his visitor. Brown noticed that His Lordship was large and
bovine, and reserved his smile exclusively for entering and depart-
ing visitors. Asked about the Briand proposal, Cushendun said he
would have done the same thing as Briand in regard to the original
offer had he been representing France, and he would feel the same
way as the French felt now about the American attempt to extend
the pact to other countries. Cushendun said that he decidedly had

21. For Claudel's conversation with Olds, see below, pp. 168–169.
22. Who later, as acting foreign secretary, signed at Paris the antiwar treaty.

no use for gestures, that they meant nothing and would not be worth the paper they were written on; any country, he observed, would break such a contract if the national interest required it.

Brown, astonished, ventured the remark that even though the Outlawry proposals remained merely resolutions they at least would have value if they broke the connection between militarism and patriotism.

Cushendun stared. Hmmm, well, perhaps so some day, but the time had not yet come.

Brown countered that at least there was an incentive for helping it come—namely, that if it did not appear soon then civilization would wipe itself out.

Well, yes, that might happen.

Cushendun thought that he had read Morrison's book—he fancied that Lady Astor had given it to him. If not he would let Brown know.

His Lordship thereupon shook hands very warmly and beamed upon his visitor.

Harrison Brown did not beam when he afterward wrote to Levinson. How, he asked, could salvation come from such people as the Cushenduns? [23]

All was not lost, for salvation suddenly appeared at the American State Department. Secretary Kellogg came to the rescue of Outlawry. In a new note, dated January 11, 1928, and given to Ambassador Claudel two days later, Kellogg said he was gratified by the French Government's acceptance of the multilateral idea "in principle." But the secretary did not think France and the United States should sign first. A treaty, even though acceptable to France and the United States, Kellogg declared, might for some reason be unacceptable to one of the other great powers. In such event the treaty could not come into force and "the present efforts of France [sic] and the United States would be rendered abortive. . . . I have no doubt that your Government will be entirely agreeable . . ." As for the "aggression" idea, Kellogg noticed that the French draft of June 20, 1927, did not so stipulate but provided rather for unconditional renunciation of war as an instrument of

23. Brown to Levinson, Jan. 8, 1928, Levinson MSS.

national policy; the secretary adhered to Briand's original suggestion.[24] Kellogg stood firmly by his proposal of December 28, 1927.
He would not budge.

To the Quai d'Orsay the American secretary of state's new-
found zeal for renunciation of war was proving very embarrassing.
For good and sufficient reasons Briand could neither refuse nor
accept a multilateral treaty. Kellogg abruptly had turned down
Briand's proposition of sign-first and stipulation for renouncing
wars of aggression. What further course of action was available to
the harassed French foreign minister?

III

It was not a simple matter for Briand to decide what next to do.
For a short time he seemed without any plan at all.

Meanwhile Ambassador Claudel spoke in New York at the
Union League Club during a dinner in honor of Ambassador Herrick. The American ambassador was about to return to France.
Claudel used the occasion to say that "no country in the world is
able to do war" if the United States disapproved. He then declared that France and the United States must take the leading part
in the new international era of peace which was just beginning.
"My dear Ambassador," said Claudel to Herrick that night,
". . . You have many times explained France to America, you will
have once more to explain America to France. She will believe you,
for, to use an American expression, she knows that Myron Herrick
is the man 'who delivers the goods.' " Herrick, however, refused to
make any affirmations that evening about delivering the goods and
spoke rather on the pressing problem of making America's foreign service a career service, a service of dedicated experts instead
of volunteers.[25] Perhaps Herrick, speaking of volunteers, thought of
certain individuals whom President Coolidge not so long before
had called by that term.

24. Kellogg to Claudel, Jan. 11, 1928, *FR: 1928*, I, 3–5. Wrote Castle,
apropos this note: "Wednesday [Jan. 11] was largely taken up with discussions
with the Secretary and Olds about an answer to the latest Briand note. This
was finally sent on Friday and was pretty good . . ." Castle diary, Jan. 14, 1928.
25. New York *Times*, Jan. 14, 1928.

The morning after the Union League dinner there appeared an indication that the State Department might be thawing out. The Department, for some reason, on January 14, 1928, lifted its ban against flotation of French industrial securities in the United States, a ban which had been in force for more than three years as a result of the failure of France to refund her war debt. This announcement followed recent notification to France that the Department would place no obstacle in the way of the French Government's plans to refund in the United States its old eight-per-cent bonds so as to permit a lower interest rate. Perhaps these moves—permission to refund, and also to float industrial securities—were only a quid pro quo, for observers noticed that recent French tariff discriminations against American goods were temporarily in abeyance. Perhaps also the improvement in Franco-American relations occasioned by airplane diplomacy and Briand's overtures of friendship—an improvement which if not noticeable in the State Department was evident among the American people in general—made this move expedient.[26]

While financial experts speculated on the changing pattern of Franco-American refunding operations and while Ambassadors Herrick and Claudel were thinking about delivering the goods, in Washington there convened the Third Conference on the Cause and Cure of War. Mrs. Carrie Chapman Catt, graying in the serv-

---

26. The effectiveness of governmental bans on foreign loans evidently was slight, for they were honored mostly in the breach. It was a simple matter to export funds by roundabout means. This certainly had occurred in the United States in spite of the State Department.

The French money market at this time, moreover, was very easy; Poincaré only a few days before the American move had raised the then existing ban on French capital export abroad (the ban had been in effect since the war). France probably had no need of American industrial loans. In the spring of 1928 the Republic had upwards of a billion dollars in credits in the United States, and this huge balance hardly indicated need of French companies for American capital.

French governmental circles appear to have welcomed the new American attitude because sooner or later there might follow a lifting of the ban against *new* French Government flotations in the American market. This action might prove highly important if the French Government decided to stabilize its currency after the May 1928 elections. Hence the State Department announcement of Jan. 14 held important promise.

ice of women's rights but still brimful of energy, presided at the conference's deliberations. When Mrs. Catt's formidable figure appeared at any gathering those in attendance knew they were in for action—that she would have some kind of goods of her own to deliver. There was no pussyfooting about Mrs. Catt.[27] To the hundred delegates from nine national women's organizations she now declared war on the war system. Secretary of War Dwight F. Davis, Admiral Frank H. Schofield, and Assistant Secretary of State William R. Castle spoke to the conference. All three speakers were unanimous in asserting that there was no nation more instinctively opposed to all thought of war than the United States.

Particularly interesting was Assistant Secretary Castle's speech. He declared that peace, to be real, must be a state of mind. Concerning the antiwar treaty with France, Castle became specific. "We felt," he said, "that an agreement that under no circumstances would we attack France might cause irritation and unrest in other nations. It would almost inevitably have been looked upon by them as something closely approaching a defensive alliance." Castle then illustrated to his audience—with some bravery, considering the recent activities of that audience—how professional peace makers and agitators had sought to influence the State Department in favor of the Briand treaty. One person called Castle on the telephone and said: "It is an outrage that our Government should hang back in a matter of this kind. I am going to make speeches about it and I warn you that I shall attack the Department of State as it deserves. I am absolutely in favor of the Briand treaty. Will you tell me what is in it?" [28] ". . . let me assure you," Castle warned, "that there is far more danger in peace pacts based on muddled thinking than there is in refusing to sign new pacts at all." [29]

The following day Mrs. Catt addressed the delegates. She told

27. Mrs. Catt never allowed any shillyshallying by her followers in respect to whatever issue she was advocating. In personal relations she was an awesome, revered figure. No one ever called her "Carrie." The women always referred to her as "Mrs. Catt" or, if on terms of relative intimacy, "C.C.C."

28. Evidently this incident occurred before publication of Kellogg's note of Jan. 11, 1928, which revealed the text of Briand's original proposal.

29. New York *Times,* Jan. 16, 1928.

them the next war was moving down upon them with the pitiless certainty of an avalanche. Unless there were "rock-ribbed" treaties pledging the civilized nations, led by the great powers, to agree to renounce war among themselves, peace would not last. Mrs. Catt predicted that a rock-ribbed treaty such as the Kellogg proposal would break the backbone of present-day war.[30]

A slight commotion upset the fervor of the conference. Miss Annie Matthews of New York stood up and declared Secretary Kellogg insincere in his peace efforts, and that his proposal to France was a futile gesture, equivalent to the project for universal disarmament which Russia recently had presented to the League of Nations.[31] But Miss Matthews had hardly sat down when Mrs. Catt went into action, squelched Miss Matthews properly, and steered through the conference a resolution endorsing the Kellogg proposal.[32]

During these days the diplomatic picture went out of focus and blurred. It began to clear up again as the Quai d'Orsay prepared a new French note to answer Kellogg. The Havana International Conference of American States was in session, and the French press had a field day scoring United States imperialism. Reports from Paris indicated an anti-American press assault more harsh than even the Sacco-Vanzetti campaign during the summer of 1927. Appropriately, Chargé Sheldon Whitehouse during these critical days told the members of the Paris American Club at their regular Thursday luncheon that "too much soft soap" did not help Franco-American relations.[33] Certain it was that the French Foreign Office had issued no press instructions for soft soap.

In this acrimonious setting Ambassador Claudel delivered [34] Briand's latest reply to Secretary Kellogg.

Perhaps Poincaré himself had collaborated with his foreign minister, for Briand this time seemed to have lost all his usual literary flair. The note was stiff and irritable. "The American Govern-

30. New York *Times,* Jan. 17, 1928.
31. See above, p. 126 n.
32. New York *Times,* Jan. 19, 1928.
33. New York *Times,* Jan. 20, 1928.
34. *Ibid.,* Jan. 21, 1928.

ment," it announced, ". . . considered . . . for reasons of its own
which the French Government has not failed to take into account,
that it would be opportune to broaden this manifestation against
war . . . The Government of the Republic was not opposed to
this expansion of its original plan, but it could not but realize . . .
that the new negotiation as proposed would be more complex and
likely to meet with various difficulties." As for the question of the
two countries signing first, suggested by Briand, this according to
the new note was simply a matter of procedure; France offered to
sign first "only because of its desire more speedily and more surely
to achieve the result which it seeks in common with the United
States." As for the question of renouncing wars of aggression,
France's commitments under the Covenant and Locarno had inspired this formula. The French Government also reminded the
United States of the League resolution of September 1927 against
wars of aggression. In conclusion the note doggedly affirmed that a
bilateral pact still would be best.[35]

This frigid note appeared to mark the end of negotiations. The
New York *Times* reported [36] the virtual death of the antiwar treaty.
Even so well-disposed a critic as Professor Shotwell, in his notable
study of the antiwar pact written during the summer of 1928, felt
moved to declare that this French reply appeared to be "an effort
to withdraw from the whole negotiation." [37]

IV

Washington bided its time. In a few days the French Government shifted to a new line. The Franco-American arbitration treaty
was being prepared for signature on February 6, the one-hundred-

35. Claudel to Kellogg, Jan. 21, 1928, *FR: 1928,* I, 6–8. "Another French
note on the Briand proposal came in this morning," wrote Castle in his diary.
"It gets us no furtherer. The Ambassador, in talking with me about it, said that
he thought we ought to stop note writing and talk things over. He is entirely
right, especially, as I reminded him, as the French Foreign Office leaks always
even before we receive the notes. The note had not a single new argument but
made the French position a little more precise." Castle diary, Jan. 21, 1928.
36. New York *Times,* Jan. 22, 1928.
37. James T. Shotwell, *War as an Instrument of National Policy,* p. 133.

fiftieth anniversary of the first Franco-American treaties, and the French decided to make the most of the occasion. Briand hoped to head off the Outlawrists and renunciationists, now so zealously led by Secretary Kellogg toward a multilateral treaty, by blowing trumpets for the bilateral arbitration treaty.

The French Embassy sounded the first blare by indicating to the press that because of the arbitration treaty's preamble there now would exist a moral obligation between France and the United States not to go to war. The preamble read as follows: ". . . Eager by their example . . . to demonstrate their condemnation of war as an instrument of national policy in their mutual relations . . ." [38] Someone at the State Department, however, stopped this music by insisting that the preamble was not legally binding.[39]

The Department seems indeed to have been well aware of Briand's attempt to play up the arbitration treaty and perhaps make it the substitute for his proposed bilateral treaty for the renunciation of war between the United States and France. Herrick on February 1 had talked with Briand, who then remarked that negotiations for the arbitration treaty were proceeding satisfactorily. While the preamble, the foreign minister said, did not cover in the form he had wished his original proposal of a bilateral treaty, nonetheless the preamble would contain the essentials of the proposed pact.[40] Herrick concluded that this undoubtedly was Briand's face-saving line which he would take in the Chamber of Deputies and elsewhere. The ambassador suggested some friendly comment on Briand by the Department at the time the treaty was signed so as to aid in the face-saving process.[41]

Secretary Kellogg uncooperatively went to Canada before the

38. *FR: 1928*, II, 817.

39. New York *Times*, Feb. 3, 1928. For discussion of the binding nature of treaty preambles, see above, p. 134 n.

40. The Quai d'Orsay earlier had made an attempt to cut out of the arbitration treaty's preamble Shotwell's phrase, "condemnation of war as an instrument of national policy." Briand on Jan. 7 had omitted the phrase in a French draft arbitration treaty. Kellogg's revised draft, transmitted to Claudel on Feb. 1, again embodied Shotwell's words. See *FR: 1928*, II, 811, 813, 817.

41. Herrick to Kellogg, Feb. 1, 1928, 711.5112 U.S./15.

signature of the arbitration treaty, but the ceremony in Washington was impressive. The two signatories, Claudel and Olds, seated themselves at the long ebony table in the diplomatic reception room of the Department of State. A dozen motion picture cameras surrounded the table.[42] Claudel in signing spoke of the arbitration treaty as being in the same category as the Franco-American treaty of alliance of 1778. He also sought to make it appear like a treaty for the Outlawry of war. "The first treaty [of 1778]," he said, "gave a start to a new nation; the second treaty gives the start to a new idea. Outlawry of war is a specifically American idea . . ."[43] After the ceremony Olds and Claudel, together with Jules Henry of the French Embassy, Spencer Phenix,[44] and Assistant Secretary Castle all posed solemnly standing about the arbitration treaty, and photographers took pictures.

That night in New York there was a dinner at the Waldorf.[45] Messages arrived from Coolidge, Poincaré, Herrick, and others. Claudel had hurried up from Washington, and his after-dinner address gave Senator Borah credit for "the grand word, outlawry of war." He remarked that after this phrase had been enunciated and heard in France it only remained for diplomats to frame the new principle in a treaty of arbitration. Outlawry, said Claudel, was a word the inborn virtue of which literally compelled diplomats to make way for it in the complicated game of international relations. Concerning the new arbitration treaty, Claudel asserted that "No negotiations were ever conducted in a more open light and in a freer air, an air so free and so fresh that it makes old diplomacy quiver."[46]

In Paris there was a gala fete for the new treaty. Briand and Herrick had luncheon, and with mingled emotions looked at and read the old alliance treaty of 1778 which Briand had had brought out of the Quai d'Orsay archives. The two men made informal speeches.

42. ". . . such a phalanx of cameras as I have seldom seen." Castle diary, Feb. 8, 1928.

43. New York *Times,* Feb. 7, 1928.

44. Secretary Kellogg's special assistant.

45. Held under the auspices of three leading French societies in the United States: The France-American Society, La Fédération de l'Alliance Française, and the American Society of the French Legion of Honor.

46. New York *Times,* Feb. 7, 1928.

Briand said that many treaties had been signed during the past few years and some of them might and probably would suffer the ultimate fate of Benjamin Franklin's treaty, dying in so far as the letter was concerned. But if the spirit survived, of what avail the letter? Herrick in reply stressed the dignity, reason, and deliberation which always had characterized the settlement of any small differences between France and the United States.[47] "This long experience we have had in handling the difficulties and the problems which naturally arise between two friendly nations," he maintained, "is itself sufficient to banish all fears of possible recourse to a brutal adjustment of our affairs by war." [48]

Two days after these flattering exchanges, however, newspapermen uncovered dissatisfaction at the Quai d'Orsay. It seemed that members of the Foreign Office staff the evening of February 8, seeking diversion, had endeavored in vain to find any subject for arbitration which could by any stretch of the imagination come within the scope of the new treaty. A report of the evening's discovery appeared in the New York *Times* [49] and came to the attention of Secretary Kellogg. At a State Department press conference the secretary discussed it vehemently and for the record. The treaty, he snapped, was purely an arbitration treaty of judicial questions, "the only questions I think any Government can arbitrate." The treaty was an advance over treaties hitherto made by the United States. This arbitration treaty, Kellogg proclaimed, "is not intended to take the place of the Briand proposal for an antiwar treaty." [50]

V

During all the discussion preceding and following signature of the arbitration treaty the proposed antiwar treaty remained uppermost in the mind of Senator Borah. The *New York Times Maga-*

47. He overlooked the acrimony which preceded and followed the Rives Convention of 1831.

48. New York *Times*, Feb. 7, 1928.

49. Feb. 9, 1928.

50. Interview of Feb. 11, in New York *Times*, Feb. 12, 1928. Kellogg on Feb. 2 had told Sir Esme Howard that the arbitration treaty had "nothing to do with" the antiwar treaty. Memorandum by Kellogg of a conversation with Howard, Feb. 2, 1928, 711.5112 France/144.

zine of February 5 printed a front-page article by the senator entitled "One Great Treaty to Outlaw All Wars." Written to a large extent by Levinson,[51] this article appearing under the name of the chairman of the Senate Committee on Foreign Relations became important in the later history of the antiwar negotiations. For the Levinson-Borah article suggested to France a way to honor her Continental alliances and sign the Kellogg treaty. A breach of the proposed multilateral treaty, Borah argued,[52] automatically would release the signatories from their obligations thereunder. France's commitment to Belgium, for example, would only be in suspended animation, not abrogated, so long as no nation violated the multilateral treaty. But upon violation—say by Germany—France became automatically released from the antiwar treaty and might proceed to the aid of Belgium under the terms of the Franco-Belgian alliance.

Strangely enough Ambassador Claudel a month earlier, in one of his private tête-à-têtes with Assistant Secretary Castle, had also suggested this very idea of release in case of breach. In his "strictly personal" five-point proposal Claudel had included as point five: "Any State having recourse to war in order to obtain a settlement of its differences with the other Signatories shall ipso facto place itself beyond the pale of the present Treaty." Perhaps Levinson, who kept in close touch with the French Embassy in Washington, obtained the idea of release-in-case-of-breach from Claudel himself. And supposing that Claudel's five-point proposal in reality was Briand's: Briand could have obtained the idea of release from Part I, Article 3 of the almost-forgotten Shotwell-Chamberlain draft treaty. Then what a tortuous route this release idea may have taken: Shotwell to Briand to Claudel to Levinson to Borah.[53]

Reports from Borah's office said he had received scores of telegrams commending his *Times* article and that a friend had arranged for printing three thousand copies.[54] The article received

---

51. See J. Stoner, *Levinson,* pp. 347–350. Stoner prints Levinson's draft and Borah's article in parallel columns.

52. This idea was Levinson's.

53. And later to Kellogg (see below, pp. 173–174, 187.

54. New York *Times,* Feb. 7, 1928.

wide distribution, appearing abroad in British and Continental periodicals. Even Professor Shotwell could not contain his enthusiasm for Borah's new formula and in a long letter to the editor of the New York *Times* declared "Senator Borah has cleared away much of the obstruction in the path of negotiations." Outlawry and the League of Nations envisaged the same goal, Shotwell wrote: the community of nations should outlaw a nation which ran amok; and self-defense was always justifiable, individual or collective.[55]

In spite of the favorable response to Borah's *Times* article three weeks elapsed with almost no development in the Franco-American negotiations. Each side seemed to be watching the other to see who would make the first move. Finally Secretary Kellogg grew tired of waiting and on February 27 gave Ambassador Claudel a new American note.

"A Government free to conclude . . . a bilateral treaty," Kellogg held, "should be no less able to become a party to an identical multilateral treaty since it is hardly to be presumed that members of the League of Nations are in a position to do separately something they cannot do together." [56] Kellogg declared he desired no definitions of aggression in the treaty, for such might virtually destroy the antiwar proposal itself; definitions would lead to reservations, and thus the governments would be only "recording their impotence, to the keen disappointment of mankind in general." Kellogg for the third time—December 28, January 11, and now February 27—proposed a multilateral treaty.[57]

It was evident that up to this point Briand had achieved nothing in his maneuvering with Secretary Kellogg. In two formal notes [58] he had failed to break off the antiwar negotiations. Attempting next to shift Outlawry and renunciation on to the Franco-

55. *Ibid.*, Feb. 6, 1928.

56. Kellogg had wanted to put in his note a statement that if the French believed a multilateral antiwar treaty was contrary to the ideals of the League it would prove that the League was a military alliance. Wrote Castle in his diary, Feb. 17: "I think we have got him to give up the phrase which would certainly lead to an outburst. We can intimate the same idea without saying it in that blunt fashion."

57. Kellogg to Claudel, Feb. 27, 1928, *FR: 1928*, I, 9–11.

58. Those of Jan. 5 and Jan. 21.

American arbitration treaty, he failed again. Briand then received the new note from the United States Government insisting upon Kellogg's original multilateral proposal.

Kellogg's persistent antiwar diplomacy by now had very much discomfited the French foreign minister, who apparently was going to have to choose between his loyalties as a Frenchman and his public reputation as a man of peace. As Assistant Secretary Castle summed up the situation, "I do not think the French will agree [to the multilateral treaty proposal], but I think they will have an awful time not to agree." [59]

VI

At approximately this time there appeared a certain transformation in Secretary Kellogg's attitude toward the proposed multilateral antiwar treaty. One of the reasons Kellogg originally had made his multilateral proposition was to appease the American peace movement, enthusiastic over Briand's suggestion for Franco-American perpetual friendship. This had been achieved. As Assistant Secretary Castle on February 28, 1928 wrote in his diary with obvious satisfaction: "After all we have done what we set out to do. We have made a big, peaceful gesture and we have public opinion fairly solidly behind us." In proposing his multilateral treaty Kellogg also undoubtedly looked forward to placing Aristide Briand in a diplomatic dilemma. The French foreign minister had highly embarrassed Kellogg by offering a bilateral treaty between the United States and France, and we may be certain that Kellogg enjoyed Briand's equal embarrassment at the prospect of a multilateral treaty. But having accomplished all this the American secretary of state began to undergo a momentous change of heart: *he began to believe that a multilateral treaty really would be a great gift to the world.*

Not that Kellogg was ready to advocate such a treaty unreservedly.[60] There were certain contingencies when the secretary deemed the United States Government might need to resort to

59. "We have Monsieur Briand out on a limb and we might just as well keep him there." Castle diary, Feb. 28, 1928.

60. See below, Chapter XII.

force—for instance, self-defense, or the Monroe Doctrine. But even with these reservations Kellogg began to feel that a multilateral anti-war treaty would constitute a magnificent boon to world peace. The secretary of state was an elderly man, at the end of a long public career. He was planning to retire on March 4, 1929.[61] What better than to grace his final months in office with signature of a grand treaty renouncing war as an instrument of national policy? Such a treaty might become the consummation and crown of his life's work.[62]

When he observed this change in Kellogg's attitude Assistant Secretary Castle was flabbergasted. As he wrote in his diary: "For weeks the press has chorused approval of F.B.K.'s exchange of notes with Briand on outlawing war . . . actually it is futile. It appealed enormously to the Pacifists and the Earnest Christians but . . . I think it is about time for the correspondence to stop. The political trick has been turned and now we should take a well deserved rest. *The funny thing is that Olds and the Secretary seem to take it all with profound seriousness . . .*"[63]

Such was the new prospect when the foreign ministers of France,

61. Kellogg to Herrick, Mar. 19, 1928, Herrick MSS.
62. Such it became. In Professor Bryn-Jones' biography of Kellogg, written with Kellogg's approval and active assistance, there occurs the following passage: "And of all the experiences and recollections of those years [of public service], none shine out more brightly in retrospect than those that were connected with the project which Mr. Kellogg always regarded as the consummation and crown of his labors—the Pact of Paris." *Kellogg*, p. 251.

Below the Kellogg window at the National Cathedral in Washington, where Kellogg's ashes are buried, is the following inscription:

IN GRATEFUL MEMORY OF
FRANK BILLINGS KELLOGG, LL.D.
1856–1937
SENATOR OF THE UNITED STATES FROM MINNESOTA
AMBASSADOR TO THE COURT OF ST. JAMES
SECRETARY OF STATE
A JUDGE OF THE PERMANENT COURT OF INTERNATIONAL JUSTICE
JOINT AUTHOR OF THE KELLOGG-BRIAND PACT
IN FIDELITY TO AMERICAN IDEALS HE SERVED HIS NATION
WITH CONSPICUOUS ABILITY AND SOUGHT EQUITY AND PEACE
AMONG THE NATIONS OF THE WORLD.
HIS BODY RESTS IN THIS CATHEDRAL

63. Castle diary, Mar. 6, 1928. Italics inserted.

Britain, and Germany gathered at Geneva early in March for a meeting of the League Council. Rumor had it that to the ministers Kellogg's proposal appeared, with the help of Borah's *Times* article, in a new light. Instead of continuing to exchange polemical notes between Paris and Washington, the new policy was to ascertain just what Kellogg wanted and thus what reservations would be necessary to make his proposal acceptable.[64] On the train back from Geneva to Paris the ubiquitous James of the *Times* asked Briand for a statement on the Kellogg peace plan. "There is every possibility," Briand said, "of the conclusion of this treaty suggested by the United States, provided we can find a formula which is fair and square. I am convinced we shall be able to find it. And such is the sentiment of other European nations." [65]

What Briand had told his colleagues at Geneva was rather interesting. Upon Stresemann's return to Berlin, Ambassador Jacob Schurman inquired just what had happened. Stresemann responded that the big five (Germany, France, Britain, Italy, and Japan) had discussed the war-prevention treaty only once, and then informally: Briand had said to his colleagues, in a lighter vein, that when he had proposed to America a treaty providing that France and the United States should renounce war as an instrument of their national policy toward each other he had meant it rather as a gesture, but now that the secretary of state's reply had invested it with importance he might wish in the future to consult them on the subject; that in the meantime he wished only to ask them one question, Had the American Government communicated with their governments in regard to it? To this inquiry Chamberlain, Adachi (the Japanese representative on the League Council), and Stresemann said that it had.[66]

Meanwhile Secretary Kellogg had given in New York a speech before the Council on Foreign Relations.[67] Kellogg made his posi-

64. Edwin L. James, Geneva, Mar. 6, in New York *Times*, Mar. 7, 1928.

65. Dispatch from Paris, Mar. 11, in New York *Times*, Mar. 12.

66. Schurman to Kellogg, Mar. 16, 1928, *FR: 1928*, I, 15. Kellogg on Jan. 6 authorized communication to the great powers of the text of Briand's June 20, 1927, draft and the American counterproposal of Dec. 28. *FR: 1928*, I, 3.

67. An eminent organization with headquarters in New York whose avowed purpose was to study international aspects of American political, economic, and

tion very clear—as he already had done in three previous notes and numerous conversations and interviews. ". . . I cannot state too emphatically," he said, "that . . . [the United States] will not become a party to any agreement which directly or indirectly, expressly or by implication, is a military alliance." He added that the American Government always was ready to conclude "appropriate" treaties for arbitration, for conciliation, and for the renunciation of war.[68]

Kellogg strengthened the effect of his speech by citing a resolution renouncing war as an instrument of national policy which seventeen American members of the League of Nations recently had signed at the Havana Inter-American Conference.[69] The secretary of state in his speech stressed in three different places the fact that League members had signed this antiwar resolution. If seventeen American members of the League could sign such a statement, contended Kellogg, then why all the hesitation and talk in Europe about squaring the proposed peace treaty with the obligations of the League?

Perhaps it was not exactly to the point for Kellogg to chide France by citing the Havana resolution. The resolution renounced war only in its preamble, and moreover the resolution had no more binding effect than had the Polish resolution at the Eighth Assembly of the League of Nations in September 1927. The American states, meeting periodically in conference, never failed to release a shoal of pious resolutions which often were not worth the paper and ink necessary to print them.[70] It may be, however, that Secretary

financial problems. Formed after the World War the Council soon began publishing a quarterly *Foreign Affairs*, a *Political Handbook of the World*, a yearly survey of American foreign relations, and other individual volumes on special international questions.

68. For this speech of Mar. 15, 1928, see *American Journal of International Law*, 22 (1928), 253–261.

69. For the text of this resolution of Feb. 18, 1928, see Carnegie Endowment for International Peace, *The International Conferences of American States: 1898–1928* (New York, 1931), p. 437.

70. Intervention of the United States in Latin American affairs was the principal issue at the Havana conference. The Latin-American governments sought valiantly to persuade the United States to renounce such intervention.

Kellogg in citing the Havana resolution was hinting ever so delicately to European statesmen that, after all, he was not interested in unreservedly renouncing war, but rather in what one of his detractors, Miss Annie Matthews, so improperly had termed a "futile gesture" and what a skeptical American senator [71] later was to describe as an "international kiss."

Just how fervent an international kiss should properly be was a matter for the Emily Posts of diplomacy. Senator Borah gave his own opinion in an interview to Kirby Page, editor of *The World Tomorrow*. Talking with the senator soon after Secretary Kellogg's speech, Page reported Borah's eyes "glistening with enthusiasm" as he watched him at the private luncheon table in the Senate building. Borah said he had spent hours seeking to find a definition of aggression, but failed. Outlawry, of course, did not mean disarmament. But to attack the war system by outlawing war was "an incalculable contribution" to the security of the nations. In telling the joys of Outlawry Borah quite forgot the bowl of milk toast before him. He declared (and this declaration was the cause of some later embarrassment) that it was inconceivable that the United States should stand idly by in face of a flagrant violation of an Outlawry agreement.[72] "Of course, in such a crisis we would consult with the other signatories and take their judgment into account. But we should not bind ourselves in advance to accept their decision if it runs counter to our own conclusion." [73]

Ambassador Claudel called on Undersecretary Olds and again made an offer—again a "strictly personal" one—to sink the antiwar negotiations with an international declaration of principles. Claudel this time gave Olds the actual text of the five-point declaration

---

Renouncing war as an instrument of national policy probably was one means to this end.

There was another resolution, also dated Feb. 18, 1928, declaring aggression illicit and prohibited. For the text, see *ibid.,* pp. 441–442.

71. Reed of Missouri, *Congressional Record,* Jan. 5, 1929, p. 1186.

72. In the Senate, Jan. 7, 1929, he denied having said this. *Congressional Record,* Jan. 7, 1929, pp. 1281–1282.

73. New York *Times,* Mar. 25, 1928.

previously mentioned.[74] Olds told Claudel that public opinion in the United States would insist in the long run upon everything possible being done to outlaw war—in other words the American Government was not simply building a perfunctory official record on this subject but meant business. Claudel protested that his chief, Briand, was equally earnest and sincere and meant business, but that there were difficulties. The ambassador said that in the end a declaration of principles might be best. Olds insisted that public opinion the world over would regard anything short of a treaty as a confession of failure.[75] And so the dejected Claudel left the text of his own five-point declaration and gave up the struggle against Outlawry.

As the month of March drew to a close Aristide Briand surveyed the last three months of diplomatic maneuvering and knew that, although he had not yet lost, he was very close to losing. Perhaps the time had come to accept, at least nominally, Kellogg's suggestion for a multilateral antiwar treaty. Simultaneously it would be possible to add reservations to Kellogg's multilateral proposal, and the maneuvering then could commence again. Ambassador Claudel, March 30, presented a new note to the American secretary of state. "If Your Excellency really believes that greater chances of success may be found in this [multilateral] formula," Briand painfully began, ". . . the French Government would hesitate to discuss longer the question of its adherence to a plan which the American Government originated and for which it is responsible." Briand would insist only on "three fundamental points": (1) the treaty must be universal; (2) a breach would release the signatories; (3) the treaty would not prejudice the right of self-defense. France, averred its foreign minister, was "always ready to associate itself without ambiguity or reservation [sic], with any solemn and formal undertaking tending to ensure, strengthen or extend the effective solidarity of the Nations in the cause of peace." [76]

74. Above, pp. 151–152. Claudel in January had only read the declaration to Castle.

75. Memorandum by Olds of a conversation with Claudel, Mar. 24, 1928, 711.5112 France/225.

76. Claudel to Kellogg, Mar. 30, 1928, *FR: 1928*, I, 15–19.

Chapter Twelve: MODIFICATIONS,

QUALIFICATIONS, CONSIDERATIONS,

INTERPRETATIONS

After three months of evasive delay Aristide Briand finally had accepted the principle of a multilateral treaty renouncing war as an instrument of national policy. Briand, however, had no intention of omitting reservations in the proposed pact.

Nor did Secretary Kellogg himself desire an unconditional treaty. The secretary at about this time was becoming enamored with the grand idea of renouncing war; but Frank B. Kellogg could be counted upon never—not for even one moment—to lose sight of American national interests. Those interests required American reservations to any antiwar treaty. Kellogg knew this.

The reader should not conclude that Briand and Kellogg were now in perfect agreement, that in a short time they could come together and decide on the nature and form of their respective reservations. Briand remained intensely annoyed that the American secretary of state had jockeyed him into so embarrassing a position that he was forced to consent to the principle of a multilateral antiwar treaty. The French foreign minister undoubtedly would have been most happy at any time to withdraw from the negotiations. Kellogg, in turn, had been enormously disgusted by the manner in which Briand had placed pressure upon him for a bilateral pact of perpetual friendship. And now that the American secretary of state had with new zeal begun to advocate a multilateral treaty he felt deeply offended by Briand's almost undisguised efforts to stop the negotiations. Clearly, although both Kellogg and Briand wished reservations, it would be no easy task for them to agree as to precisely how the conditions should be attached to the proposed treaty. Kellogg, taken with the idea of renunciation of war, perhaps would not want to see too many reservations attached too obviously. Briand, disliking the entire affair, probably would continue his covert attempts at sabotage.

The first step in this new, "reserving" phase of the negotiations required some sort of new draft treaty over which to negotiate. Secretary Kellogg had not yet proposed an actual text of a multilateral antiwar treaty. Neither had Briand.

I

Kellogg submitted to Italy, Japan, Germany, and Great Britain on April 13, 1927, an official invitation to enter the antiwar discussions, and the invitation took the form of a draft treaty. The draft's two substantive articles were almost the same as those of Briand's original Pact of Perpetual Friendship offered nearly a year before. What changes appeared were only those necessary to transform the original bilateral pact into a multilateral instrument. The preamble had suitable amendments, as did the third article of ratification.[1]

Exactly one week later Aristide Briand made a countermove. He offered the powers a new, French-style draft of a multilateral antiwar treaty.

The French draft in Article 1 reserved legitimate self-defense, together with action under Locarno or the Covenant. Article 2 was almost identical with Article 2 of Briand's draft of June 20, 1927 (providing that settlement of international disputes never should be sought except by peaceful means). Article 3 was similar to Claudel's fifth "personal" suggestion of January 7, 1928; it released all signatories in the event of a treaty breach. Article 4 reserved rights and obligations of prior international agreements (meaning French treaties of alliance with Belgium, Poland, Czechoslovakia,

1. For text, see *FR: 1928*, I, 23–24.

Rumania, and Yugoslavia). Article 5 provided that the treaty to be binding must secure accession of all the nations—unless there should be specific agreement to the contrary. Article 6 contained details of ratification.[2]

2. Following are the substantive articles of Briand's draft, dated Apr. 20, 1928:

ARTICLE ONE

The High Contracting Parties without any intention to infringe upon the exercise of their rights of legitimate self-defense within the framework of existing treaties, particularly when the violation of certain of the provisions of such treaties constitutes a hostile act, solemnly declare that they condemn recourse to war and renounce it as an instrument of national policy; that is to say, as an instrument of individual, spontaneous and independent political action taken on their own initiative and not action in respect of which they might become involved through the obligation of a treaty such as the covenant of the League of Nations or any other treaty registered with the League of Nations. They undertake on those conditions not to attack or invade one another.

ARTICLE TWO

The settlement or solution of all disputes or conflicts of whatever nature or origin which might arise among the High Contracting Parties or between any two of them shall never be sought on either side except by pacific methods.

ARTICLE THREE

In case one of the High Contracting Parties should contravene this treaty, the other Contracting Powers would *ipso facto* be released with respect to that Party from their obligations under this treaty.

ARTICLE FOUR

The provisions of this treaty in no wise affect the rights and obligations of the Contracting Parties resulting from prior international agreements to which they are parties.

ARTICLE FIVE

The present treaty will be offered for the accession of all Powers and will have no binding force until it has been generally accepted unless the signatory Powers in accord with those that may accede hereto shall agree to decide that it shall come into effect regardless of certain abstentions.

The complete text is in *FR: 1928*, I, 32–34.

Ambassador Claudel felt abashed by having to deliver such a draft treaty. He later confided to Assistant Secretary Castle that the draft was utterly stupid. The ambassador explained that Briand evidently had told the Quai d'Orsay's legal expert, Henri Fromageot, to prepare something, and that he had produced nothing but *fromage*.[3]

When Secretary Kellogg saw this *projet au fromage* he became quite excited. No one has recorded what he said at the time, but as he held a doctor's degree in profanity [4] it would not be especially difficult to guess the substance of his remarks. Even when he had cooled a little he still considered the French draft wholly unacceptable to the United States: ". . . it cannot in any respect be regarded as an effective instrument for the promotion of world peace. It emphasizes war, not peace, and seems in effect to be a justification rather than a renunciation of the use of armed force. . . . if the present draft represents the limit to which the French Government is prepared to go in renouncing war by treaty, it is idle for the United States to endeavor to seek an agreement with France, the respective positions of the two Governments in that event being totally irreconcilable."

It is most curious to discover that Kellogg made the above strictures in a dispatch of April 23 to American embassies in Paris, Tokyo, London, and Rome, and later in this same dispatch accepted, almost point for point, the French reservations.[5] This though he had castigated the French draft as not in any respect an effective instrument for world peace, that it emphasized war, and that it was idle for the United States to seek such an agreement. Kellogg of course did not refer to French reservations. The secretary avowed rather that the United States Government was willing to discuss modifications [6] or qualifications [6] to the antiwar pact, and he undertook to deal seriatim with what seemed to be the six major considerations [6] which the French Government had

3. Castle diary, May 1, 1928.
4. See above, p. 81.
5. For text of Kellogg's acceptance of the French reservations, see *FR: 1928*, I, 36–38.
6. Kellogg's word, used in the note of Apr. 23.

emphasized in its correspondence and in its draft treaty: (1) self-defense; (2) the Covenant; (3) the Locarno treaties; (4) certain unspecified treaties of neutrality (the alliances); (5) release in case of breach; (6) universality. There was nothing in his proposed treaty, Kellogg argued, which conflicted with the first five of these vital points. In the case of (1) self-defense he declared such a right "inherent in every sovereign state" and "implicit in every treaty"; "Every nation is free at all times and regardless of treaty provisions to defend its territory from attack or invasion and it alone is competent to decide whether circumstances require recourse to war in self-defense."[7] One by one Kellogg discussed and accepted the other French considerations. The League Covenant, the French point (2), imposed no "affirmative primary obligation" to go to war; hence there could be no conflict between the Covenant and an antiwar treaty. Resort to war by any state in violation of the Locarno treaties (3) and the French alliances (4) would also be a breach of the multilateral antiwar treaty; and the parties to the latter treaty would thus be automatically released from their obligations thereunder, free to fulfill their Locarno and alliance commitments. There could be no question about relations with a treaty-breaking state (5), Kellogg repeated, for violation of a multilateral treaty against war would release the other signatories from their obligations to the treaty-breaking state. Only in the case of (6) universality—that the treaty before going into effect should include all the nations—did the secretary dissent; some obstructionist state, he contended, might block agreement or delay ratification in such a way as to render abortive the efforts of all the other powers. With this sole exception of universality, Kellogg thus managed to interpret the position of the United States Government so as to agree to all the considerations found in the French draft treaty of April 20.

7. It appears that as early as Apr. 21 Kellogg had prepared his views on self-defense—if not on the other points of Briand's draft. The secretary on that date told Sir Esme Howard that "there was nothing in the treaty which Briand had originally proposed to me and which is the one I proposed to the five other powers in any way restricting the right of self-defense; that that right of self-defense was inherent in every sovereign state and implicit in every treaty." Memorandum by Kellogg of a conversation with Howard, Apr. 21, 1928, 711.5112 France/280.

The secretary's dispatch, however, was for the personal information of the American ambassadors, and only for oral communication to the respective foreign ministers if deemed necessary.

Ambassador Houghton soon afterward cabled the substance of a conversation with Chamberlain. The latter had confessed he had not yet been able to give the proposed multilateral treaty any real study, but was sympathetic of course. He thought a meeting of the foreign secretaries might be necessary at some later date and hoped to meet Kellogg. Chamberlain asked about the Monroe Doctrine and assumed that he and Kellogg were agreed on the necessity of self-defense. Houghton repeated to Sir Austen his instructions from Kellogg: "That right [of self-defense] is inherent in every sovereign state . . ." Houghton in his cable to Kellogg suggested that the secretary give to the press the six-point discussion of April 23, 1928.[8]

The day after Chamberlain gingerly asked about self-defense Foreign Minister Gustav Stresemann in Berlin handed to Ambassador Schurman an official note formally accepting, in the name of the German Government, the American antiwar proposal. In the course of his note Stresemann deftly inserted three reservations —self-defense, release after violation, universality as the ultimate goal—but the German note if read uncritically sounded like an unconditional acceptance.[9] Chamberlain had cabled Stresemann asking the latter to hold back his reply until Chamberlain could discuss it with him; but Stresemann had answered that the government's reply had been accepted by the German Cabinet and could not be delayed.[10] Germany, by a skillful diplomatic stroke, thus had wasted no time in accepting the proposed treaty against war, American version. By moving speedily Stresemann had associated Germany with the United States, against the other great powers, in the campaign against war.

No less startling was the next development. Secretary Kellogg spoke in Washington April 28 at a dinner of the American Society of International Law. He had planned to speak extemporaneously.

8. Houghton to Kellogg, Apr. 27, 1928, *FR: 1928*, I, 39–41.
9. Stresemann to Schurman, Apr. 27, 1928, *ibid.*, 42–44.
10. Houghton to Kellogg, May 3, 1928, *FR: 1928*, I, 50.

But after reading Ambassador Houghton's cable of the day before he decided to use in his speech practically word for word the six numbered paragraphs of his April 23 cable.[11] Kellogg in such manner proclaimed publicly, if not officially, his acceptance of the French reservations. The secretary of state had not actually accepted the French draft treaty itself, but he had accepted what amounted to the same thing—the American draft with addition of certain interpretations:[12] self-defense, the League Covenant, the Locarno treaties, the French alliances, release in case of breach.

Kellogg thus had made it quite plain to his French opposite that there was no essential difference between them regarding what reservations should be placed in the antiwar treaty. It remained, however, to get Briand's express consent and to determine the exact form in which the conditions, if consented to, should appear. And perhaps some of the other invited powers—Britain, Germany, Italy, Japan—might have ideas of their own. For Secretary Kellogg there was much difficult negotiation yet ahead.

But no worries troubled American peace workers in the early spring of 1928. These were halcyon days for the cause.

II

". . . my inside information," Levinson wrote exultingly to Harrison Brown, "is that everybody [in Washington], from the President on, is 18K fine on Outlawry. Oh, the miracle of it!"[13]

The National Committee on the Cause and Cure of War sent forth a call for forty-eight state conferences with a view to influencing the Senate in favor of renunciation of war. Numerous local conferences would precede the state meetings. Twelve million women,

11. Kellogg used the six paragraphs verbatim except the last sentence in paragraph two concerning Germany; this sentence he omitted, for Stresemann had desired the German Government's views on the proposed pact to be confidential.

12. Kellogg's word, used in an address delivered at a banquet in New York City, June 11, 1928. New York *Times,* June 12. Already the secretary had spoken of modifications and qualifications and considerations.

13. Apr. 27, 1928, J. Stoner, *Levinson,* p. 293.

the committee announced, had affiliated to study war's cause and cure.[14]

The Women's International League for Peace and Freedom on May 5, 1928, adopted a resolution commending Secretary Kellogg for his peace activities. President Coolidge later received Jane Addams, president of the League, with a delegation representing ten states.[15]

At the annual meeting of the trustees of the Carnegie Endowment for International Peace President Nicholas Murray Butler told of the "literally enormous progress" which the antiwar treaty had just made, progress which showed the power of public opinion. The trustees re-elected Dr. Butler as president of the Endowment.[16]

The American Peace Society, meeting in Cleveland at its Centennial Conference, passed a resolution commending Coolidge and Kellogg for the multilateral antiwar negotiations. The two statesmen were admonished to continue their labors. A copy of the society's resolution went to every member of Congress.[17]

Meanwhile—as Levinson's hopes surged higher and higher—the diplomatic temperature at the Quai d'Orsay suddenly reached boiling point over an incident in Germany at Heidelberg University, May 6, 1928.

On that day Ambassador Jacob Schurman and Foreign Minister Gustav Stresemann had received honorary degrees, and the two statesmen had made short and, they believed, felicitous addresses. The eminent visitors, dressed in morning coats (academic costume was for faculty only), obtained a thunderous greeting as they took their places on the platform in the great assembly hall of the university. The ovation, one should add, was really thunderous, for in accord with Heidelberg tradition the students pounded their feet on the antique floor. Stresemann spoke inspiringly and felicitously on "New Ways to Understanding among the Nations." Ambassador Schurman emphasized the proposed pact against war;

14. New York *Times*, Apr. 8, 1928.
15. New York *Times*, May 6, 1928.
16. *Ibid.*, May 11, 1928.
17. *Ibid.*, May 12, 1928.

and noting that of all the nations Germany alone had accepted the American proposition, Schurman managed to step heavily on what at that time was probably the French Foreign Office's most sensitive nerve: he orated that, apropos the antiwar negotiations, Germany and the United States together were "marching forward in a great and noble adventure in the cause of humane civilization." [18]

The Quai d'Orsay winced in pain. Germany and America leading France and the other nations down the road to peace! And how would the French have felt had they known that Schurman in composing his speech had thought of picturing Germany and the United States marching "hand in hand"? [19] For some reason the ambassador avoided this familiarity.

Responding to French entreaties Secretary Kellogg told a press conference that the State Department had had nothing whatever to do with the ambassador's speech. Kellogg declined further comment. But officials at the Department simultaneously made it known that the American Government was glad that Germany quickly and unreservedly had responded to the antiwar proposal.[20]

The French Foreign Office having been humbled for its lax interest in peace, the turn now came for the British Foreign Office —albeit Sir Austen Chamberlain underwent his ordeal in Parliament at the hands of the Labor and Liberal opposition.

Lloyd George during a debate on May 10 declared that after Kellogg's speech of April 28 he did not see any point in making reservations. The astute wartime premier deemed the antiwar proposal especially valuable because it came from America: "America

18. For Schurman's and Stresemann's speeches, see *Addresses at the Ceremony of Conferring Honorary Degrees upon the Foreign Minister Dr. Stresemann and the Ambassador of the United States Dr. Schurman in the Convocation Hall of Heidelberg University May 5, 1928* (Heidelberg, 1928).

19. Schurman MSS, in Cornell University's Collection of Regional History.

20. New York *Times*, May 8, 1928. All this maneuvering disgusted the sophisticated French journalist, Stephen Lauzanne. In an article in the May 9 *Bulletin des Actualités* he regretted the day when Briand proposed an antiwar compact to the United States. Lauzanne found that the idealists had gotten their dreams all entangled in practical international politics, and the result was confusion. Edwin L. James, dispatch from Paris, May 8, 1928, in New York *Times*, May 9.

is the only great country—let us say it quite frankly—that has in-creased its Army and its Navy in comparison with what they were before the war, and, when a country that does that actually comes and offers to outlaw war, we ought by all means to accept it the very first time it is done; and it might have a very useful effect, because, having outlawed war, we surely ought to have no difficulty in making arrangements about cruisers." [21] Ramsay MacDonald, the head of the Labor party, believed Britain's attitude toward the Kellogg peace note was going to influence Anglo-American rela-tions for a long time to come. "Supposing it is all nonsense so far as the avoidance of war is concerned," MacDonald also wanted no British reservations.[22]

Chamberlain began his reply for the government distinctly on the defensive, and he bumbled it almost at the beginning. Great Britain, he announced defiantly, "never has treated war as an in-strument of policy."

The honorable members cried "Never?" Commander Ken-worthy asked about the Boer War.

Replied Chamberlain: "This country did not declare war. I repeat that war has never been an instrument of the policy of this country within any time which we contemplate when we are dis-cussing the Europe of to-day. I will not go back to the Crusades." [23]

As he elaborated his subject Sir Austen grew more apologetic. The government, he said, had received the American proposal on April 13. The evening before he had left the Foreign Office for a twelve-day holiday. On returning he tackled the antiwar treaty but had to consult the Dominions. Also he considered most care-fully Britain's prior commitments under the Covenant and Lo-carno. The "remarkable and very interesting" speech delivered by Secretary Kellogg before the American Society of International Law in Washington had greatly helped the government in its con-sideration of the proposal.[24]

But a few days after this debate, on May 19, when Chamberlain

21. 217 *H.C. Deb.*, 5 s., cc. 474–475.
22. *Ibid.*, cc. 444–446.
23. 217 *H.C. Deb.*, 5 s., cc. 454–455.
24. *Ibid.*, cc. 455–458.

sent to Washington Britain's official acceptance of the Kellogg proposal, the British foreign secretary no longer was on the defensive
or apologetic. Taking cognizance of Kellogg's new zeal for peace,
Sir Austen acidly remarked that European diplomacy had been
engaged for several years in the very work which now attracted
Kellogg. Yet more important than such diplomatic thrusts was
numbered-paragraph 10 of Chamberlain's note:

> . . . I should remind Your Excellency that there are *certain
> regions of the world* the welfare and integrity of which con-
> stitute the special and vital interest for our peace and safety.
> His Majesty's Government have been at pains to make it clear
> in the past that interference with these regions cannot be suf-
> fered. Their protection against attack is to the British Empire
> a measure of self-defense. It must be clearly understood that His
> Majesty's Government in Great Britain accept the new treaty
> upon the distinct understanding that it does not prejudice their
> freedom of action in this respect. . . .[25]

Here was a reservation indeed. "Certain regions," said Sir
Austen. His note did not specify. "The Government of the United
States," he had added, as if in explanation, "have comparable interests . . ." But the Monroe Doctrine, Kellogg could have replied,
explicitly limited itself in theory to the American continents, and
in practice to North and Central America and the Caribbean.

What did Chamberlain mean by certain regions? In the House
of Commons, Mr. Thurtle asked the foreign secretary to define the
regions referred to. Sir Austen evaded the question. The British
reply, he said, was then under consideration of the American Government, and His Majesty's Government would at the proper time
be prepared to offer "any explanations which may be required to
facilitate the negotiation of the proposed pact." [26]

Chamberlain's certain regions appear to have had something to

25. *FR: 1928*, I, 68. Italics inserted.
26. *217 H.C. Deb.*, 5 s., cc. 1855–1856 (May 23). On June 5, June 6, and
June 12, 1928, Godfrey Locker-Lampson, undersecretary of state for foreign
affairs, refused to define the British "certain regions." *218 H.C. Deb.*, 5 s., cc.
18, 162–163, 815.

do with Egypt. Chamberlain on May 24 dined with Ambassador Houghton at his own suggestion and spent a long evening with the American ambassador. Sir Austen that night said he had set forth his "British Monroe Doctrine"—as the press was beginning to call it—only to reassure Parliament over Egypt.[27] But why, one might ask, did not Chamberlain refer specifically to Egypt instead of vaguely to certain regions?

The answer lies in Chamberlain's cold dislike for Outlawry in general and particular, and in his determination not to sacrifice one iota of British imperial interests just to please what he deemed a politician-secretary of state. Sometime during the spring of 1928 Chamberlain wrote in his diary that "I can see many disadvantages in doing anything which Mr. Kellogg may regard as a rebuff, but I confess that I don't think the world will gain anything by merely helping Mr. Kellogg over his electoral fence. How to deal with his proposals in these circumstances is as knotty a problem as he could have found for us." [28] The way to deal with this knotty problem was

27. Houghton to Kellogg, May 25, 1928, *FR: 1928*, I, 72–74. The Egyptian problem recently had been in the forefront of British diplomacy. Just three weeks before Chamberlain sent to Kellogg the British note of acceptance, the British Government handed the Egyptian Government a forty-eight hour ultimatum demanding withdrawal of a public assemblies bill. The Egyptian nationalists were intensely anti-British, and Chamberlain had great difficulty seeking to maintain the semblance of native government in Egypt while at the same time safeguarding Britain's thoroughfare at Suez.

In addition to Egypt there was the problem of the optional clause to the World Court protocol. By adhering to Article 36 of the protocol, nations undertook to submit all *legal* controversies (as defined in that article) to the Court. The British Government was almost ready to adhere to the optional clause and, in adhering, intended to make reservations of sufficient latitude to allow escaping the Court's jurisdiction if any embarrassing case might arise. Chamberlain feared being forced, by means of the antiwar treaty, into submitting to the Court's jurisdiction with no reservations. When he dined with Houghton his final statement was that at any time he might be brought before an international court where his treaty obligations would be interpreted technically and in a purely legal way; for his protection a correct phraseology in the antiwar treaty was an absolute necessity. Nothing could be taken for granted.

28. Diary, n.d., requoted from Sir Charles Petrie, *The Life and Letters of the Right Hon. Sir Austen Chamberlain* (2 vols., London, Cassell, 1940), II, 322. And again: "I do not think that there is any reality behind Kellogg's move.

a British Monroe Doctrine. And if it was true [29] that Secretary
Kellogg, pushing his antiwar treaty, merely was endeavoring to
get over an electoral fence, then certainly no one would say that
Austen Chamberlain gave Kellogg much of a boost.

While Chamberlain in London was defending himself before
Parliament, setting forth in his note to Kellogg a British Monroe
Doctrine, and confiding his more intimate thoughts to his diary,
Secretary Kellogg went ahead with the treaty against war. In Chamberlain's certain-regions note there was a request that the United
States Government invite the British Dominions and India to become original signatories of the treaty. Kellogg quickly assented.[30]
The Government of Poland intimated to the American minister
in Warsaw, Stetson, that Poland as an ally of France should be an
original signatory, and Stetson transmitted this request to Washington with the suggestion that Kellogg include the Locarno powers.[31] Kellogg replied [32] that he had no objection (Poland, Czechoslovakia, and Belgium on June 23 officially received invitations to
become original signatories). And on May 26 came acceptance from
the Japanese Government, with reservations of self-defense and
"agreements guaranteeing the public peace." [33]

So ended another stage in the complicated negotiation of the

His long delay in replying to Briand's proposal, as well as the character of his
answer when made, combined to produce upon my mind the impression . . .
that Kellogg's main thought is not of international peace but of the victory of
the Republican party. It is one more instance of the common practice of the
State Department to use foreign politics as a pawn in the domestic game."
Chamberlain diary, Feb. 13, 1928, ibid.

29. It does not appear so. See above, pp. 164–165.

30. Invitations went on May 22, directly to Ottawa and Dublin, indirectly
(by means of Houghton and Chamberlain) to Australia, New Zealand, South
Africa, and the Government of India.

31. Stetson to Kellogg, May 14, 1928, FR: 1928, I, 63–64.

32. Kellogg to Stetson, May 15, 1928, ibid., pp. 64–65.

33. Tanaka to Ambassador MacVeagh in Japan, May 26, 1928, ibid., 75.

The Italian Government had replied on May 4, mentioning no reservations
but merely offering, although "very willingly," its "cordial collaboration towards reaching an agreement." Mussolini to the American ambassador in Italy,
Henry P. Fletcher, May 4, 1928, ibid., pp. 55–56. The Italian reservations came
in a later note (see below p. 190 n.).

multilateral treaty outlawing war. After three months of argument
—January, February, and March—France finally, and with bad
grace, gave in. But the French insisted on reservations which they
put down succinctly in a draft treaty dated April 20. Although Kellogg found this draft "entirely unsatisfactory," he soon accepted
the French position, albeit in the strange form of the American
draft treaty with the addition of certain interpretations.[34] The task
then was to get the powers' acceptance of the American draft and
interpretations. Germany had accepted even before Kellogg had
time to interpret. Britain on May 19 accepted with a reservation
which almost amounted to rejection. Japan agreed a few days later,
with two strings attached. Kellogg sent invitations to the members
of the British Commonwealth and Empire. Meanwhile, during all
this inviting and accepting, Aristide Briand—he whom Sir Austen
Chamberlain characterized as "that great Frenchman and friend
of peace"—said not a word.

III

Briand had been silently maneuvering from the Quai d'Orsay,
seeking to bring together a conference of jurists to examine the
proposed antiwar treaty. There was even thought of a conference
of foreign ministers.[35] And whatever sort of conference Briand
should manage to convene, there was a good chance that the treaty
against war, going into conference in one piece, would come out in
several.

Kellogg learned about this activity when the British ambassador
in Rome told his American colleague, Ambassador Henry P.
Fletcher, that Britain had suggested to the Italians that the meeting of juristic experts include an American expert, to avoid the
appearance of a united European front against the United States.[36]
The American secretary of state testily commented, in a dispatch
to Herrick in Paris, that if Germany and the United States could

34. Those in the explanatory dispatch of April 23.
35. Chamberlain on Apr. 27 had broached the subject with Houghton. See
above, p. 175.
36. Fletcher to Kellogg, May 2, 1928, *FR: 1928,* I, 45.

come out for an antiwar treaty without a conference, he failed to see why Britain and France could not do likewise.[37] Meanwhile the French ambassador in Tokyo called at the Japanese Foreign Office and officially requested that the Japanese Government send a legal expert for the ensuing conference; the ambassador added that he understood the American Government was favorable to the proposal.

Secretary Kellogg, alive to the dangers of conference, quickly told Ambassadors Claudel, Howard, and Prittwitz [38] that he desired no such thing. The German ambassador was very agreeable and said to Kellogg that his government meant to cooperate fully with the United States. But in London Chamberlain soon was telling Houghton that he was highly gratified to be advised by Howard that Kellogg did not wholly exclude a conference of jurists. Houghton quickly set Chamberlain right on this point.[39] So ended Briand's fond hopes to smother the proposed treaty in the disputations of an international conference of jurists.

The month of May passed into June before Briand made another move. First Germany, then Britain, then Japan had accepted the treaty against war. New Zealand accepted on May 30 as did Canada and the Irish Free State, Australia on June 2, India on June 11, and the Union of South Africa on June 15.[40] France still had not entered the procession.

The increasing number of acceptances made Secretary Kellogg more and more confident of the final success of his antiwar treaty.

37. Kellogg to Herrick, May 2, 1928, 711.5112 France/294.

38. The German ambassador, Friedrich W. von Prittwitz und Gaffron.

39. Houghton to Kellogg, May 9, *FR: 1928*, I, 57. Kellogg, however, did not categorically refuse a conference. In reply to Houghton's cable the secretary said he thought a jurists' conference neither necessary nor desirable, but had been careful to refrain from stating flatly that the United States would decline representation at such a conference. Kellogg to Houghton, May 9, 1928, *ibid.*, pp. 57-58.

40. New Zealand accepted with no reservations; Canada, the Covenant; Irish Free State, the Covenant; Australia, no reservations; India, no reservations; Union of South Africa, self-defense, release in case of breach, Covenant. For texts, see *FR: 1928*, I, 76, 77, 87-90. New Zealand, Australia, and India made their reservations later (see below, p. 190 n.).

Day by day his deeply lined face became more radiant with enthusiasm, and his occasional irascibility was less frequent. But at least
two of Kellogg's subordinates did not share their chief's optimism.
Ambassador Houghton, home on leave from London, early in June
dined with Assistant Secretary Castle in Washington. As Castle
recorded in his diary, "Houghton and I talked until nearly midnight. He had a great deal to say about the multilateral treaties
and doubts very much whether negotiations are as near completion
as F.B.K. thinks. He will remind the Secretary that the British
acceptance at the moment does not go beyond the actual words of
the British note and that it is not likely to accept the American
proposition as drafted unless or until the French accept it. In other
words, he does not agree with Kellogg's idea that everybody is
straining at the leash to sign up." [41]

Perhaps Houghton was too pessimistic. Sir Austen Chamberlain, on his way through Paris to Geneva, stopped off to see his
good friend Aristide Briand, whom illness prevented from attending the forthcoming meeting of the League Council. Afterward
Briand received reporters. Asked if he and Chamberlain had discussed the proposal to outlaw war, the French foreign minister

41. Castle diary, June 4, 1928. A few days before, on a Sunday, Castle had
gone to his State Department office "to clear up a few things." There he found
Kellogg in the adjoining office discussing multilateral treaties. Somewhat annoyed, Castle immediately set down the following entry in his diary: "They
think that they are remaking the world and actually it is nothing but a beautiful
gesture while the Jugoslavs tear down Italian consular flags and the Chinese
fight and the Japanese stand at attention. The gesture is worth while if it is
made just right and with a little guidance in wording the Secretary would make
it right. . . . [But otherwise it] may seriously tie our hands, as the originators
of the plan, if the time comes when as honorable people we must step in with
force. . . . words can never take the place of actions . . . the only way to
achieve peace is by quietly and steadily standing for the right and the fair thing.
We could change the whole sentiment of Latin America toward the United
States by getting other nations to cooperate with us in our police measures. We
have stood for moderation in China and we can be careful not to suspect and
offend the Japanese. We can learn courtesy in our dealings without losing any
of our firmness. We cannot remake humanity in a day. We cannot abolish
war with a pen but we can take the lead in making war unnecessary." Castle
diary, May 30, 1928.

made a most interesting, if somewhat disingenuous, declaration. He thought that regarding renunciation of war the powers were bordering upon success. "What did we [France] propose at the beginning of this question? We proposed a bilateral compact which could serve in some way as a preamble to our new treaty of Franco-American friendship." But because Kellogg had enlarged the scope of France's initial propositions, "the most elementary integrity commands us to express certain reservations . . . This end aimed at has been attained. The powers consulted since and Mr. Kellogg himself, one need only to read his recent speech, have come to our point of view." All that remained was to find a formula. Briand was certain there would be no delay.[42]

The foreign minister next expressed to Ambassador Herrick his satisfaction with Kellogg's speech of April 28; he thought it gave all the desired appeasement not only to France but also to other countries. Briand believed it would be comparatively easy to cast this general harmony of views into concrete form either by way of a protocol accompanying the treaty, or through a "more matured" preamble, or by some other method.[43]

And Briand soon found a way to "mature" the preamble. M. de Fleuriau, French ambassador in London and reportedly a close friend of Briand, asked Chamberlain that Sir Esme Howard in Washington support the following proposal: the French reservations—(1) maintenance of existing treaties and (2) release in case of breach—should appear in the treaty's preamble; and then (for the sake of greater clarity, said Fleuriau) Article 2 of the proposed treaty should receive an additional phrase, "in conformity with the principles enunciated in the preamble." The French Government, Fleuriau declared, preferred that its reservations appear in the body of the treaty; if this were impossible, then in a protocol of equal value with the treaty; and if this were not acceptable, then as above.[44]

Receiving the Briand-Fleuriau suggestion in the form of an

42. New York *Times*, June 3, 1928.
43. Herrick to Kellogg, June 6, 1928, *FR: 1928*, I, 79–80.
44. Aide-Memoire by the British Embassy in Washington to the Department of State, June 18, 1928, *FR: 1928*, I, 86–87.

aide-memoire from the British Embassy in Washington, Kellogg acted with dispatch. On June 20, two days after the date of the memoire, he cabled a circular note to London, Brussels, Prague, Berlin, Dublin, Rome, Warsaw, and Tokyo.[45] For communication to the respective governments, the note contained verbatim the explanations in Kellogg's speech of April 28,[46] thus making Kellogg's public explanations official.[47]

Kellogg enclosed in his note a new draft treaty. The new American proposal had a revised preamble which named individually the British Dominions, India, and the Locarno powers as signatories, and also contained a clause denying the benefits of the treaty to any violator.[48] In Kellogg's long six-point explanatory dispatch of April 23, 1928, this suggestion of release in case of breach of the treaty had figured as point (5). The secretary of state had at that time insisted that, "as a matter of law," such release was implicit in the proposed antiwar treaty. "Any express recognition of this principle," Kellogg added, "is wholly unnecessary." But the unnecessary now had proved necessary, apparently because Briand so deemed it. This idea of release in case of breach, of course, cleared the way —as Kellogg in his explanatory note had pointed out—for resort to war under terms of the Covenant, Locarno, or the French alliances. Briand, insisting upon express recognition of the idea of release, was taking no chances with France's vitally important international commitments. Nothing must in any way harm the cherished instruments of French sécurité.

But if the American secretary of state believed he now had

45. Dated (and for communication on) the 23d, the note was for publication on the 25th.

46. Which in turn were the almost verbatim explanations of Kellogg's confidential note, dated Apr. 23, to Herrick, Houghton, et al.

47. *FR: 1928*, I, 90–95. Borah, rarely able to keep a State Department secret, wrote to Levinson June 23 (two days before Kellogg's date of publication) and announced "There may be an expression in the preamble to satisfy the situation in regard to one particular matter." Levinson MSS.

48. ". . . any signatory Power which shall hereafter seek to promote its national interests by resort to war should be denied the benefits furnished by this treaty . . ." For the possible ancestry of this idea of release, see above, p. 162.

allayed Briand's fears, he was wrong. The French foreign minister was not that easy to deal with. Kellogg ever since December 28, 1927, had been talking treaty to Briand, and on several occasions it seemed that Briand was ready to agree. Each time, however, something happened. Now it was a matter of incorporating reservations in the treaty. Kellogg patiently explained to Claudel, June 29, that he would not put any interpretations into a preamble or into an exchange of notes as part of the treaty.[49] A few days later Briand blandly told Herrick that he desired a separate protocol to the effect that the antiwar treaty did not conflict with the obligations of existing treaties.[50]

Meanwhile Briand had busily arranged an informal meeting of legal experts of foreign offices. Sir Cecil James Barrington Hurst (Britain), Henri Fromageot (France), and Dr. Friedrich Gaus (Germany) met at the latter's home in Berlin and earnestly examined the antiwar pact. The London *Times* of July 13 asserted the three jurists had agreed that Kellogg's note of June 23 covered almost every possible eventuality, and this seems to have been the substance of their conclusions.[51]

49. Kellogg to Herrick, June 29, 1928, *FR: 1928*, I, 100. Kellogg told the British chargé the same.

50. Herrick to Kellogg, July 5, 1928, *ibid.*, 101–102. Briand said he had read the note of June 23 to the Council of Ministers. The government approved in principle but could not give too much attention because of preoccupation with the parliamentary situation.

As for the separate protocol, the diplomatic correspondent of the London *Daily Telegram* reported July 3 that the French Government was asking Great Britain about a separate protocol which might be treated as an annex to the Kellogg pact. The correspondent understood that Britain was somewhat friendly to the proposition.

51. A German diplomat chummily told Atherton, the American chargé in London, that at the jurists' meeting Gaus had argued against the necessity of a protocol of interpretation of existing commitments (Locarno, League, et al.). This diplomat gave Atherton to understand that the German Foreign Office would be embarrassed vis-à-vis German public opinion if any further changes in the proposed treaty were made in deference to Anglo-French conversations. Atherton added that he had heard from "well-informed sources" that Philippe Berthelot, secretary general of the French Ministry of Foreign Affairs and the ministry's *éminence grise*, in a recent London conversation with Chamberlain

Apparently the three powers represented had made a gentlemen's agreement to withhold acceptance of the new Kellogg draft until after the Berlin meeting. Sir Cecil Hurst returned to London on Monday, July 9, and by the following Saturday Sir Austen's draft reply to Kellogg was complete. But on July 11, while Sir Austen still was fussing over his reply, Germany became the first power to accept the new Kellogg draft. Again Germany and the United States together were, to use Ambassador Schurman's phrase, marching forward, almost hand in hand, in a great and noble adventure in the cause of humane civilization.[52]

So stirring a scene was too much for Ambassador Paul Claudel and his chief, Aristide Briand. Claudel hurried to the State Department, called on Secretary Kellogg, and announced that the French Government, within a few days, would itself transmit a favorable reply to the antiwar proposal. Kellogg must have sighed in anticipation.

In three days it came. Considering the general tenor of accept-

---

had pointed out to Sir Austen that British influence over Europe was much greater with France as a friendly medium, and that France and England might in the future be bound by economic ties against United States competition in world markets. Atherton to Kellogg, July 11, 1928, 711.0012 Anti-War/77. The secretary of state at the Wilhelmstrasse, Schubert, talked with Ambassador Schurman July 22 and told the latter that Fromageot and Hurst had made "the most astonishing proposals" in regard to the reply which the European governments should send to Kellogg on the antiwar pact. Gaus, however, according to Schubert, represented the German view (of no formal reservations) so effectively that he converted his two colleagues. Schurman to Kellogg, July 23, 1928, 711.0012 Anti-War/84 1/2.

Briand, talking with Herrick, said that Hurst and Gaus had recognized the rightness of the French view of the pact, and that consequently there was no possibility that Germany, sometime in the future, might contend that the pact formed a novation of existing treaties (that is, Versailles; the French had professed to fear that the Germans might claim the Rhineland occupation no longer necessary after German signature of the antiwar pact). Herrick to Kellogg, July 12, 1928, 711.5112 France/368.

52. That the German Government was endeavoring to group itself with the United States was perfectly obvious. Schubert told Schurman on the day Germany accepted the new draft that he thought there was evidence that the British and French Governments were coming nearer to "our" position on the antiwar pact. Schurman to Kellogg, July 11, 1928, 711.6212 Anti-War/50.

ances received from the other powers, [53] the French note was quite reasonable. France, Briand avowed, was in accord with the new stipulations found in the preamble of the American revised draft of June 23. The Government of the Republic observed that the following points were not contrary to the proposed pact: self-defense, the League Covenant, Locarno, the treaties of neutrality (the French alliances), automatic release in event of violation, signature to be as near as possible to universality. Briand then paid homage to the generous spirit of the Government of the United States and to the treaty against war, that "long-matured project," that "new manifestation of human fraternity." [54]

But the reservations were still there despite the seductive twang of Briand's lyre. It is now proper to pause and examine the mean-

53. The British reply, dated July 18, recalled the certain-regions doctrine: "As regards the passage in my note of the 19th May relating to certain regions of which the welfare and integrity constitute a special and vital interest for our peace and safety, I need only repeat that His Majesty's Government in Great Britain accept the new treaty upon the understanding that it does not prejudice their freedom of action in this respect." Chamberlain to Atherton, July 18, 1928, *FR: 1928*, I, 113.

The Japanese Government, July 20, repeated its qualifications to Kellogg's first draft (self-defense, Covenant, Locarno, and "agreements guaranteeing the public peace"). *FR: 1928*, I, 123–124.

The Italian reply of July 15 declared that the Italian Government would sign the antiwar treaty on the premise of the interpretation in Kellogg's June 23 explanatory note. *FR: 1928*, I, 108.

Belgium, July 17, reserved the Covenant and Locarno. Poland, July 17(?): self-defense, release in case of breach, Covenant. Czechoslovakia, July 20(?): Covenant, Locarno, the neutrality treaties, "the obligations contained in existing treaties which the Czechoslovak Republic has hitherto made," release in case of breach, self-defense. *FR: 1928*, I, 117–118, 119, 121–122.

New Zealand associated itself, July 18, with Chamberlain's reply of the same date (see above). India, July 18, adhered also to the British reply. Australia, July 18, reserved self-defense, release in case of breach ("the preamble in this respect is to be taken as a part of the substantive provisions of the treaty itself"), and the Covenant. *FR: 1928*, I, 114–115, 116–117.

Canada, July 16, reserved the Covenant. The Irish Free State, July 16, reserved self-defense and the Covenant. The Union of South Africa, July 18: self-defense, release in case of breach, treaty open to accession by all powers, Covenant. *FR: 1928*, I, 109, 111, 115–116.

54. Briand to Herrick, July 14, 1928, *FR: 1928*, I, 107–108.

ing of those reservations. For Secretary Kellogg soon would be strangely writing that "this [pretreaty] correspondence does not in any way limit the application of the treaty." [55]

55. Kellogg to John Bakeless, editor of the *Living Age,* Oct. 1, 1928, 711.0012 Anti-War/424. Bakeless had asked if the reservations had been officially communicated to all signatory powers. Kellogg replied that since there were no reservations his question was answered.

Chapter Thirteen: THE FORCE OF INTERPRETIVE

NOTES IN INTERNATIONAL LAW

Secretary of State Kellogg always held that the notes received from the various governments were only unilateral declarations, lacking the force of formal reservations because, although communicated, the other governments did not expressly accept them.[1] In a very technical sense this was a good argument.

Uninformed folk in America and Europe nonetheless read only the two-article text of Kellogg's proposed antiwar treaty and thought that the treaty meant what it said. The unsophisticated, and there are many in this world, began to believe the millennium was approaching. So the result of Kellogg's argument—good though it might be in theory—the result was confusion, close to delusion, among broad masses of the American people. When postmasters hung up the great red, white, and blue texts of the treaty in

1. Kellogg had telegraphed Levinson July 23 concerning the British Monroe Doctrine: "I note your telegram about the so-called indefinite Monroe Doctrine reservations proposed by British. I have not been asked by them to make any reservations in the treaty and am not going to make any reservations in the treaty at all and the British notes are only unilateral declarations. . . . Great Britain does not ask us to change the treaty or to make any specific declaration to her note . . . I do not think it is necessary for us to pay any attention to this discussion or any of the other discussions which appear in the various notes since they call for no change in the simplicity of the treaty itself." J. Stoner, *Levinson,* pp. 303–304.

post offices all over the United States,[2] they did not affix to the texts the numerous notes exchanged during the spring and early summer of 1928. To do so would have papered the post-office walls.

As a result of this official stressing of the antiwar treaty's two substantive articles, the importance of the interpretive notes was lost from sight. If anyone sought to acquaint the general public with the import of those notes, he met with disbelief. Carrie W. Ormsbee of Brandon, Vermont, wrote to Senator Frank L. Green of Vermont that she had participated in a discussion group at the Williamstown Institute of Politics and there heard Professor Borchard of Yale. Borchard, she said, had asserted that the British and French interpretations of the antiwar treaty constituted an integral part of the treaty, greatly changing its meaning; but she was certain that Professor Borchard erred, for Secretary Kellogg had said the opposite in a statement of August 8.[3] (Kellogg then had said that the interpretations to the multilateral treaty were in no way a part of the pact and could not be considered as reservations.) Carrie Chapman Catt, who likewise was at the Williamstown meeting, wrote her friend Laura Puffer Morgan that, having watched Professor Borchard's mental reactions on other matters, she considered him one of those legalistic individuals who always saw legal flaws in every question. When a normally conservative point of view was added to a legalistic attitude, Mrs. Catt affirmed, the result was precisely such empty talk as Borchard's.[4]

But there can be no doubt that the meaning of the treaty lay not in its two grand substantive articles, but in those two articles together with the exchanged notes and also the treaty's preamble (for many of the notes referred to the clause in the preamble which denied the treaty's benefits to a transgressor). It did not make much difference whether the exchanged notes technically were reservations or mere unilateral declarations. David Hunter Miller, long

2. This was a private venture in public post offices. The National Council for Prevention of War obtained authorization from the Post Office Department. Arthur Charles Watkins of the NCPW designed the poster and attended to the printing and mailing.

3. Letter of Sept. 29, 1928, NCPW files.

4. Letter of Sept. 20, 1928, NCPW files.

the Department of State's treaty expert, has asserted flatly that "The explanations and statements of the Parties are as much a part of the meaning of thé agreement among them as is the text of any one of the Articles of the Treaty proper. . . . Whether it be called explanation or interpretation or qualification or reservation, everything that the Parties themselves agreed that the Treaty means, it does mean. Any suggestion to the contrary is erroneous." [5] As Dr. Philip Marshall Brown, professor of international law at Princeton, wrote in the pages of the *American Journal of International Law*, no rule of international law was more firmly established than the rule of interpretation of treaties in the light of the intent of the negotiators. That intent, emphasized Brown, might appear in any interpretations, clarifications, understandings, constructions, qualifications, or actual conditions set forth during the negotiations prior to ratification.[6] Brown's opinion received support from no less an authority than John Bassett Moore, the dean of American international lawyers. In a letter to Raymond L. Buell, Judge Moore declared the "immemorial and constant practice of governments," including that of the United States, was to recur to the diplomatic correspondence as a means of explaining and determining the nature and extent of mutual obligations under treaties.[7]

5. David Hunter Miller, *Peace Pact of Paris*, pp. 95–96. Professor Borchard, who in the interpretation of many international matters was at the opposite pole from Hunter Miller, nevertheless agreed exactly on this point: "Governments do not make such declarations or reservations as idle gestures not to be taken seriously; on the contrary, the reservations constitute the frank and honest avowal of the governments' understanding of the obligations contracted. They constitute as inherent and essential a part of the treaty obligations as if they had been written into Article I of the Pact." E. M. Borchard, "The Multilateral Treaty for the Renunciation of War," *American Journal of International Law*, 23 (1929), 117.

6. Philip Marshall Brown, "The Interpretation of the General Pact for the Renunciation of War," *Am. J. of Int. L.*, 23 (1929), 378.

7. "It cannot be supposed that the governments, in making to the United States the official communications above mentioned [that is, the antiwar communications], considered themselves to be performing an idle and empty act, which, according to international law, would have no international force. The vital import of some of the declarations would preclude such a supposition, even if common sense and international practice would permit us to indulge it." John Bassett Moore to Raymond L. Buell, Sept. 29, 1928, NCPW files.

In the annals of American diplomacy, moreover, there was precedent for considering pretreaty correspondence as binding. The American Government on November 25, 1850, concluded a treaty of commerce with Switzerland. Nearly fifty years later, in 1898, the Swiss Government contended that the clauses of the treaty providing for most-favored-nation treatment were to be considered as unlimited, although this was contrary to the settled American rule of construction of such clauses.[8] When the United States Government then examined the pretreaty correspondence it discovered that there actually had been an understanding waiving in favor of Switzerland the restrictive construction. This understanding had been communicated to both the governments in 1850. Under these circumstances the United States in 1898 accepted the contention of Switzerland. Secretary of State John Hay wrote to the Swiss minister on November 21, 1898: "Both justice and honor require that the common understanding of the High Contracting Parties at the time of the executing of the Treaty should be carried into effect." [9]

All this notwithstanding, Secretary of State Kellogg in negotiating his multilateral antiwar treaty steadfastly refused to consider the pretreaty correspondence as, in any sense, in the nature of reservations. As we have seen,[10] he chose to denominate it rather as modifications, qualifications, considerations, and interpretations. It is interesting though to observe that Kellogg slipped on at least one occasion and used the word "reservation." Putting down for State Department records an account of a conversation on June 27, 1928, with Ambassador Claudel, Kellogg wrote that "I impressed on him that I could not make *any further reservations* . . . in the matter." But then the secretary reverted to his customary words: "I told him [Claudel] . . . we had taken care of the two points" (release after breach, and the Locarno and alliance treaties). Kellogg concluded that "I certainly made it plain that we could not make any further concessions." [11]

8. With very few exceptions the United States until the year 1923 construed its most-favored-nation treaty-clauses as limited—that is, as operative only in case of exchange of a specific quid pro quo.

9. Hay to the Swiss minister, Pioda, Nov. 21, 1898, *FR: 1899*, p. 748.

10. Above, Chapter XII.

11. Memorandum by Kellogg of a conversation with Claudel, June 27, 1928,

Perhaps out of solicitude for Secretary Kellogg, the other signatories to the antiwar treaty also avoided the word "reservation"
and in the main adopted Kellogg's alternate wording. Sometimes
they even improved upon it. From London in August 1928 Harrison Brown wrote Levinson that the Foreign Office fondly was calling the British reservation of certain regions its "caveat." [12]

Secretary Kellogg seems actually to have considered that his own
interpretation—the long, numbered exegesis which he prepared in
April 1928 and communicated two months later [13]—was the treaty's
one true interpretation (not, of course, a reservation), and that if
the other powers adhered to this they then could "unconditionally"
accept the antiwar treaty. For example, when the German Government accepted the antiwar proposal by referring to Kellogg's explanatory note, the secretary of state wired President Coolidge that
"Germany accepted the multilateral treaty yesterday without condition." [14] And even when powers in their "unconditional" accept

711.5112 France/352. Italics inserted. On another occasion Kellogg almost
called the interpretive notes "reservations." At a hearing of the Senate Committee on Foreign Relations, Dec. 7, 1928, someone asked Kellogg about the
reservations. "As to the reservations," replied the secretary of state, "of course
I can not go over all the discussions on this treaty . . ." U.S. Sen., 70th Cong.,
2d Sess., *Hearings before the Committee on Foreign Relations, on the General
Pact for the Renunciation of War* (Washington, 1928), I, 4.

12. Brown to Levinson, Aug. 19, 1928, Levinson MSS. The British Government early in August sent the antiwar correspondence to the League of Nations—which in a sense registered it as binding. Kellogg, interestingly enough,
himself also transmitted the correspondence to the League. In a conversation
with the Italian ambassador on Aug. 13, 1928, he explained that while the
United States Government did not file its treaties with the League officially, it
always sent treaties to Geneva for the League's information. The League, said
Kellogg, did the same with the United States. The Secretary added that he had
no objection to Britain's sending the correspondence. Memorandum by Kellogg
of a conversation with the Italian ambassador, Nobile Giacomo de Martino,
Aug. 13, 1928, 711.0012 Anti-War/252.

13. For this, see *FR: 1928*, I, 36–38.

14. Kellogg to Coolidge, July 13, 1928, 711.6212 Anti-War/55. Once during
the negotiations Sir Esme Howard remarked to Kellogg that he did not see
any reason why, as the secretary of state had expressed his understanding of
the treaty, the other countries could not do likewise, and all this then could be
made a part of the treaty itself. "I said," wrote Kellogg afterward, "that the

ances ventured to mention matters other than those with which Kellogg had dealt specifically in his long interpretive note, such matters easily could be considered—and Kellogg himself always so considered them—as mere aspects of what the secretary of state in his note had termed the "right of self-defense."

For Kellogg, we recall, had defined that right in a very latitudinarian way.[15] The secretary's definition in fact was so general that one could well assume that all the pretreaty correspondence was only a long, complicated explanation of self-defense. Professor Charles Cheney Hyde, a most distinguished student of international law, has written that "Examination of the preparatory work [of the treaty] reveals what is equivalent to an additional explanatory article, in a definite acknowledgment that the agreement should not curtail the freedom of the parties to have recourse to defensive measures." [16]

Self-defense, however, although stretchable to include numerous contingencies, could not possibly have covered all the eventualities reserved in the exchanged notes. Chamberlain's explanation of "certain regions," which both Chamberlain and Kellogg declared was only self-defense,[17] was a reservation of imperial pro-

---

trouble about [that] was that if each country went to tacking on [sic] to this treaty understandings which would be in the form of reservations or provisos or stipulations as to what it means, each country would have a different construction and different reservations and different provisos and we would end up by having so many that the treaty would be a joke. I said that I was not prepared to do it and I could not agree to any such proceeding; that if my construction of the treaty was correct, they can say that that was their understanding . . ." Memorandum by Kellogg of a conversation with Howard, May 29, 1928, 711.4112 Anti-War/107.

15. "There is nothing in the American draft of an anti-war treaty which restricts or impairs in any way the right of self-defense. That right is inherent in every sovereign state and is implicit in every treaty. Every nation is free at all times and regardless of treaty provisions to defend its territory from attack or invasion and it alone is competent to decide whether circumstances require recourse to war in self-defense." *FR: 1928*, I, 36.

16. Charles Cheney Hyde, *International Law Chiefly as Interpreted by the United States* (Boston, Little, Brown, 1945), III, 1683.

17. Said Chamberlain in Parliament, July 30, 1928: ". . . our doctrine is exactly comparable to that of the American Government [that is, the Monroe

portions. Then there were France's alliance treaties; France had reserved those agreements with all their unknown details. Surely self-defense under such imprecise interpretation was ambiguous. And even had there been no gaping reservations such as the British Monroe Doctrine and the French alliances, the fact remained that Kellogg in his explanatory note had held that "Every nation . . . alone is competent to decide whether circumstances require recourse to war in self-defense." This was open invitation to license. As Edwin M. Borchard has written: "In view of the fact that the treaty apparently leaves each country contemplating or exercising measures of force the judge of what is 'self-defense,' who could assert that any signatory, going to war under circumstances which it claims require 'self-defense,' is violating the Pact? Has any modern nation ever gone to war (and without any suggestion of bad faith) for any other motive? How then could this Pact ever be legally violated?" [18]

In spite of all this, some international lawyers have continued to minimize the importance of the prepact correspondence. Professor Hersch Lauterpacht, whose editions of Oppenheim's *International Law* are the best general treatises on the subject, maintains that "In law, the scope of . . . [the Kellogg treaty's] exceptions is small when compared with the magnitude of the change effected by the Pact in the system of International Law." [19] But while Lauterpacht is very explicit in naming the treaty's exceptions (self-defense, League and Locarno wars, war between a signatory and a nonsignatory, war with a violator of the pact),[20] he is tantalizingly vague in detailing the magnitude of the pact's influence on

Doctrine], that it is not a doctrine of aggression, that it is not a desire for territorial expansion, but a pure measure in self-defense . . ." *220 H.C. Deb.*, 5 s., c. 1842. Said Kellogg to the Senate Committee on Foreign Relations, Dec. 7, 1928: ". . . Great Britain was talking about nothing but self-defense." U.S. Sen., 70th Cong., 2d Sess., *Hearings before the Committee on Foreign Relations, on the General Pact for the Renunciation of War*, I, 11.

18. Edwin M. Borchard, "The Multilateral Treaty for the Renunciation of War," *Am. J. of Int. L.*, 23 (1929), 117.

19. H. Lauterpacht, ed., L. Oppenheim, *International Law* (2 vols., London, 1935–37), II, 166–167.

20. *Ibid.*, p. 153.

international law. Resort to war, he explains, is no longer a discretionary prerogative of states signatories of the pact, but rather an act for which a justification must be sought in one of the four exceptions permitted by the pact.[21] One of Lauterpacht's exceptions, of course, was self-defense.

Another minimizer of the antiwar treaty's reservations, Professor Quincy Wright of the University of Chicago, has admitted that "it can not be said that the interpretative notes are without weight." Wright thought, however, that the notes should be treated "merely as evidence of the sense of the text and not as modifications of or exceptions from it, or even as conclusive interpretations." [22] One nonetheless has difficulty distinguishing between, on the one hand, "evidence of the sense of the text" and, on the other, "modifications" and "exceptions" and "conclusive interpretations." How does the first category differ from the second, third, and fourth? It would seem that Wright rather confused than clarified the situation. But not content with this, he confounded confusion by next explaining that use of force in self-defense was not a resort to war as an instrument of national policy.[23]

From all this welter of comment by the international lawyers one fact stands out: of the writers we have cited—Miller, Hyde, Moore, Brown, Borchard, Lauterpacht, and Wright—only the latter considered the pretreaty correspondence as not in the nature of reservations. And even Wright would agree that the meaning of the treaty lay not simply in its two substantive articles—its "post-office articles"—but rather in those articles together with the exchanged notes and also the treaty's preamble (Wright would call the notes and preamble "evidence of the sense of the text").

The present writer believes it would have been better had Secretary Kellogg accepted the French draft of April 20, 1928, which candidly put the reservations into the body of the treaty. Kellogg, however, chose to retain and negotiate his own two-article treaty and to describe any differences therefrom as modifications,

21. *Ibid.*, pp. 166–167.
22. Quincy Wright, "The Interpretation of Multilateral Treaties," *Am. J. of Int. L.*, 23 (1929), 104.
23. *Ibid.*, p. 106.

qualifications, considerations, or interpretations. The result was that the secretary of state, when he finally "delivered the goods," delivered a great amount of wrapping paper.

It is not possible at this point in our narrative to discuss the benefits of the Kellogg-Briand antiwar treaty. Suffice to end this present discussion with some remarks Senator Borah addressed to his good friend Salmon O. Levinson on August 2, 1928.[24]

"Levinson," Borah wrote, "I may be extremely obtuse, but I am unable to understand how talks and suggestions on the side can have the slightest effect upon the terms of the treaty as it will be signed. . . . I had a letter yesterday from Professor Borchard in which he seemed to think that these statements made by the British Government and by France would have the same effect upon the treaty as if they were reservations to the treaty. If there is any such doctrine or principle as that, the treaty would not be worth a damn."

24. J. Stoner, *Levinson,* p. 306.

Chapter Fourteen: "THE MIRACLE HAS COME"

> Lift up your heads, ye peoples,
> The miracle has come.
> No longer are ye helpless,
> No longer are ye dumb.

S o wrote Robert Underwood Johnson, creator of New York University's Hall of Fame,[1] who in August 1928 had arrived in Paris to see with his own eyes the signing of the treaty against war.[2]

1. New York *Times,* Aug. 26, 1928. Johnson published much poetry. See, for example, his *Poems of the Longer Flight: Chiefly Odes and Apostrophes, with Prefatory Consideration of Obstacles to Poetry in America* (New York, 1923).

As for the Hall of Fame, there is the remark Mr. Dooley made one day to Mr. Hennessey: "A Hall iv Fame's th' place where th' names iv the most famous men is painted, like th' side iv a bar-rn where a little boy writes th' name iv th' little girl he loves. In a week or two he goes back an' rubs it out."

2. Somewhat different was Ambassador Herrick's view of the miracle. Herrick wrote from Paris, July 3, 1928, to Robert Woods Bliss, his colleague at the American Embassy in Buenos Aires: "We seem to be gradually approaching better times universally and Briand's peace efforts, aided and enlarged by those of our chief seem to be nearing accomplishment. I suppose treaties are somewhat like children's games. When some child does not want to play any longer, he breaks up the game and that's the end of it. Some day, if the world continues to grow better, say in 100 or 500 years, people may become so good and kind and peaceful, and so loath to be 'joggled' out of their everyday avocations, in

Paris from the start had seemed the proper place to sign the treaty. The French capital was rich in memories of the World War— of the great ministry of Clemenceau, who at times seemed to hold off the German hordes by sheer will power; of the hurried parleys of Allied statesmen and generals who on several occasions momentarily expected a breakthrough by Hindenburg's gray veterans; of a poignantly memorable day in November 1918; of miles of ranks of cuirassiers with sunlit regimental colors gleaming as, on June 28, 1919, President Wilson and the Allied leaders passed slowly through packed streets toward Versailles. No other city could boast such memories.

I

As early as June 23 Secretary of State Kellogg suggested to Ambassador Paul Claudel that the nations sign the antiwar treaty in Paris, and Claudel received the suggestion with "obvious emotion." [3] A month later President Coolidge at his summer residence near Superior, Wisconsin, was reported to approve of Paris; the president did not regard Washington as a feasible place for holding such a conference, it being manifest that to send official representatives and their staffs from Europe to the American capital would cost much more than to send them to the French city. [4]

Paris, however, had one drawback—its relative proximity to Moscow. There was real danger that the Bolsheviki might show up at the Paris ceremonies and make a scene. Cables flew back and forth between Paris, Berlin, London, and Washington as statesmen sought some way to deal with the matter. Herrick informed Kellogg that if the powers even asked Russia to adhere to—not to sign but to

other words, the force of economic considerations may become so great and they so good that there will be no more war and there will then no longer be any need of armies. It is possible that you and I and Mildred [Bliss' wife] may not live to see this but if Mildred's faith is strong, as I am constrained to think it is, she may feel that we may be perched somewhere where we may observe the consummation of this delectable dream." Herrick MSS.

3. Memorandum by Olds of a conversation between Kellogg and Claudel, June 23, 1928, *FR: 1928*, I, 97–98.

4. New York *Times*, July 21, 1928.

adhere to—the treaty, she might seize upon the occasion to write an intemperate answer.[5] Kellogg heard that Sir Austen Chamberlain personally would not make the slightest effort to obtain Russia's participation;[6] and in Parliament Sir Austen repeated that if the American Government proposed an invitation to Russia he would not support it, neither would he object to it.[7] The German Government, although in treaty relations with the Bolsheviki, at that moment was engaged in an argument with Moscow; the Soviets had imprisoned some German engineers, and the Wilhelmstrasse was lukewarm to Russian participation in the treaty to outlaw war. Eventually the powers solved the ticklish problem: only the great powers, the Dominions and India, and the Locarno powers signed at Paris, the other nations of the world sending their adherences to Washington. The United States not having recognized the Bolshevik Government, the French ambassador in Moscow received the Russian instrument of adherence and then transmitted it antiseptically via Paris to Washington.

Statesmen were discussing the Bolsheviki when a matter of even greater unpleasantness burst into the newspapers: the French and British Governments announced conclusion of what amounted to an anti-American naval agreement. While Paris and London had negotiated with Kellogg they simultaneously had conferred behind his back about a new disarmament scheme to throttle the American Navy.

The agreement sounded very abstract and technical, merely a plan to limit building of

(1) Capital ships, i.e. ships of over 10,000 tons or with guns of more than 8 inch calibre.

(2) Aircraft carriers of over 10,000 tons.

(3) Surface vessels of or below 10,000 tons armed with guns of more than 6 inch and up to 8 inch calibre.

(4) Ocean going submarines over 600 tons.[8]

5. Herrick to Kellogg, July 26, 1928, *FR: 1928*, I, 127.

6. Atherton to Kellogg, July 26, 1928, *ibid.*, p. 128.

7. 220 *H.C. Deb.*, 5 s., c. 1771.

8. The British chargé in Washington, Chilton, to Kellogg, July 31, 1928, *FR: 1928*, I, 265.

These four classes of warships, however, did not include 6-inch cruisers or submarines of less than 600 tons—the very types in which Britain and France respectively were interested. Moreover, the two powers were proposing, in class (3) above, limitation of 10,000-ton 8-inch cruisers—and this was the very type which the United States Navy desired most to build. American desire for large cruisers and British preference for small cruisers, we recall, had resulted already in the acrimonious breakup of the 1927 Geneva Naval Conference. Ray Atherton of the American Embassy in London remarked to Sir Ronald Lindsay at the Foreign Office that the proposed naval limitations affected only vessels in which the United States was interested. "Yes, that is true," replied Lindsay. Atherton asked if Sir Ronald had any explanation. Sir Ronald weakly answered that he hadn't, except that no further military disarmament seemed possible in Europe especially because of Russia, yet some sort of disarmament had to be accomplished and hence the Anglo-French discussion.[9]

From Superior, Wisconsin, President Coolidge on August 3 advised Kellogg: "I have your wire relative to the British naval proposals. What I desire to have done in relation to these at present is nothing at all. . . . I do not especially like the meeting that is to be held in Paris. While it is ostensibly to sign the treaty, I can not help wonder whether it may not be for some other purpose not yet disclosed. Of course, so far as this Government is concerned, it will neither discuss nor decide any other question of any kind or nature at the Paris meeting." [10]

Secretary Kellogg the next day replied to the president. "I am also very sorry," he wrote to Coolidge, "that I agreed to go to Paris to sign the treaty." Kellogg then told how he originally had decided to go because the French so desired it. "Nevertheless," he repeated, "I am sorry I agreed to go to Paris." [11]

Although the Anglo-French naval agreement thus heartily disgusted both Kellogg and Coolidge, it appears that Coolidge's annoyance went far deeper than his secretary of state's. As Assistant

9. Atherton to Kellogg, Aug. 4, 1928, 500.A15 Franco-British/4.
10. Coolidge to Kellogg, Aug. 3, 1928, *FR: 1928*, I, 270.
11. Kellogg to Coolidge, Aug. 4, 1928, 500.A15 Franco-British/10 1/2.

Secretary Castle recorded in his diary, "The President . . . was annoyed that we even asked the British to explain vague statements in the note [the British note of July 31 detailing the agreement] and orders us to do nothing more about it whatsoever. . . . All I am afraid is that he will get so angry that he will tell the Secretary he cannot go to Paris after all. This would be an utterly impossible situation and the Secretary says that if it should by any chance arise he would have to tell the President that he must either go or resign." [12]

Sir Austen Chamberlain had spoken in Parliament on July 30, and in addition to announcing the Anglo-French naval agreement he had made some announcements about the Kellogg treaty. Sir Austen was not sure what importance the treaty would have in the future. "It may mean much, very much for the peace of the world. It may mean not much, even very little." Everything depended on what part the United States would take in international affairs. Chamberlain assumed that the American Government would take no engagements in advance, but if American public opinion ranged itself behind its own treaty "then, indeed, the signature of this treaty will be an additional and most formidable deterrent of war." [13] In that spirit, Sir Austen said, His Majesty's Government was signing the treaty.[14]

12. Castle diary, Aug. 7, 1928.

13. Mrs. Ben Hooper of Oshkosh, Wisconsin, chairman of international relations of the General Federation of Women's Clubs, read about Chamberlain's remark that American public opinion would have to range itself behind the Kellogg treaty. Mrs. Hooper wrote to Mrs. Otis G. Wilson, Aug. 2, 1928: "I think that little quotation tells us in the clearest, most definite form that the women of these nine great organizations [in the National Committee on the Cause and Cure of War] have undertaken the biggest and most important piece of work for the benefit of our country and all the world that has ever been attempted by any group. We just must make good for the sake of the boys and girls who are coming up. . . . I wish I could be every place at once. My whole heart is in this work." Hooper MSS.

14. 220 H.C. Deb., 5 s., cc. 1842–1843. Chamberlain undertook to calculate his antiwar zeal for the information of dubious M.P.'s: "Mr. Kellogg took six months to reply to M. Briand. I took six weeks to reply to Mr. Kellogg. Mr. Kellogg took six weeks to reply to me and I took between three or four weeks to answer again, to send my final reply to his Government." c. 1838.

This statement did not sound enthusiastic. Nor was it meant to be. Sir Austen, in fact, was in a quandary. "I can form some opinion," he wrote in his diary,

> as to what France or Germany or Italy may be likely to do in this or that contingency. Except in a narrow field the course which will be taken by the United States is a riddle to which no one—not even themselves—can give an answer in advance. But perhaps this is only saying that the United States has no foreign policy. The ship drifts at the mercy of every gust of public opinion. Take the Kellogg proposal for example. Who could guess when they left Briand's suggestion unnoticed for months that it would suddenly become the cardinal feature in their attitude to the rest of the world? And what do they mean it to be even now on the eve of signature—a "moral" gesture, *vox et praeterea nihil,* or a new Monroe doctrine? It will be the one or the other according as the trend of American opinion makes the rest of the world think that they are in earnest or the reverse. I end as befits the whole correspondence with an enormous mark of interrogation.[15]

As if to answer Chamberlain, Professor Shotwell, described as an expert on renunciation of war, undertook in the New York *Times* to tell "How the Anti-War Compact Binds Us." Shotwell thought that the United States itself must now make good its offer to the world to renounce war as an instrument of national policy. "There can be," he wrote, "no two opinions on this point." But when someone brought Chamberlain's Parliament speech to Kellogg's attention the secretary of state said that the treaty contained no sanctions and no commitment for the United States to go to war. The treaty, he was sure, did not involve the United States in European affairs.[16]

15. Chamberlain diary, n.d., in Sir Charles Petrie, *Life and Letters of the Right Hon. Sir Austen Chamberlain,* II, 324.

16. New York *Times,* July 29, Aug. 2, 1928. Kellogg on July 21 had said that the antiwar compact would not draw the United States into European affairs any more than the various arbitration treaties which this country had negotiated with European governments. *Ibid.,* July 22, 1928.

Reports nevertheless kept flowing out of Europe that the European nations accepted the Kellogg treaty as a means to let or get the United States into world councils; [17] and Frank H. Simonds, the distinguished journalist, felt himself compelled to write to the editor of the New York *Times* that because the European interpretation of the antiwar compact was so different from the American interpretation the Senate would be justified in refusing to ratify the treaty.[18]

The problem of the pact's interpretations soon bobbed up again as an object of comment, and on August 8 Secretary Kellogg said to the press that interpretations of the multilateral treaty to renounce war were in no way a part of the pact and could not be considered as reservations. The interpretations, he announced, would not be deposited with the text of the treaty.[19] Senator Borah reassured Colonel Robins, telling him that the so-called reservations were nothing more than the expression "of a personal opinion, I presume largely for local use." Certainly, Borah added, they were in no sense a modification of the treaty or reservations to the treaty; the friends of the treaty need not be disturbed.[20]

Although Kellogg and Borah thus had to reassure some of their followers, others were undisturbed. Senator Capper on August 5 was describing the treaty as "the most telling action ever taken in human history to abolish war." [21] Colonel E. M. House, once Woodrow Wilson's alter ego, said that the Kellogg peace plan was the greatest move toward peace the world had ever attempted.[22]

Meanwhile President Coolidge in Wisconsin told the press he did not anticipate any reduction in the army and navy by reason of the Kellogg treaty. He viewed the army and navy purely as defensive weapons.[23] French Government officials, according to sub-

17. See, for example, Edwin L. James' dispatch from Paris, July 29, in New York *Times*, July 30, 1928.

18. *Ibid.*, Aug. 8.

19. New York *Times*, Aug. 9, 1928.

20. Borah to Robins, Aug. 6, 1928, Borah MSS.

21. New York *Times*, Aug. 5, 1928.

22. *Ibid.*, Aug. 11, 1928.

23. *Ibid.* The president developed his ideas on international affairs, the army, and the navy to the accompaniment of a red-coated boys' brass band from

sequent newspaper reports, received the president's words with great satisfaction, declaring that France and her allies had expected a new disarmament drive, especially against land armaments, as a result of the treaty.[24] In London Walter Bridgeman, first lord of the Admiralty, lauded the treaty and hoped it would pave the way for disarmament. He added that Britain would not modify her Singapore naval base plans in consequence of the multilateral compact.[25]

A few days later President Coolidge spoke at Wassau, Wisconsin, and spared no words in praise of the Kellogg treaty. Secretary Kellogg, busily preparing to sail for Europe, must have blushed as he later read the president's remarks. Coolidge stood in a canopied pavilion, facing a large grandstand filled to capacity and behind which rose a shield of tall pines. Observers estimated the crowd to be between 15,000 and 20,000 persons. "Had an agreement of this kind [the Kellogg treaty] been in existence in 1914," said the president, "there is every reason to suppose that it would have saved the situation and delivered the world from all the misery which was inflicted by the great war. . . . It holds a greater hope for peaceful relations than was ever before given to the world. If those who are involved in it, having started it will finish it, its provisions will prove one of the greatest blessings ever bestowed upon humanity. It is a fitting consummation of the first decade of peace." [26] Careful readers of the president's speech might have detected some presidential doubts about the treaty, but no one remarked them, and Coolidge did not undertake to elaborate them.[27]

Two days after he spoke at Wassau the president telephoned the

_____

Cumberland, Wisconsin, which stood on the lawn outside and played "Under the Double Eagle"—reminiscent of an empire that fell to ruin in 1914–18 after having tried war as an instrument of national policy.

24. New York *Times*, Aug. 12, 1928.

25. *Ibid.*

26. Dispatch from Wassau, Aug. 15, in New York *Times,* Aug. 16, 1928.

27. Telegrams from all over the United States and cables from abroad reached Coolidge the next day, praising his speech at Wassau. The president was delighted. Sources close to Coolidge said the president was more keenly anxious to learn the reaction to this speech than to any other he had made in years. New York *Times,* Aug. 17, 1928.

State Department in Washington and commented on the itinerary of Secretary Kellogg's forthcoming visit to Europe. After signing the antiwar treaty in Paris Kellogg had planned to stop briefly in England and Ireland.[28] Coolidge, however, now said over the telephone that Kellogg could not go to England. Reason: the president was still intensely disgusted with the Anglo-French naval agreement.[29]

II

Lying along one of the great piers of lower Manhattan the *Ile de France* bustled with activity on the night of August 18, 1928, for the secretary of state of the United States, the Honorable Frank Billings Kellogg, was coming aboard to sail shortly after midnight for France. The secretary, his small but burly figure distinguished by his shock of white hair, briskly strode up the gangplank. A small but distinguished company of friends watched and waved when, at 12:30 A.M., tugs began pulling the huge French liner out into midstream. The only incident was an abortive demonstration by some one hundred members of the All-American Anti-Imperialist League. Getting to the dock almost too late, they feverishly began pulling out signs reading "Hands Off Nicaragua," "Down with American Imperialism," and "Down with Kellogg's Fake Peace

28. Kellogg to Herrick, July 30, 1928, *FR: 1928*, I, 129–130.
29. Castle diary, Aug. 17, 1928. There later was much newspaper speculation as to why Kellogg did not visit England. On the very day the nations in Paris were signing the antiwar treaty Assistant Secretary Castle had to tell the Washington newspaper correspondents half-truths about Kellogg's itinerary: "This morning has been a hectic one and the press pretty vicious on account of a story Wilmot Lewis [correspondent of the London *Times*] telegraphed to London that the Secretary was not going to England because the President prevented it to show his disgust at the Franco-British naval agreement. Of course I gave the various reasons why he did not go and of course the correspondents did not believe I told the whole story—as I did not. Perhaps the President will now announce that he told the Secretary not to go. That would make trouble worse confounded. The President did wrong in issuing his order because it could only lead to bad feeling and because he should have trusted Kellogg not to talk about the agreement. It cannot be helped now." Castle diary, Aug. 27, 1928.

Treaty." Watchful police herded the leaguers off the pier and there were no arrests. Newspapermen otherwise found little that was spectacular about the secretary of state's departure. Before going aboard Kellogg had been almost uncommunicative about his mission, saying merely that signing the treaty was his only purpose. The Kellogg party included, in addition to Mrs. Kellogg, William H. Beck, Kellogg's private secretary, Michael J. McDermott, chief of the State Department's press relations, and Spencer Phenix, former assistant and a close friend and advisor to Kellogg. J. Theodore Marriner, chief of the Department's Division of Western European Affairs, already was in Paris arranging preliminary details of the ceremony of signature.

Some doubt had arisen as to whether many or any of the foreign ministers would come to Paris for the ceremony. Stresemann had been severely—and, as it proved later, fatally—stricken in the summer of 1928, and for days his doctors were uncertain if he could make the trip. Chamberlain suffered something close to a nervous breakdown about the first of August and had to retire temporarily from the Foreign Office, turning his duties over to Lord Cushendun. Premier Mussolini of Italy, who was also his own foreign minister, found his time occupied by army maneuvers in Northern Italy (he also was war minister).[30] Nor could he spare his assistant at the Palazzo Chigi, Dino Grandi. The best Mussolini could offer was his ambassador in Paris. As we have seen, Kellogg himself wished after the Franco-British naval agreement that he had never offered to go to the French capital. For a while it looked as if Aristide Briand might sign the treaty with the various ambassadors at Paris. Even Briand's presence was somewhat in doubt. The French foreign minister was in delicate health that summer of 1928,[31] and might well have been taken ill and become unable to sign for France.

30. A versatile person, Mussolini in addition presided over the ministries of marine, aviation, interior, and labor. Simultaneously he was commander-general of the Fascist Militia. Probably the reason he personally would not go to Paris was not busyness but rather the possibility of anti-fascist demonstrations and the problem of police precautions. So guessed Ambassador Fletcher in a dispatch to Kellogg, July 22, 1928, 711.6512 Anti-War/66.

31. He had been very ill early in the summer.

Secretary Kellogg rejoiced in his ocean voyage. Mrs. Kellogg told reporters on the boat that for the first time since her husband became secretary of state he slept until ten o'clock in the morning. Afterward he paced the deck with an old gray slouch cap pulled down over his eyes.

While the secretary enjoyed himself little problems of ceremonial procedure troubled the Quai d'Orsay. First, there was the pen which Kellogg should use to sign the treaty. The city of Le Havre, where the secretary planned to come ashore in France, decided to offer him a solid gold pen, twelve inches long, nearly half an inch thick, and surmounted by a large aquamarine stone suitably inscribed "F.B.K." The pen bore the legend *Au Grand Artisan de la Paix, Son Excellence M.* Frank Billings Kellogg: *la ville du Havre, Aôut, 1928.* The city encased this magnificent pen in a green leather box bearing the words *Si Vis Pacem Para Pacem.*

Unfortunately another pen was available. Robert Underwood Johnson in mid-June had offered Kellogg the use of perhaps the most distinguished pen in America, excepting the pen with which Lincoln signed the Emancipation Proclamation. This pen Johnson had fashioned from a feather, plucked in 1890 from a live eagle in the National Museum. Presidents Harrison, Taft, and Wilson had used the pen for various occasions.[32] Nearly a month later William H. Beck, Kellogg's efficient secretary, replied that Kellogg would "keep the pen in mind." [33] Not to be put off so easily, Johnson took his eagle feather to Europe so that Kellogg could use it if he desired. The secretary of state desired to use the Le Havre gold pen. This nonetheless was not the end of the tale of the Johnson pen, for after the Paris ceremonies Johnson hurried around and persuaded each of the fourteen signatories to sign a sheet of paper for the archives of the American Academy of Arts and Letters. Not satisfied with this signal achievement, Johnson then had the idea of each one of the adhering powers signing the sheet of paper— using of course the famous eagle-quill pen. He believed the sheet

32. Robert Underwood Johnson to Kellogg, June 14, 1928, 711.0012 Anti-War/218.

33. William H. Beck to Johnson, July 10, 1928, 711.0012 Anti-War/221.

of paper then would be a unique souvenir.[34] It certainly would have been. But the director of New York University's Hall of Fame eventually had to give up this scheme. He began to realize that the paper and pen would have to travel from Afghanistan to Venezuela and some forty-odd other places. Perhaps pen and paper would have been lost somewhere between Caracas and Kabul.

The problem of the pen disposed of, there arose the question of the chair. What chair should Kellogg sit in? The signing was to take place at the Quai d'Orsay in the Salle de l'Horloge, and in that very room was a chair which Woodrow Wilson had used during the Paris Peace Conference. Should Kellogg use Wilson's chair?

Soon it was announced that Kellogg would not sit in Wilson's chair. The reason however was quite proper and unsensational. Wilson had had a special chair with a high carved back; and according to Quai d'Orsay protocol such chairs were reserved for use of heads of state, which is to say kings and presidents. Thus Kellogg could not have sat in Wilson's chair even if he had wanted to.

The *Ile de France* on August 23 touched at England and rode at anchor in Plymouth harbor for half an hour, discharging passengers and mail. A deputation of local dignitaries had time to clamber aboard and visit Secretary Kellogg, congratulating him on his treaty against war. It being necessary to say something in return, Kellogg said he believed the treaty was "a great step forward in civilization—a great moral step." [35]

Early the next morning the *Ile de France* docked at Le Havre and Kellogg underwent his first ceremonial introduction to France. Accompanied by Canadian Prime Minister Mackenzie King, who had sailed with the Kelloggs from New York, the secretary of state stepped ashore and received a greeting from a company of French infantry rendering a military salute. A committee representing the city of Le Havre presented Kellogg with the foot-long pen, so heavy that he handed it to Admiral Burrage to hold. Mrs. Kellogg received a large bouquet of roses, and Mackenzie King a gold medal. Said Kellogg to the assembled crowd: "This treaty

34. Johnson to Assistant Secretary of State Wilbur J. Carr, Oct. 23, 1928, 711.0012 Anti-War/483.

35. New York *Times*, Aug. 24, 1928.

had its inspiration in the grand idea of M. Briand, your distinguished Foreign Minister. It was an idea which appealed to the statesmen of the world, and I am very glad that the consummation is to take place in Paris." [36] After this solemn declaration the Kellogg party proceeded to their special train, escorted between troops lined at attention. A special detail of fifty French bicycle police followed the secretary to the city limits, pedaling vigorously to keep up with the train. Newspapermen noted that the entire ceremony took only twenty minutes.

As a precaution against possible Communist demonstration the Kellogg train slipped into Paris forty-five minutes early. One lone reporter was there; Ambassador Herrick received just fourteen minutes' notice before the train arrived. Only M. de Fouquieres, director of the protocol of the French Republic, was on the platform. Kellogg drove quickly to the American Embassy with five hundred policemen as a guard of honor. Later he went out to the American hospital at Neuilly and inquired for Marriner, ill with pleurisy; Marriner's condition was serious, and Kellogg could not see him. The secretary lunched with Ambassador Herrick. He had a chat with Briand at four o'clock. There followed dinner with the Herricks and then early to bed.

The next morning the secretary received at the Embassy nearly two hundred American and foreign correspondents. "As you know," he told them, "I am here simply to sign a treaty which I hope, and I know all nations of the world hope, will be a forward step in the interest of world peace. It was the grand conception of M. Briand which led to the making of this treaty. The United States and I personally feel under great obligation to him . . ." Kellogg then bowed to the journalists, indicating the interview was over.

"I hope it will be well with the American Senate," came from a Hungarian correspondent in the back row. Everyone strained eagerly for the secretary's reply.

"That is a matter entirely up to the Senate, and I do not feel I can say anything on the point," Kellogg quickly answered. He then bowed again as if to end the meeting.

The reporters made further attempts to draw him out, but be-

36. New York *Times*, Aug. 25, 1928.

yond stating that those countries which were not signing the treaty would receive on the following Monday individual invitations to adhere to it, Kellogg would say nothing and withdrew hurriedly.[37]

Shortly after noon of the same day Kellogg and Herrick drove to the Arc de Triomphe, where the secretary laid a wreath of roses on the tomb of the unknown soldier. Although there had been no announcement a large crowd had gathered. Walking ahead of the ambassador, Kellogg placed the flowers on the grave and then knelt in prayer—first on one knee and then on both. This little ceremony became the subject of much friendly comment in afternoon Parisian newspapers. After lunch the two American diplomatists had a round of golf at the St. Cloud country club.

On the evening of August 26, the day before the ceremony of signature, Secretary Kellogg played host to the signatories. They all came except Stresemann who was too sick for social activities. Servants set up a huge horseshoe-shaped table in the American Embassy. The most distinguished gathering of diplomats since the days of the Versailles Peace Conference enjoyed an elaborate menu, featuring delicacies such as *aiguillette de boeuf Richelieu*. There was an "impressive" list of French wines and champagne, the details of which—unlike other items of the menu—were not announced.[38] After dinner the guests strolled through the Embassy gardens, illuminated for the occasion by hundreds of small colored electric lights buried in flower beds and bushes and placed in trees. A twenty-five piece band from the cruiser *Detroit,* then anchored at Le Havre, played the latest American jazz tunes.

Secretary Kellogg, surveying his laughing, jostling guests, and catching occasional strains of jazz from the *Detroit*'s band, must have mused silently over the many events of the past few months. From the enthusiastic activities of a group of people whom Kellogg once had called "——— ——— pacifists," and from the exigencies of the French Foreign Office, had come—months ago—a proposed Franco-American Pact of Perpetual Friendship. The American

37. New York *Times,* Aug. 26, 1928.

38. Although American Embassies abroad were exempt from the provisions of the Volstead Act, most foreign service officers undertook to make their convivialities as inconspicuous as possible.

secretary of state quickly had caught the implications of this innocent-sounding treaty. Only after half a year of ingenious stalling did Kellogg decide to answer the French Government—with his counterproposal of a multilateral, universal pact instead of a bilateral Franco-American treaty equivalent to a negative alliance. And after Coolidge's laconic "We can do that, can we not?" Kellogg did it with a vengeance. Then for three months Aristide Briand painfully sought to wiggle off the hook, but finally had to accept Kellogg's proposal in principle. After nearly four months more of observing and qualifying, the great powers, the Locarno powers, and the British Dominions and India had sent their plenipotentiaries to Paris. At that fleeting moment on the evening of August 26 Secretary Kellogg, standing in the Embassy gardens, might have agreed with Robert Underwood Johnson—that the treaty against war really was something of a miracle.

III

Flags of all the nations of the world hung from public and other buildings in Paris on August 27, 1928. The hammer and sickle even waved from the Quai d'Orsay itself. This was the day for the renunciation of war as an instrument of national policy. This was the day for which Salmon O. Levinson and James T. Shotwell, Nicholas Murray Butler and Charles Clayton Morrison, Colonel Raymond Robins and Senator William E. Borah all had waited. At 2:30 P.M. diplomats began to gather in Briand's office at the Quai d'Orsay, ready to walk to the Salle de l'Horloge where they would sign the treaty. A large crowd lined the streets opposite the Foreign Office and cheered the statesmen as they arrived. Newspaper reporters estimated that several thousand Americans were there who seemed to enjoy themselves greatly. Fully half of them were women.

The famous clock room was crowded. It was not a big room, and in addition to the signatories and several hundred invited guests it had to hold six huge klieg lights, placed so that all the people of the world might see the ceremony. Ushers clad in blue and gold trimmed coats, red velvet breeches, and white silk stockings directed guests to their seats. One of them helped Harrison Brown who at the last minute had, as he put it, wangled a ticket. Brown thought it scandalous that Chamberlain, who was not nearly so ill as Stresemann, should not have come to sign,[39] but at that moment in the afternoon of August 27, 1928, he was too busy examining the beautiful rococo decoration of the Salle de l'Horloge to bother much with scandals.

Harrison Brown was fortunate to have wangled a ticket, for less than seventy-five Americans witnessed the great ceremony in the clock room.[40] Twenty of them were members of Secretary Kellogg's official party. Several hundred people had sought, or fought, at the American Embassy to get tickets. For two weeks Mrs. Carter Murray of the Embassy staff listened to "the man who knew Coolidge," to "friends of the Administration." Even after Mrs. Murray had distributed the few tickets there was trouble. At the last minute it turned out that Robert Underwood Johnson, who as one-time American ambassador to Rome could claim a ticket, had not gotten one. Because he had failed to pick up his ticket Mrs. Murray had given it to Justice Pierce Butler of the Supreme Court. There ensued a wild scramble and finally the Embassy came up with another ticket for the former ambassador.

William Allen White, on hand to report to American newspaper readers on what he called "the first treaty renouncing war ever signed on this planet," counted only twenty-three silk hats out of three hundred headpieces at the Quai d'Orsay check room. He saw half a hundred gray business suits among the invited guests in the audience. "It was," he wrote, "the middle class speaking through the treaty." Business demanded and needed peace, wrote the famous and sophisticated editor of the Emporia *Gazette,* and the treaty was an expression of this demand and need.[41]

Among other Americans present that afternoon were Senator and Mrs. Walter E. Edge of New Jersey, Hamilton Fish Armstrong of the quarterly *Foreign Affairs,* Secretary of Labor James J. Davis,

39. Brown to Levinson, Aug. 27, 1928, Levinson MSS.

40. Fifteen nations had to divide about a thousand tickets.

41. New York *Times,* Aug. 28, 1928. See also White's *A Puritan in Babylon* (New York, 1938), p. 410.

former Undersecretary of State Robert E. Olds,[42] Dr. Earl B. Babcock of the Carnegie Endowment for International Peace, and Dr. Hugh Young, the famous Johns Hopkins surgeon. Europeans among the audience looked askance when Mrs. John W. Morrison of New York, representative of the American League of Women Voters, entered the clock room unescorted. "Naturally, an American," was the whispered comment, for no European lady would have thought of arriving alone for such a notable ceremony. While there were fully twenty other American women present, all of them were wives of Embassy officials and other prominent Americans and were accompanied by their husbands.

As the hands of the ornate gilt clock pointed to three, a Swiss guard with a halberd led a distinguished group of diplomatists into the room, where they seated themselves around a horseshoe-shaped table. There was the president of the Irish Free State, William Thomas Cosgrave, and the premier of the Dominion of Canada, the Right Honorable W. L. Mackenzie King. There were the six foreign ministers, Dr. Gustav Stresemann of Germany, the Honorable Frank B. Kellogg of the United States, Aristide Briand of France, Dr. Eduard Beneš of Czechoslovakia, Paul Hymans of Belgium, and A. Zaleski of Poland. There was Britain's acting secretary of state for foreign affairs, the Right Honorable Lord Cushendun, who signed also for India. Then there were the five special plenipotentiaries: the Honorable Alexander John McLachlan of Australia, the Honorable Sir Christopher James Parr of New Zealand, the Honorable Jacobus Stephanus Smit of the Union of South Africa, Count Gaetano Manzoni of Italy, and Count Uchida of Japan. A most distinguished gathering.

At 3:02 Briand began to speak. Contrary to his usual custom he read his speech—and this meant he had prepared it with care and calculation. Briand described the treaty to his audience. Some people, he said, insisted the treaty was not realistic for it had no sanctions. Then Briand the orator contradicted those individuals, for the treaty bore the sanction of "moral forces, among which is that of

42. Early in the summer of 1928 Olds had resigned from the Department. J. Reuben Clark took his place.

public opinion." What nation, he asked, could safely oppose such forces? Briand told his audience the history of the negotiations which had brought them that historic day into the clock room. "When, on the 20th of June, 1927," he said, "I had the honor of proposing to the Hon. Mr. Kellogg the form of words which he decided to accept and embody in the draft of a multilateral pact, I never contemplated for one moment that the suggested engagement should only exist between France and the United States. . . . It was, therefore, a source of gratification to me to see Mr. Kellogg from the beginning of the active negotiations that he was to lead with such a clearsighted and persevering mind, advocate extension of the pact and assign to it that universal character that fully answered the wishes of the French Government." In his mind's eye Briand looked beyond the walls of the clock room and over all frontiers whether on land or on sea. He was sure that, with this wide communion of men surrounding the signatories, they sincerely were entitled to reckon that there were more than fourteen around the table in the clock room. Gentlemen, Briand said, in a moment the awakening of a great hope would be signaled to the world along the wires. "Peace is proclaimed. That is well; that is much; but it still remains necessary to organize it." Briand closed by proposing that the signatories should dedicate the treaty to the dead, to all the dead, of the Great War.[43] The audience listened to the foreign minister's words with rapt attention. In the midst of the speech reporters saw tears trickle down the cheeks of Secretary Kellogg.

When Briand had finished Professor Camerlynk translated his speech into English. As the professor ended his translation, a whisper of "l'Américain, l'Américain" ran through the audience, for they expected Kellogg to speak. Instead Briand rose and read the preamble and text of the treaty.[44] Then one by one the diplomats began signing.

43. New York *Times,* Aug. 28, 1928.

44. A day or so before the ceremony Kellogg made known his decision not to make a speech, and this made it improper for the other signatories to deliver speeches. Unfortunately they already had prepared their speeches. The Quai d'Orsay had twenty-four strenuous hours of work persuading the statesmen not to speak.

Quai d'Orsay officials had spread the treaty on a small table inside the horseshoe table. Already the treaty bore fifteen wax wafers, each marked with the seal of the signer; the Foreign Office had requested each of the plenipotentiaries to lend it his seal so that the wafers might be stamped in advance.[45]

Stresemann as representative of *l'Allemagne* signed first. Looking gaunt and unwell, the German foreign minister rose from his seat and walked to the small table. Seated before the treaty and facing the audience in the clock room, he wielded the foot-long pen without difficulty. Next was the turn of Kellogg, representative of *l'Amérique, les États-Unis.* Kellogg started to sign his name but had trouble with the gold pen and had to dip it in the famous inkwell provided for the ceremony.[46] The other signatories who followed Kellogg had the same difficulty with the big golden pen, but otherwise everything went off without incident. At three minutes to four it was all over. The Swiss guard banged his halberd on the floor and the signatories filed out behind him through Briand's office into the gardens of the Quai d'Orsay Palace. After half an hour's conversation over tea and cake they scattered to their respective embassies.

That night the French Government illuminated all public buildings in Paris. Newspapermen from abroad still were busy sending out details of the afternoon's ceremony. Typesetters of great morning dailies in London, Berlin, Rome, Tokyo, New York, and elsewhere were beginning to put into print the day's events in Paris. There were festivities in the French capital that evening, and Harrison Brown, sitting down in a Paris hotel to typewrite a letter to Levinson, wrote that Dr. and Mrs. Morrison had gone to a soiree at the Quai d'Orsay.[47]

45. Kellogg used the aquamarine stone inscribed "F.B.K." set at the top of the great gold pen given him by the citizens of Le Havre.

46. The inkwell used by Franklin and Vergennes in signing the Franco-American alliance of Feb. 6, 1778.

47. Levinson MSS.

That evening after the pact had been signed a certain anonymous "onlooker" wrote the following: "The deed cannot be doubted. I saw it done. I heard the words spoken. I looked into the grave faces of the men who were impowered to sign. I handled the finished pact. I read again the unambiguous words of re-

Next morning American newspapers carried texts of messages between President Coolidge and President Gaston Doumergue of France. Coolidge had written that the new treaty was a great forward step, and Doumergue replied expressing the thanks of the civilized world. As he had done on other occasions, Aristide Briand sent another message to the American people through the Associated Press. "It has been a year and a half," he recalled, "since, in a message conveyed through The Associated Press, I let fall this fragile germ of a suggestion sufficiently discreet, anticipating nothing more than the spontaneous sympathy of the American people. . . . The harvest has not deceived my hopes . . ." [48]

---

nunciation. I looked at the signatures and seals. I cannot do otherwise than to command my pen to write these words: Today international war was banished from civilization." "Words of an Onlooker," Hooper MSS.

48. New York *Times,* Aug. 28, 1928.

Chapter Fifteen: TRAVAIL IN WASHINGTON

Aristide Briand in his new message to the American people had spoken of a harvest which had not deceived his hopes. The treaty against war apparently had delighted the foreign minister of France. But to speak of a harvest was premature, for the American Senate had not yet voted upon the pact of Paris: according to the Constitution of the United States the president had power "by and with the Advice and Consent of the Senate, to make Treaties, *provided two thirds of the Senators present concur.*" [1] Sometimes—as Europeans sadly learned after negotiation of the Treaty of Versailles—the Senate chose to withhold its advice and consent. It was thus almost in the nature of things that there should have to be a fight for American ratification of the antiwar treaty. The American peace forces girded themselves for battle against recalcitrant or wavering senators. For Professor Shotwell and Dr. Butler, Salmon O. Levinson and Colonel Robins, there would have to be travail in Washington.

Let us now follow the fortunes of the Kellogg antiwar treaty as, immediately after its signature, Secretary of State Kellogg carefully stored it in his bedroom at the American Embassy in Paris; as he nervously carried it with him on the cruiser *Detroit* to Ireland and back; as he watched the purser of the *Leviathan* stow it away in the great ship's safe; and as, back in Washington, he proudly stood guard over the precious parchment in his office at the Department of State.

1. Art. II, Sec. 2, par. 2. Italics inserted.

I

It is not possible to describe in detail Secretary Kellogg's official activities in France and Ireland during the days after signature of the antiwar treaty. The secretary had luncheon with the president of the French Republic in the splendid presidential chateau at Rambouillet. Kellogg received the freedom of the city of Paris; Georges Lemarchand, president of the Municipal Council, welcomed him at a grand ceremony, declaring Paris was proud that the antiwar treaty forever would bear the name Pact of Paris. (Kellogg, however, already had accepted a suggestion of Ambassador Herrick that the treaty be known as the General Pact for the Renunciation of War.) [2] After the secretary left France for Ireland, August 29, accompanied by President Cosgrave of the Irish Free State, he sent a message to Briand thanking him for the "delightful visit." "I feel sure," Kellogg declared, "that the work accomplished will mark a new epoch in international relations." [3] Briand, "profoundly touched," replied that he too hoped the work accomplished would mark the beginning of a new era. [4]

Arriving in Dublin, Kellogg and Cosgrave faced dense crowds

2. Kellogg to Herrick, Aug. 16, 1928, 711.0012 Anti-War/272. Nearly a year later, July 11, 1929, the Treaty Division of the Department of State proposed the designation Treaty for the Renunciation of War. 711.0012 Anti-War/839. The treaty has had many names: Pact of Paris, Paris Pact, Multilateral Treaty for the Renunciation of War, Treaty for the Renunciation of War, Kellogg-Briand Pact, Briand-Kellogg Pact, Kellogg Pact, Peace Pact of Paris. Kellogg-Briand Pact probably is the most accurate title, historically.

The present writer recently asked the Department of State for the correct title of the treaty. The Department replied that the treaty itself has no title but that, in accordance with the wording of the preamble, the accepted and proper designation is "Treaty providing for the renunciation of war as an instrument of national policy."

3. New York *Times*, Aug. 30, 1928.

4. *Ibid.*, Aug 31, 1928. Already the French foreign minister had written a thank-you to Nicholas Murray Butler: "I do not forget the effective part you have played in the vast movement of ideas which have paved the way and assured the success of the pact signed today. And I cannot refrain from sending you my most cordial greetings upon this day." *Ibid.*, Aug. 30, 1928.

of enthusiastic workmen, children, mothers, and colleens. Seumas Murphy, chairman of the City Commissioners, fairly outdid himself in extending the city's greetings. Said Mr. Murphy to Mr. Kellogg: "There are many names on the world's register of fame, placed high by deeds of courage and acts of wisdom and honored for administrative genius and artistic qualities. With confidence we can say there is none imbued with finer nobility. In you the angels of peace have come to minister to men again. With your advent in Europe has come the birth of what may be termed the second era of peace—peace on earth to men of good will." Surrounded by local Dublin dignitaries, Secretary Kellogg—small, stoop-shouldered, white-haired, seventy-one years of age—was so moved by this tribute that he faltered several times in replying.[5] A few days later, after enjoying himself thoroughly in the blarney-famed land of the shamrock, he sailed away on the *Detroit* for Cherbourg, and there, September 4, 1928, he happily boarded the *Leviathan* for home.

Yet one must not presume that the European political scene in the late summer of 1928 was as irenic as it appeared to Secretary Kellogg. European politics were not confined to official receptions and complimentary speeches.

Gustav Stresemann, while in Paris for the ceremonies of the Kellogg-Briand Pact, conferred with Premier Poincaré of France. The two statesmen did not range over the general beauties of peace but confined themselves to more specific matters, such as the still occupied German Rhineland, the Saar basin (then under a fifteen-year guardianship of the League of Nations), and international debts. In regard to the latter Stresemann and Poincaré made some highly interesting comments, thereby illuminating one of the factors in Secretary Kellogg's successful negotiation of his cherished antiwar pact.

"To meet our economic needs," Stresemann said, "we have borrowed many milliards of gold marks, especially from America, both in long-term and short-term loans. The moment it becomes generally known that Germany is not meeting her international obligations, these American loans will be called in. And in that moment we could no longer feed the 64 millions of our population. . . ."

5. *Ibid.*, Aug. 31, 1928.

"I am much interested," Poincaré replied, "in the situation in Germany in regards the United States of America. All of us in Europe are suffering from the situation in which we find ourselves as regards the United States." [6]

There were other contemporaneous events which pointed ominously toward the future, for in spite of unceasing efforts of diplomats and peoples, peace in Europe in 1928 was not well organized.

The delicacy of Franco-German relations appeared in a truly startling manner at the September meeting of the League of Nations in Geneva. There Briand, famous as the conciliator and man of peace, suddenly became angry after listening to a speech by the German Chancellor Hermann Müller. The chancellor, referring to the unilateral nature of disarmament—i.e., that the disarmament provisions of Versailles seemed to apply only to Germany—tactlessly had spoken of the "double face" of international politics. Briand retorted with a sweeping attack on German good faith. Germany, said the aroused French foreign minister, had not fulfilled her disarmament obligations. This angry exchange raised up a storm of denunciation on both sides of the Rhine and threatened to undo all the effects of Briand's previous conciliatory policy toward the German Republic.

It is not without interest that early in September 1928 important decisions were made in Paris relative to fortifying France's eastern frontier. The 1928 French budget already had appropriated 200,000,000 francs for the fortifications, at the request of the former minister of war, André Maginot.

Such developments did not bother Secretary Kellogg as he sailed home to the United States. A reporter on the *Leviathan*, who had seen Kellogg daily for the past two years, could not help remarking how the trip to Europe had changed the secretary. The reporter believed that Kellogg looked immensely pleased with himself and his treaty. A tired, worn, elderly man had gone to Europe only to return home buoyant, ruddy-complexioned, radiant.[7]

6. Notes by Stresemann of a conversation with Poincaré, Aug. 27, 1928. Eric Sutton, ed., *Gustav Stresemann*, III, 388. It is curious that this conversation should have occurred the very day of the signing of the Kellogg pact.

7. New York *Times*, Sept. 7, 1928.

II

Meanwhile in the United States political leaders were eyeing the forthcoming 1928 presidential election. It was a foregone conclusion that the Kellogg treaty would become an issue in the campaign. For the Republican party, embarrassed for years with its negative record on foreign policy, the antiwar pact was heaven-sent. Leaders of the Grand Old Party realized with fond anticipation that the Coolidge Administration—a Republican administration—had "outcovenanted" [8] Woodrow Wilson himself.

Originally there had been a strange reluctance among certain Republicans to use the antiwar treaty in the campaign. The Republican National Committee in May 1928, while the treaty negotiations still were in progress, zealously had begun collecting potential campaign planks. But when Assistant Secretary of State Castle on May 16 telephoned James White of the National Committee that Kellogg was a little delayed in getting in the foreign relations plank—which Castle had composed a few days before— "Jim asked [Castle wrote in his diary] whether it would be necessary to talk about this outlawry of war negotiation. I said it would. He then said he hoped it could be avoided as C.C. was bored with it and considered it foolish. I immediately went to the White House and asked Ted Clark [9] whether this was the case. He was much disturbed as to where White had got this information and said he thought it was not correct. I only wanted to know because if White was correct I wanted to cut out as much as possible. Jim White, of course, is working in the interests of C.C. and he ought to know. There are an infinite number of wheels within wheels." [10]

A few days later White visited the State Department and discussed with Castle the various planks of the Republican platform. White said that the platform, as far as he had it, was "dry as dust." He thought it needed "a little jazzing up," for the Democratic platform would be "very lurid." [11]

8. The good word is Samuel Flagg Bemis'. See his *Latin American Policy of the United States,* p. 219.

9. One of Coolidge's secretaries.

10. Castle diary, May 16, 1928.

11. *Ibid.,* May 22, 1928.

But when Castle went to Kansas City in June to help Senator Smoot with the platform, the foreign relations plank remained almost as Castle originally had written it.[12] Thus it came to pass that the Republicans fervently endorsed the proposal of the secretary of state, an idea which "has stirred the conscience of mankind and gained widespread approval, both of Governments and of the people, and the conclusion of the treaty will be acclaimed as the greatest single step in history toward the conservation of peace."

Outlawry and renunciation having become an issue in the campaign, American peace leaders resolved that politicians should not forget promises. Frederick J. Libby of the National Council for Prevention of War suggested to his peace workers that "Now is the time to ask your Congressman and Senators whether they support unreservedly their Party platform . . . Don't take as a sufficient answer the promise to 'study' the subject or to 'give the subject careful consideration when it arises.' "[13]

But Outlawry and renunciation were such easy paths to follow. In fact, they were not only easy but convenient. Dr. Hubert Work and Mrs. Alvin T. Hert, chairman and vice-chairman of the Republican National Committee, soon were hailing the treaty as an outstanding achievement of the Coolidge Administration. Said Mrs. Hert, with obvious inspiration: "Never in all history has there been taken a step of so profound significance to mankind." Both she and Dr. Work announced that Herbert Hoover would continue this policy if elected.[14]

Although the Democrats in their party platform also had adopted the Kellogg antiwar treaty (at Houston, Texas, they had resolved for "outlawry of war and an abhorrence of militarism, conquest and imperialism"), a leading Democrat, Franklin D. Roosevelt of New York, found occasion to criticize the antiwar pact. "If the vision of real world peace, of the abolishment of war, ever comes true," Roosevelt declared in his speech nominating Alfred E. Smith at Houston, "it will not be through the mere mathematical calculations of the reduction of armament program

12. *Ibid.,* Kansas City, June 10, 1928.
13. Frederick J. Libby, in NCPW, *News Bulletin,* 7 (Aug. 1, 1928), p. 3.
14. New York *Times,* Aug. 28, 1928.

nor the platitudes of multilateral treaties piously deprecating armed conflict." [15] Levinson anxiously wrote Kellogg about this attack on Outlawry, but Kellogg replied with assurance. "I am quite familiar with Franklin Roosevelt's statement at the Convention," he wrote. "I also knew that Mr. Morgenthau had proposed stumping the country against the treaty but many Democrats had dissuaded him from doing it. . . . The country is almost unanimous for the treaty." [16]

While Secretary Kellogg still was aboard the *Leviathan* coming back to the United States, Herbert Hoover himself undertook to make the new treaty redound to the greater glory of the Republican party. At his regular Friday press conference, September 7, Hoover broke his rule against being quoted and agreed to speak for the record. He announced that the Washington Disarmament Conference of 1921–22, the Dawes reparation plan, and the new Kellogg treaty (that "great treaty for the renunciation of war," that "magnificent step toward world peace") were "the greatest steps toward international peace by any country since the signing of the peace treaty ending the great war." [17]

But the mixing of politics with the antiwar treaty was doomed to failure.

Secretary Kellogg repeatedly had stated that the pact belonged to the nation, and not to the Republicans. A group of reporters accompanying Kellogg aboard the *Leviathan* therefore engaged in a conspiracy to remove the antiwar treaty from politics.

To Frederick T. Birchall, the managing editor of the New

15. New York *Times,* June 28, 1928. Roosevelt made another attack on the treaty in the pages of *Foreign Affairs:* "Today our Secretary of State is working on a glorified multi-powered declaration solemnly resolving against war. . . . It is of the utmost importance that this nation realize that war cannot be outlawed by resolution alone. . . . Practical machinery must be erected and kept in good working order. Secretary Kellogg's plan, even if approved by the leading nations, still fails in two points. It leads to a false belief in America that we have taken a great step forward. It does not contribute in any way to settling matters of international controversy." Franklin D. Roosevelt, "Our Foreign Policy: A Democratic View," *Foreign Affairs,* 6 (July 1928), 585.

16. Kellogg to Levinson, Oct. 25, 1928, Levinson MSS.

17. New York *Times,* Sept. 8, 1928.

York *Times,* Drew Pearson, one of the conspirators, sent the following radio: SUGGEST SENDING ME FOLLOWING QUERY QUOTE ASK KELLOGG WHETHER HE INTENDS TO LET HIS TREATY BECOME FOOTBALL OF POLITICS OR WHETHER HE BELIEVES IT SHOULD REMAIN COMPLETELY NON-PARTISAN ISSUE UNQUOTE. Birchall radioed as suggested. The reporters then showed a copy of the radiogram to Kellogg who, as Pearson later wrote, "gobbled the bait." The pact of Paris, the secretary said vehemently, was not to become a political issue in the presidential campaign. Kellogg's eyes snapped when he said this. He did not know that Hoover already had declared that the pact was an achievement of the G.O.P. The next morning the New York *Times* carried a lead: "Aboard the SS *Leviathan:* Secretary of State Kellogg does not approve the attempt of Mr. Hoover to claim the renunciation of war treaty as a great achievement of the Republican Party, and he has decided to do his best to prevent the treaty from becoming a political issue in this presidential campaign."

Kellogg did not waver in his determination to ensure the nonpartisan status of his treaty. As he left the *Leviathan* in lower New York harbor and steamed toward the Battery in a special tug, he received the press.

"Well, have you got the paper in your pocket?" asked a reporter.

"What paper?"

"You know, that paper you signed over in Paris."

Kellogg, disconcerted by this reception, fumbled in his pocket for several small slips of paper. Slowly he gave a slip to each reporter.

They read: "I do not think the treaty for the renunciation of war should be made a party issue either in the campaign or in the Senate, and I cannot conceive that it will be." [18]

When Secretary of State Frank B. Kellogg returned to Washington all unpleasant thoughts of politics had vanished from his mind. Undersecretary J. Reuben Clark and the four assistant secretaries [19] greeted him at the train station. Having already lunched on the

18. Drew Pearson and Constantine Brown, *American Diplomatic Game,* pp. 40–42.

19. William R. Castle (western Europe), Nelson T. Johnson (Far East), Francis White (Latin America), Wilbur J. Carr (administration).

train, Kellogg proceeded directly to the Department. There he happily showed his colleagues the treaty and the gold pen. Assistant Secretary Castle later recorded that the secretary of state talked about all of his experiences "like a pleased child." [20]

III

The antiwar treaty placed above the reach of Republican political leaders, there once more arose the problem of Soviet Russia. Did Russia's adherence to the pact of Paris automatically involve recognition by the United States Government? "By this act," later wrote the learned jurist and international lawyer, John Bassett Moore, "we necessarily recognized the Soviet government; for, by the hornbooks—the very primers of the kindergartens—of international law and diplomacy, recognition may be implied as well as express, and one of the stock examples of implied recognition is the entrance into conventional relations." [21] But the State Department would not so much as glance at these hornbooks and primers. The Department steadfastly refused to acknowledge that Russian adherence to the treaty had resulted, automatically, in American recognition of the Bolshevik regime.

Yet the Department recently had recognized Nationalist China by concluding a bilateral commercial treaty with the Nationalist

20. Castle diary, Sept. 10, 1928. En route to Washington there occurred a humorous incident. Kellogg's secretary, William H. Beck, was in charge of the Kellogg-Briand Pact, which Beck carried locked in a special suitcase purchased in Paris. Kellogg warned his secretary never to let the treaty out of sight. At Pennsylvania Station in New York Beck desired to repair to a telephone booth to telephone his family in Washington. Kellogg willingly assented but reminded him of his responsibility concerning the pact of Paris. Whereupon Beck repaired to the booth taking the suitcase along, much to the amusement of Secretary and Mrs. Kellogg. (Mr. Beck to the writer.)

21. *The Collected Papers of John Bassett Moore* (7 vols., New Haven, Yale University Press, 1944), VI, 349. In this connection one recalls the unsuccessful mission of Francis Dana to St. Petersburg in 1780 to secure American adherence to Catherine II's league of armed neutrals; such adherence, Congress then thought, would constitute implicit recognition of the United States by the members of the league.

government.[22] There was as a consequence some support within the Department for the idea that a *bilateral* (not a multilateral) treaty should constitute recognition. The Department's Treaty Division, however, was not prepared to accept as a general rule even such a proposition as this. The Treaty Division canvassed the entire question of recognition in an official memorandum of November 15, 1928, entitled "Recognition by Means of Treaty." "Practical convenience," proposed the division, "will, it would seem, be best served by confining the acts which may constitute recognition as narrowly as possible to express statements that one country recognizes the other. Where recognition does not follow from any other act or statement, the nervousness lest certain acts not intended to constitute recognition may nevertheless do so, may be avoided." [23]

The Government of Soviet Russia surely was difficult to treat with. Although the great powers after much discussion had arranged to exclude Russia from the Paris ceremony of signature,[24] this could not prevent the Soviets from giving a sarcastic note to M. Herbette, the French ambassador in Moscow, for transmission through Paris to Washington. Maxim Litvinoff as acting commissar for foreign affairs called attention in the note to Russia's proposals for general and total disarmament [25] and pointed out the "total impotence" of the League of Nations in rejecting these proposals. The British reservation of "certain regions" he declared a shabby attempt at imperialism. "But the said note of the British Government is not communicated to the Soviet Government as an integral part of the Pact or an annex thereto, therefore it can not be considered as binding on the Soviet Government, just as the other restrictions concerning the Pact mentioned in the diplomatic correspondence, are not binding on the Soviet Government." After

22. The commercial treaty, moreover, did not contain an explicit clause of recognition. See text in *FR: 1928*, II, 475–477.

23. "It may be recalled," the memorandum continued, "that during recent years most of the recognitions of new Governments by this Government have taken place through definite statements to that effect, and have not been left to be implied or presumed from some other act or statement." 711.9412 Anti-War/74.

24. See above, pp. 202–203.

25 See above, p. 126 n.

several hundred words of sharp criticism of the pact and its authors,
Litvinoff in the second to the last sentence of his long note expressed the Soviet Government's desire to adhere to the antiwar
treaty.[26] (But a few weeks later K. E. Voroshiloff, Soviet war commissar, said in a speech in Kiev that the Soviet Government had
never considered the Kellogg pact seriously and had adhered to it
merely for tactical purposes in order to prevent other powers from
accusing Soviet Russia of "Red imperialism.") [27]

The Soviet Russian Government nonetheless had the honor
of being the first state formally to adhere to the treaty against war.
The French Embassy in Washington, September 27, 1928, presented the State Department with Russia's instrument of adherence. Most of the other nations of the world, although having signified their intention of adhering, chose to withhold formal adherence until such time as the United States Senate should advise
and consent to American ratification.

IV

The great popular campaign for ratification of the antiwar
treaty did not get under way until after the campaign to elect a

26. Litvinoff to Herbette, Aug. 31, 1928, *FR: 1928*, I, 170–175.

27. Dispatch from London, Sept. 24, 1928, quoting a Riga dispatch in the
London *Times*. New York *Times*, Sept. 25.

According to Louis Fischer, *The Soviets in World Affairs* (2 vols., Princeton,
Princeton University Press, 1951), II, 774–775, a sharp struggle in Bolshevik
ranks preceded Russia's decision to adhere to the Kellogg pact. The party
theorist, Nikolai Bukharin, favored adhering. The foreign minister, Georgi
Chicherin, opposed. Chicherin argued that it would open the way to outside
dictation to Moscow. President Mikhail Kalinin remarked that the pact
"amounts to nothing. Instead of a real abolition of war—some more talk. . . .
Will the cause of peace be advanced a single metre? It will not." Why, asked
Kalinin, did the nations do such things? To trick the workers and masses into
acquiescing in larger armies and navies, he believed. "This is the only purpose." Prime Minister Alexei Rykov replied that the Kellogg pact would help
deprive the leaders of the "anti-Soviet bloc" of the formal possibility of an
attack on the Soviet Union. With all its faults the pact constituted a moral
obligation, Rykov believed, and therefore obstructed, to some small extent, the
psychological preparation for war. The then secretary general of the Communist party, Joseph Stalin, seems to have said nothing.

president of the United States. Only after that great quadrennial milestone of American political life—the first Tuesday after the first Monday in November—had passed, did the antiwar cohorts begin the fight for ratification. Carrie Chapman Catt's Committee on the Cause and Cure of War, the World Peace Foundation, the Carnegie Endowment for International Peace, the American Committee for the Outlawry of War, the Commission on International Justice and Goodwill of the Federal Council of Churches of Christ in America, the World Alliance for International Friendship, together with a veritable host of churches and women's clubs—all these then swept forward in grand alliance. No senator in Washington escaped the imperious request of these organizations: that the antiwar treaty receive promptly and without reservation the Senate's advice and consent for ratification. Salvos of resolutions, letters, and telegrams fell on the heads of the senators in Washington.

In this strenuous campaign for ratification Mrs. Catt's cause-and-cure committee was especially effective. Battle-hardened in the fight for women's rights, Mrs. Catt knew how to exert pressure on the American Government. As she told her friend Laura Puffer Morgan, she was writing to her representatives in the various states for a report on how their senators stood. That of course, Mrs. Catt added, was merely a start. She had never considered that a senator's attitude was assured unless he had become an all-out advocate, and unless he had been interviewed by several people and had said to each one the same thing.[28]

Mrs. Catt already had spread across the entire country an intricate network of state and local conferences on the cause and cure of war. The ladies, announced Mrs. Catt from her office in New York, were working with immense enthusiasm, furthering the movement for peace which was sweeping over the world. One woman drove her car eight hundred miles for a single interview with an important female in her state, and another said that she arose at four o'clock in the morning to take an early train to arrange for the meeting of cooperating organizations preceding the formal cause-and-cure conference in her state. At one conference

28. Letter of Sept. 20, 1928, NCPW files.

a representative of the American Legion was making the chief address. Patriotic women's organizations were joining in the peace movement in several states, and a number of colleges had decided to sponsor reading courses and extension lectures supplementing the peace conference programs.[29]

The cause-and-cure committee held more than 10,000 meetings. A standard resolution was presented and adopted at each meeting imploring the Senate to pass the antiwar treaty. Minnesota was the most resolute state, adopting the resolution over a thousand times.[30] The mere list of all the resolutions throughout the nation, wrote Mrs. Catt triumphantly to Senator Borah, "weighs 1 pound and 9 ounces and the resolutions themselves, if placed end to end, would measure nearly 2 miles." Mrs. Catt placed the resolutions on file, for inspection purposes, at the committee's headquarters in New York. "We are convinced from our experience of the past six months," she concluded, "that the women of this Nation are more united in their endorsement of this treaty than we have ever known them to be on any other question." [31]

The women of the nation however experienced disappointment on Armistice Day 1928—ordinarily a day of thoughts of peace— for President Coolidge made it an occasion for requesting new heavy cruisers for the American Navy. Coolidge spoke in the Washington Auditorium at exercises held under the auspices of the American Legion. "We meet to give thanks for ten more years of peace," he began auspiciously. But soon he turned to the Anglo-French naval agreement. "During last summer France and England made a tentative offer," the president said, "which would limit the kind of cruisers and submarines adapted to the use of the United States, but left without limit the kind adapted to their use. The United States, of course, refused to accept this offer." Coolidge concluded bluntly: "It is obvious that . . . world standards of defense require us to have more cruisers." [32] It appeared as if the

29. New York *Times*, Nov. 4, 1928.

30. Mrs. Ben Hooper to Mrs. Oce Curtis, Jan. 26, 1929, Hooper MSS.

31. Carrie Chapman Catt to Borah, Dec. 28, 1928, *Congressional Record*, Jan. 3, 1929, p. 1022. Borah introduced this letter into the record.

32. New York *Times*, Nov. 12, 1928. In his Armistice Day speech the presi-

president—having in past months made many flattering remarks about the antiwar treaty—now was inaugurating a world naval race.

Yet the peace movement held the center of the stage in New York City. There on Armistice Day Secretary Kellogg spoke at the Metropolitan Opera House before the World Alliance for International Friendship. The secretary of state maintained that the best way to abolish war as a means of settling international disputes was to conclude treaties of arbitration, conciliation, and renunciation. This, he inferred, the United States faithfully had done, under Secretaries Elihu Root, William Jennings Bryan, and himself.[33]

After the secretary's speech there followed a two-day Goodwill Congress. Not all of the speakers championed the Kellogg antiwar pact. Rabbi Stephen S. Wise, for example, described the Paris pact as a wishbone of peace rather than a backbone. But both Rabbi Wise and Carrie Chapman Catt strongly criticized for its militarism President Coolidge's Armistice speech.[34]

Senator Borah spoke in Carnegie Hall on the night of November 13 at the final meeting of the Goodwill Congress. He pledged his support to the Kellogg treaty against war. He promised to do all in his power to expedite it through the Senate. At the same time he declared himself in favor of an appropriation for heavy cruisers and added frankly that he would not fight such a measure: failure of a naval bill would, he believed, jeopardize passage of the antiwar treaty. But this advocacy of heavy cruisers could not brand Senator Borah as a militarist: the American Navy, he was certain, would

dent did not fail to praise the Paris treaty: "While this [antiwar pact] leaves the questions of national defense and limitation of armaments practically where they were, as the negative supports of peace, it discards all threat of force and approaches the subject on its positive side . . . . it is the most complete and will be the most effective instrument for peace that was ever devised . . . . this is the best that mortal man can do. . . . The progress that the world has made in this direction in the last ten years surpasses all the progress ever before made."

33. Frank B. Kellogg, *The Settlement of International Controversies by Pacific Means.* The cost of distributing this speech in Europe was $2,520.00. Norman Armour, American chargé in Paris, to Kellogg, Dec. 18, 1928, 711.0012 Anti-War/572.

34. New York *Times,* Nov. 13, 1928.

be used only as a defensive weapon. And the sole war admissible under the Kellogg treaty, said Borah, would come under the "higher law of self-defense, which can never be given or taken away from a nation by treaty." At this point when Borah began to discuss the higher law, there was an interruption. A well-dressed individual marched down the side aisle and stepped across the stage to where Borah was standing. Taking his place before the microphones of station WOR, which was broadcasting the evening's speeches, the man announced that he was bringing a message on world peace which he had received from the Kingdom of Heaven. Someone sitting on the platform escorted the messenger off the stage, and Senator Borah completed his speech without further ado.[35]

During the general public acclaim of the new treaty, Secretary of State Kellogg in Washington was eagerly anticipating arrival from Europe of a portrait of the Salle de l'Horloge, by the eminent artist Phillip de Laszlo. The portrait was to be hung in the White House. Becoming impatient, the secretary inquired of Chargé Atherton in London whether the portrait showed the likenesses of the signers, and, if so, did it show "me" signing the treaty? Atherton cabled that Laszlo had painted only an interior of the *salle,* with no figures. Crestfallen, Kellogg decided that a mere picture of the clock room would be rather disappointing.[36]

The secretary's disappointment was only momentary. He could not help feeling encouraged, even elated, by the way peace workers throughout the United States were supporting his Paris pact. Typical were the labors of Mrs. Fred Pittenger of Idaho, chairman

35. New York *Times,* Nov. 14, 1928. There were many other Armistice speeches throughout the country, and it is impossible to treat them at any length. Ambassador Herrick, home in Cleveland on leave, made a speech praising the Kellogg treaty and declared it destined "to go down into history as the final act toward removing that great burden [of war] from the shoulders of men." *Ibid.,* Nov. 13, 1928. Herrick's public declaration, that the treaty was "the final act," was not quite in harmony with what he had written privately July 3, 1928, to Robert Woods Bliss. See above, pp. 201–202.

36. Kellogg to Atherton, Nov. 13, 1928, 711.0012 Anti-War/494. Atherton to Kellogg, Nov. 14, 1928, 711.0012 Anti-War/506. Kellogg to Atherton, Nov. 15, 1928, 711.0012 Anti-War/511.

of the department of international relations of the Idaho Federation of Women's Clubs. Writing to her senator, William E. Borah, Mrs. Pittenger poured out her heart. Since last seeing Borah she had been faithfully working for the Kellogg treaty. It had become a personal matter with her. Through her efforts and others' the treaty now was before every federated women's club in Idaho. What, she asked, was the prospect? She thought that she would go into an early decline if the senators in Washington failed to do their duty by the treaty. Was there any message which Senator Borah had for the women of Idaho? Was there anything else she herself might do? [37] Borah hastened to assure Mrs. Pittenger that "I feel that when we get to a vote, it [the treaty] will be ratified. It would be simply awful if it were not ratified." [38]

Other eminent senators were feeling the ground swell of public opinion in favor of the treaty against war. Senator Arthur Capper, speaking November 23 at the Hotel Astor in New York before a thousand members and guests of the Academy of Political Science, hailed the signing of the antiwar pact as "the greatest turning point in the history of nations." He promised his whole-hearted support.[39] Soon came another advance for the peace movement: Senator Claude Swanson of Virginia, the ranking Democrat on the foreign relations committee, announced his support of the Kellogg pact.[40]

Congress assembled on December 3, and President Coolidge in his Annual Message proudly described the country in the midst of an era of prosperity more extensive and of peace more permanent than it ever before had experienced. The president in his message gave nearly three times as much comment to national defense as to the peace treaty, but what he did say about the Kellogg treaty was flattering enough. The treaty, Coolidge declared, was "the most solemn declaration against war, the most positive adherence to peace, that it is possible for sovereign nations to make. . . . The observance of this covenant, so simple and so straightforward,

37. Nov. 19, 1928, Borah MSS.
38. Nov. 23, 1928, Borah MSS.
39. New York *Times,* Nov. 24, 1928.
40. *Ibid.,* Nov. 27, 1928.

promises more for the peace of the world than any other agreement ever negotiated among the nations." [41]

By the time President Coolidge was delivering his Annual Message the peace movement's campaign for ratification was surging to ever greater heights. All of the various American peace organizations were at work, and their labors were herculean. Phil Harris Jr., an official of the National Council for Prevention of War, wrote to Professor Shotwell about astonishing "recent developments" in Kentucky. "The letterhead on which this is written," Harris informed Shotwell, "was drawn up after little more than three days' work in this State. An office, established at the Y.W.C.A., in Louisville, has employed a staff and has sent out seven thousand letters. We have a speakers' bureau, a weekly release to ministers, a weekly service to editors and contacts with the colleges and other groups of young people. . . . Petitions have been signed in great numbers . . ." [42] Miss Dorothy Detzer, the executive secretary of the Women's International League for Peace and Freedom (American Branch), wrote to Emily Balch, the WILPF-US's president, of a plan to push through ratification of the treaty by Christmas. Miss Detzer had become acquainted with Ludwell Denny, chief editorial writer of the Scripps-Howard newspaper chain of twenty-five papers. Denny had volunteered his cooperation. When Miss Detzer arrived home one evening she discovered that Denny had been attempting to get in touch with her all that day. She offered "Lud" a number of leads, and Denny kept at the long distance telephone for most of the night. [43]

The ratification campaign rolled on. The National Council for Prevention of War was receiving countless requests such as: "Enclosed find check for 60¢ for which send me 100 fliers & 5 broadsides and 10 petitions." [44] Shrewdly the council advised cor-

41. For the text of this message, see *FR: 1928,* I, vii–xxvi.

42. Phil Harris Jr. to James T. Shotwell, Dec. 3, 1928, NCPW files. The NCPW opened a special office in Tennessee, which between Nov. 5 and Jan. 14 sent out approximately 18,000 letters containing 33,700 pieces of literature. Minutes of the executive board meeting, NCPW, Feb. 20, 1929, NCPW files.

43. Dorothy Detzer to Emily Balch, n.d. (late Nov. 1928?), Balch MSS.

44. Dwight Arnold, of Arcanum, Ohio, to NCPW, Nov. 17, 1928, NCPW files.

respondents to write individual letters to Coolidge, Borah, and
Swanson, rather than prepare typed letters and then collect signatures under them. Laura Puffer Morgan of the council informed
Jane Addams how the Western European Division of the State
Department was "completely swamped with our letters and petitions. There is no doubt," Mrs. Morgan added proudly, "that our
methods are effective." [45] In the meantime Dorothy Detzer of the
WILPF-US had discovered that the State Department was answering all letters with the following form: "The General Pact for
the Renunciation of War will be submitted promptly after the convening of Congress." Miss Detzer called upon Prentiss Gilbert, acting chief of the Division of Western European Affairs, who had
been signing the forms. She asked a pointed question: Could he
interpret the word "promptly"? Prentiss Gilbert, with some embarrassment, said he could not.[46]

Letters and petitions continued to pour into Washington.
Secretary Kellogg on December 1 wrote to Senator Borah, giving
the chairman of the foreign relations committee a list of various
organizations and societies which had sent in resolutions expressing commendation of the pact (the Department had received no
petitions against the pact). Kellogg wrote again three days later:
"I am sure that you will be interested to know that . . . some
2,200 further communications have been received, addressed both
to the President and to myself . . . These communications have
come in from all the states, from the large cities, as well as from
small towns. . . . I believe that a conservative estimate would
indicate that the persons who have sought to express themselves
through the letters and resolutions to which I refer exceed 50,000 in
number, and I might furthermore add that the volume of such
communications, at present about 300 daily, seems to be increasing rather than diminishing." [47]

A few days afterward President Coolidge announced that the

45. Laura Puffer Morgan to Jane Addams, Nov. 30, 1928, NCPW files.
46. Report of the executive secretary, WILPF-US, Oct.–Nov. 1928, WILPF-
US files.
47. Kellogg to Borah, Dec. 4, 1928, 711.0012 Anti-War/564.

White House was receiving letters at the rate of 200 a day, and the State Department at the rate of 600.[48]

48. New York *Times,* Dec. 8, 1928. "Are the letters coming in uniformly favorable?" asked a reporter at Coolidge's press conference. Replied the president: "I haven't seen one that is in opposition. Of course some of them are in the nature of propaganda, evidently having been made by people that were asked to write, but a great many of them are voluntary expressions of their own desire to see a treaty of that kind." Transcript of Coolidge's press conference, Dec. 7, 1928; transcripts deposited in The Forbes Library, Northampton, Mass.

Chapter Sixteen: THE TREATY AND THE SENATE

Before Secretary Kellogg had gone to Paris to sign the treaty against war, Senator Borah had predicted to his friend Colonel Robins that opposition to the treaty in the United States would come from the "militarists," those persons who thought that the United States could not get along without the institution of war.[1] It was not quite to be expected, however, that the antiwar treaty, when coming before the Senate for advice and consent, should have to fight for a place on the docket against a naval appropriation bill which called for fifteen heavy cruisers and one aircraft carrier.[2] It even appeared that this cruiser bill might come up to the floor of the Senate before the antiwar treaty. Senator Hale of Maine, chairman of the naval affairs committee, and Senator Borah, chairman of the foreign relations committee, held a conference on November 22. Afterward Hale said that the cruiser bill would come up immediately after the Boulder Dam bill, and Borah added cryptically that he would go ahead with the antiwar treaty just as if there were no naval bill pending.[3]

1. Borah to Robins, July 25, 1928, Borah MSS.
2. This bill dated back to the failure of the Geneva Naval Conference of 1927. The Wilbur bill (named after the secretary of the navy), introduced immediately after the 1927 fiasco at Geneva, had stipulated for construction of seventy-one vessels costing altogether $725,000,000. Early in 1928 a new bill replaced the Wilbur bill, and this new bill asked only for fifteen 10,000-ton cruisers and one aircraft carrier, with an aggregate cost of $274,000,000. This second bill passed the House on Mar. 17, 1928, and then went to the Senate.
3. New York *Times,* Nov. 23, 1928.

I

President Coolidge transmitted the treaty to the Senate on December 4. Three days later the Committee on Foreign Relations held its first hearing. Secretary Kellogg appeared in person to defend his treaty.

Kellogg began by describing the treaty's obligations: beyond the agreement not to go to war there were no obligations, said the secretary. The nations knew, he declared, "from the notes that I wrote, that I was not willing to impose any obligation on the United States. I knew that was out of the question." [4] Kellogg warmed to his subject. "They [the nations] knew perfectly well that the United States would never sign a treaty imposing any obligation on itself to apply sanctions or come to the help of anybody." [5] Asked about the British reservation of "certain regions," he answered: "I did not acquiesce in it at all; and if there was anything in that note contrary to the treaty they signed, it would not be a part of the treaty." [6] It was clear, however, said the secretary, that "Great Britain was talking about nothing but self-defense." [7]

"Supposing some other nation does break this treaty," asked Senator Walsh of Montana, "why should we interest ourselves in it?"

"There is not a bit of reason," responded Kellogg. [8]

Senator Reed of Missouri hypothesized an alliance between England and Japan to attack the United States. Could not the United States, suffering under this aggression, call on the other signatories of the antiwar treaty for help? Kellogg answered to the effect that the United States was big enough to take care of itself; the American Government, Kellogg said, would not be calling on other countries of the world for help. Reed replied that he thought

4. U.S. Sen., 70th Cong., 2d Sess., *Hearings before the Committee on Foreign Relations, on the General Pact for the Renunciation of War* (Washington, 1928), I, 3–4.

5. *Ibid.*, p. 7.

6. *Ibid.*, p. 8.

7. *Ibid.*, p. 11.

8. *Ibid.*, p. 14.

the United States would be calling for all the help it could get.[9]

The foreign relations committee, having satisfied itself as to the obligations of the antiwar treaty, reported the treaty to the Senate on December 19. This did not in the meantime prevent senators from debating the pact [10] or even proposing reservations to it.

Senators Reed of Missouri and Moses of New Hampshire on December 14 introduced a resolution proposing four reservations: the treaty contained no obligation of coercion; the treaty did not affect the Monroe Doctrine; it did not interfere with self-defense; it did not entangle the United States in the League.[11] This resolution did not please the chairman of the Senate foreign relations committee, for Borah told reporters it would have an "immoral" effect.[12] Secretary Kellogg himself sought to block the resolution by talking to individual senators, but when he spoke to McLean of Connecticut and Johnson of California they refused to abandon

9. *Ibid.*, p. 21.

10. Before opening debate the Senate removed the injunction of secrecy.

11. The full text of the Reed-Moses resolution is as follows: "Resolved, That the Senate of the United States declares that in advising and consenting to the multilateral treaty it does so with the understanding—

(1) That the treaty imposes no obligation on the United States to resort to coercive or punitive measures against any offending nation.

(2) That the treaty does not impose any limitations upon the Monroe doctrine or the traditional policies of the United States.

(3) That the treaty does not impair the right of the United States to defend its territory, possessions, trade, or interests.

(4) That the treaty does not obligate the United States to the conditions of any treaty to which the United States is not a party." *Congressional Record,* Dec. 14, 1928, p. 599.

When the foreign relations committee on December 19 sent the treaty to the Senate floor, it also reported out the Reed-Moses resolution, albeit without comment on the latter.

12. New York *Times,* Dec. 15, 1928. The Washington correspondent of the *Times,* Richard V. Oulahan, understood that the resolution had originated from Professor Borchard of Yale. Senator Bingham of Connecticut later read into the record a letter from Borchard in which the latter said, "This is the first time in 10 years that I have ventured to differ from Senator Borah in a matter involving our foreign policy." *Congressional Record,* Jan. 10, 1929, p. 1469.

support of the Reed-Moses resolution. The two senators, on President Coolidge's invitation, went to the White House, but Coolidge also was unsuccessful.[13]

Senator Bruce of Maryland on December 15 made a merciless attack on the treaty. Ever since the rejection of the Treaty of Versailles, Bruce said, the Republicans had been playing with peace. He cited the "profuse spawn" of conciliation and arbitration treaties with Central and South America. He cited the much-reserved adhesion to the World Court. "And now comes along this anemic peace pact of our able and amiable Secretary of State, Mr. Kellogg, which is about as effective to keep down war as a carpet would be to smother an earthquake, but which, nevertheless, has worked up all the unsophisticated humanitarians of both sexes to a high state of excitement." If President Coolidge had any real faith in the pacific virtue of the antiwar treaty, "why, pray, when Mr. Kellogg [on Armistice Day] was cooing like a gentle dove, did the President set up such a jungle roar about more cruisers?" The United States, Bruce believed, should abandon "the unreal make-believe policies of peace which find their supreme expression in the Kellogg peace pact." It must enter the World Court and the League. Bruce felt that it was really of not much consequence whether he voted for or against ratification of the antiwar treaty. But it might aid in bringing the United States to a truer world cooperation. ". . . I shall, therefore, under the determining influence of this thought, vote in favor of ratifying the mighty, multilateral Kellogg peace pact, which may the prayers of the pious induce heaven to prosper far beyond my present expectations!" [14]

Petitions for the treaty continued to pour into Washington. Senators dutifully read them into the *Congressional Record*, consuming much time thereby. Representatives of the Federal Council of Churches brought to the White House on December 17 a monster of a petition asking for prompt ratification and containing more than 180,000 signatures.[15]

13. New York *Times*, Dec. 16, 1928.
14. *Congressional Record*, Dec. 15, 1928, pp. 678–681.
15. Senator Fess of Ohio read into the *Record* a letter of Dec. 17 from the Reverend Sidney L. Gulick, which described the petition. Signatures, classified

Christmas was approaching. This meant a long congressional recess until January 3, 1929. Several senators consequently met December 20 with Vice President Charles G. Dawes and agreed that both the peace treaty and the cruiser bill would be the Senate's unfinished business on January 3, the cruiser bill in legislative session and the peace treaty in open executive session.[16] To this arrangement the Senate consented unanimously.

II

On New Year's Day, 1929, the secretary of state and Mrs. Kellogg were entertaining the diplomatic corps at a breakfast in the beautiful building of the Pan-American Union.

"Why, where is Senator Borah?" Kellogg asked the wife of the Idaho senator, as she walked up the steps of the Union.

Mrs. Borah, a gentle-mannered lady, smiled. "He said that if you asked for him I should say he was at home working on your damned treaty," she replied.

The secretary of state and Mrs. Kellogg chuckled audibly. They stood together at the head of the marble staircase. "That is all right," responded Kellogg as Mrs. Borah passed on into the hall. "I want him to work on that treaty." [17]

When the Senate reconvened January 3 Senator Hale obtained

---

by states, numbered as follows: Alabama 2; Arkansas 12; Arizona 210; California 7,632; Colorado 2,205; Connecticut 8,268; Delaware 208; District of Columbia 495; Florida 663; Georgia 284; Idaho 645; Illinois 11,427; Indiana 6,229; Iowa 5,864; Kansas 8,313; Kentucky 377; Louisiana 347; Maine 1,998; Maryland 4,710; Massachusetts 8,809; Michigan 8,253; Minnesota 4,265; Missouri 2,141; Montana 527; Nebraska 2,159; Nevada 1; New Hampshire 997; New Jersey 5,472; New York 27,793; North Carolina 369; North Dakota 936; Ohio 15,399; Oklahoma 440; Oregon 2,585; Pennsylvania 19,712; Rhode Island 1,469; South Carolina 85; South Dakota 1,771; Tennessee 483; Texas 417; Utah 96; Vermont 1,004; Virginia 699; Washington 3,772; West Virginia 727; Wisconsin 5,085; Wyoming 677; miscellaneous 4,150.

16. Diary of Charles G. Dawes, Dec. 20, 1928. C. G. Dawes, *Notes as Vice President: 1928–1929* (Boston, Little, Brown, 1935), pp. 191–192.

17. New York *Times*, Jan. 2, 1929.

the floor for a speech on the cruiser bill. He argued cogently that nothing in the Kellogg treaty prohibited self-defense, that the cruiser bill was an implement of self-defense, and that no foreign nation had changed its naval program because of the Kellogg pact. At the conclusion of Hale's rather long speech Senator George of Georgia submitted a resolution on corruption of postmasters in the South. The Senate immediately went into open executive session to consider the Kellogg pact. Borah took the floor and began a speech which because of continual interruption soon turned into a running debate.

Borah stated frankly why the United States Government had concluded a multilateral instead of a bilateral pact. A treaty of the nature originally proposed by the French Government, he said, would have been "something in the nature of an alliance." This the American Government had refused to enter.[18] Borah declared that the treaty carried no provision, express or implied, for use of force.

Senator Reed of Missouri soon managed an interruption. He sought to embarrass Borah by opening up the subject of self-defense and citing the Spanish-American War. Reed recalled how, after the *Maine* explosion in Havana harbor, the Spanish Government immediately had disclaimed the act and made great efforts to avoid war. Surely, he concluded, if the United States in 1898 had been party to a Kellogg treaty there never would have been a Spanish-American War. But Borah deftly sidestepped the argument. "The principle of the treaty," he replied, "is that we can only go to war in self-defense; if we did not do that in the Spanish-American War, then it would have been barred by this treaty." Reed made a feeble attempt to reopen the subject; Borah answered in such a manner as to twist the discussion away from the Spanish-American War. Vanquished, Reed gave up the struggle.[19]

Senator Shipstead of Minnesota asked Borah if, in some future contingency the treaty should require interpretation, the notes exchanged by the powers would have any effect.

18. *Congressional Record*, Jan. 3, 1929, p. 1063.
19. *Ibid.*, pp. 1069–1070.

Borah responded: ". . . I regard these notes in the light of the fact that they add nothing to the treaty nor take anything from the treaty as having no legal effect whatsoever."

"The notes are a part of the treaty without adding anything to it or taking anything from it?" Shipstead asked innocently.

"I say that the notes are interpretative," Borah explained.[20]

Later in the debate Shipstead [21] cleverly raised the ever-recurring question of self-defense. Probably recalling Coolidge's assertion that the Kellogg antiwar treaty, if it had been in force in 1914, would have prevented the World War, Shipstead asked Borah if it were not true that every government taking part in the World War had done so under the right of self-defense.

"Under the claim of the right; yes," answered Borah.

". . . how could this treaty have stopped the World War?" queried Shipstead.

"I do not know," Borah admitted, "that this treaty could have stopped the World War." [22]

Hiram Bingham of Connecticut then mentioned that Briand of France once had said the antiwar treaty outlawed only selfish wars. "Is it not likely," Bingham asked, alluding to the pending cruiser bill, "[that] as many cruisers are needed to fight an unselfish war as to fight selfish wars?" [23] The Senate laughed.

Debate on the treaty continued the next day, January 5. Senator McLean believed that it was high time to cease throwing peacepaper wads at the dogs of war. It was time to pull the teeth of those dogs—that is, it was time for disarmament. He would not begin by pulling the teeth of the United States' half-grown pups, however, but rather would start on the sharp teeth of the European beasts. In other words he desired a disarmament conference rather than an antiwar treaty. Changing his picturesque language McLean admonished his auditors to remember the Indians. "Mr. Briand comes to us with his new pipe of peace. We suggest that it is a good time for all the braves to gather around the international wigwam and have

20. *Ibid.*, Jan. 4, 1929, p. 1126.
21. Who was not a lawyer by profession, but a dentist.
22. *Congressional Record*, Jan. 4, 1929, p. 1134.
23. *Ibid.*, p. 1138.

a smoke. This they did, but, as might have been expected, they found a carload of coughs in the first puff of the self-defense mixture, and they declined the second puff until it was understood that it would not interfere with the free use of tomahawks and hatchets." [24]

As debate thus proceeded it became quite evident that the Senate was not in reality hostile to the Kellogg pact, but rather that some of the senators were simply humoring themselves: so long as they eventually cast their votes in favor of the treaty they saw no harm in offering sharp questions or disparaging comments. It was also clear that many senators, although favoring the treaty, considered it of questionable value. One senator told Bingham of Connecticut, confidentially, that he would vote for the treaty because it might keep American ships and men out of China and Nicaragua, where he thought they should not be. Another senator said to Bingham that he was going to vote for the treaty because he believed it meant nothing and would in no way limit the United States' freedom of action. A third senator remarked to Bingham that if the treaty meant exactly what it said there would not be a dozen senators on the floor of the Senate who would vote for it. [25]

Senator McKellar of Tennessee told his confreres that he would vote for the antiwar pact because he had voted for the Bryan treaties and for the League and did not wish to spoil his voting record. To vote against the treaty, moreover, might make his position as to war misunderstood—for McKellar was against war. He then quoted a statement by an anonymous person in the Washington *Post* of January 9, 1929: "I called on Senator McKellar, and he said the pact didn't amount to anything. He said the only way you can have peace on earth is to have a navy bigger than England's." McKellar denied having said this; he merely had contended for many years that the best way to secure peace was for the United States and Great Britain to have equal-sized navies. [26]

24. *Ibid.*, Jan. 5, 1929, pp. 1189–1190.
25. Senator Bingham, *ibid.*, Jan. 10, 1929, p. 1467.
26. *Ibid.*, Jan. 9, 1929, pp. 1414–1415. One suspects that the *Post* had published an actual statement by the loquacious Tennessee senator, and that McKellar was indulging in a diplomatic denial.

Senator Borah soon began to find his colleagues' long speeches rather boring. On January 11 he sought a limitation of debate to thirty minutes per senator, but failed to obtain the necessary unanimous-consent agreement.[27] The Senate was in a self-indulgent mood.

Some senators, moreover, were circulating a round-robin to obtain pledges that their colleagues would not vote for the treaty without an interpretive declaration. The round-robin reached formidable proportions, with twenty-five signatures and some ten more adherents. The Senate seemed stubbornly determined to place some sort of reservations to the Kellogg pact. Among the senators there was a feeling amounting almost to pique, which Senator Bruce aptly expressed as follows: England, France, even Afghanistan and Persia, have given their interpretations of the treaty; Mr. Kellogg has stated his understanding of it; why cannot the Senate of the United States do likewise? [28] Such an attitude on the part of the senators was highly distracting to Secretary Kellogg who by this time doubtless was pacing the floor in the State Department, fussing, fidgeting, calling in assistants, and in general working himself into a state of exhaustion.[29]

27. *Ibid.*, Jan. 11, 1929, pp. 1567–1568.
28. *Congressional Record,* Jan. 14, 1929, p. 1658. Bruce concluded that Mr. Kellogg was not Sir Oracle. Kellogg could not say that when he opened his mouth let no dog bark, whether a senatorial dog or otherwise. The Senate had a function to perform just as well as Mr. Kellogg. There was a need for an expression of the Senate's opinion. *Ibid.*, p. 1665.
29. Something of his feelings emerges from a telegram which he sent hurriedly to Levinson in Chicago: YOUR TELEGRAM RECEIVED THE LAST SCHEME OF THE MEN DESIRING TO DEFEAT THE TREATY IS VERY INGENIOUS IS TO GET TO THE FOREIGN RELATIONS COMMITTEE TO MAKE A REPORT INTERPRETING THE TREATY THEY ARE NOT PARTICULAR WHAT INTERPRETATION IS PUT ON IT SO THAT FOREIGN COUNTRIES WILL KNOW THAT SOME INTERPRETATION HAS BEEN PLACED UPON IT THEY KNOW OF COURSE THAT UNDER THE DECISIONS OF OUR COURTS WHILE INDIVIDUAL SENATORS REMARKS WILL NOT BE CONSIDERED IN INTERPRETING A TREATY A REPORT OF THE COMMITTEE WILL I THINK THEY HAVE MANY SIGNATURES TO THEIR ROUND ROBIN WHICH THEY WOULD NOT HAVE OBTAINED HAD THEY KNOWN THE EFFECT IT IS IMPOSSIBLE FOR ME TO SEE EVERYBODY TREAT THIS AS STRICTLY CONFIDENTIAL. Telegram of Jan. 14, 1929, Levinson MSS.

Already, however, the outlook for the treaty had begun to brighten.

III

President Coolidge on Sunday, January 13, called Vice President Dawes on the telephone and asked him to help to get the treaty ratified as soon as possible. Dawes, a peppery, resolute individual, declared he would "steam up" on Monday. The vice president wrote in his diary that Sunday evening how bored he was by the ponderous debate over the treaty: "I find myself more or less in a state of irritation . . ." [30] And so when Monday came, "Hell-and-Maria" Dawes [31] set to work.

He enjoyed a considerable support. During the next twenty-four hours—that is, between Monday and Tuesday, January 14 and 15—petitions flooded into Washington.[32] Also, over a thousand women peace leaders were in Washington attending another Conference on the Cause and Cure of War; and these militant ladies divided into forty-eight groups and descended upon the senators

---

30. Dawes diary, Jan. 13, 1929, in *Notes as Vice President*, p. 230.

31. As he was known after a flamboyant speech in 1921.

32. The Senate was overwhelmed by petitions. Senator Vandenberg of Michigan on Jan. 15 presented petitions of 70,000 citizens and 896 organizations of the state of Michigan, praying for the prompt ratification of the Kellogg-Briand peace pact. Senators Dale and Greene of Vermont presented 440 resolutions from Vermonters. Senator Frazier presented 20 resolutions from the state of South Dakota. Shipstead of Minnesota presented "numerous" resolutions from his state. Thomas of Idaho presented petitions signed by 9,000 women of Idaho. Tydings of Maryland presented "numerous" resolutions. So did Senator Sheppard of Texas. Bayard of Delaware presented 74 resolutions. Phipps presented petitions bearing the signatures of 60,000 citizens of Colorado. Neely of West Virginia presented 118 resolutions. Blaine of Wisconsin offered a resolution of the Woman's Foreign Missionary Society of North Freedom, Wisconsin. Hawes of Missouri presented petitions. Bingham, Caraway, and Burton did likewise. So did Senators Walsh, Copeland, Simmons, McKellar, Glass, Bruce, Sackett, and Smoot. It was stated finally that every senator had the right to file petitions without asking permission to do so. *Congressional Record*, Jan. 15, 1929, pp. 1709–1710.

from their home states, arguing imperatively for the antiwar treaty. The women presented 12,533 resolutions to the senators. "Do you realize that meant 12,533 meetings held in the United States at which the treaty was read, explained, discussed and voted upon?" [33] Indeed the work was so strenuous that Mrs. Carrie Chapman Catt suffered a heart attack.[34]

All this while General Dawes was putting on the steam in the Senate chamber. The vice president set out to talk personally to each recalcitrant senator: he argued that the antiwar treaty and the cruiser bill together were "the declared and unified policy of the United States," and that the antiwar pact therefore required no reservation. As set down in his diary Dawes' argument was long and complicated.[35] The general's thoughts today read slowly in print. But if accompanied by suitable Dawesean gestures and punctuation they must have been altogether convincing.

On Tuesday, January 15, events moved toward a climax. Shortly after Vice President Dawes called the Senate to order, Senator Borah asked Dawes to leave the chamber and meet him in the vice president's office. There Borah proposed that the Senate, in advising and consenting to the antiwar treaty, adopt simultaneously an explanatory report of the foreign relations committee: this re-

33. Mrs. Ben Hooper to Mrs. J. C. Zeller, Feb. 8, 1929, Hooper MSS.

34. Miss Josephine Schain to Mrs. Ben Hooper, Jan. 28, 1929, Hooper MSS.

35. "The first Senator . . . took immediately to my suggestions, which were that the Cruiser Bill and the Treaty considered together were the declared and unified policy of the United States—that if they were read together and agreed upon together by the Senate, the desire and determination to co-operate for peace would not only be properly expressed but the Treaty would be defined as not abrogating our determination to recognize our rights of self-defense, a part of which policy includes the Monroe Doctrine; that reservations detailing specific acts covered by the term 'self-defense' were unnecessary; that any Senator fearing to be called to account for his action in voting for the Treaty without reservations or their equivalent (such as the promulgation of a report by the Foreign Affairs [sic] Committee or a similar device) could protect himself by this statement to wit: that the concurrent action on the peace Treaty and the Cruiser Bill emphasized before the country and the world their true relation as a definition in combination of a unified national policy." Dawes diary, Jan. 14, 1929, in *Notes as Vice President,* pp. 231–232.

port, however, would state explicitly that it was not a modification of or reservation to the treaty.[36] Satisfied with Borah's proposal, Dawes telephoned President Coolidge. The president said that he did not wish to be publicly quoted but would say "I think you have done all you can." Then Secretary Kellogg happened to ring up the vice president while Borah yet was in Dawes' office, and Kellogg also acquiesced.[37] Thus fortified, Borah went back on the Senate floor, Dawes returned to the presiding officer's chair, and both men set about putting the treaty through that very day.

Nothing, though, could prevent Senator Carter Glass of Virginia from making a speech. ". . . I intend to vote for the peace pact," Glass announced, "but I am not willing that anybody in Virginia shall think that I am simple enough to suppose that it is worth a postage stamp in the direction of accomplishing permanent peace. I think we are about to renounce something as a national policy which no nation on earth for 150 years has ever proclaimed as a national policy. . . . But I am going to be simple enough, along with the balance of you," Glass told his fellow senators, "to vote for the ratification of this worthless, but perfectly harmless peace treaty."[38]

After Glass had finished his remarks Borah read the report from the foreign relations committee.

The report repeated the substance of the earlier Moses proposal. It reserved self-defense—and thereby the Monroe Doctrine, a part of the United States' self-defense. The report stated the foreign relations committee's understanding that the treaty did not provide sanctions, express or implied. Nor did the treaty in any respect change or qualify the United States' position or relation to any pact or treaty existing between other nations or governments. The report was made "solely for the purpose of putting upon record what your committee understands to be the true interpretation of the

36. From Senator Joseph T. Robinson of Arkansas, wrote Dawes in his diary, came the suggestion of the committee report instead of formal reservations. From Borah came the addendum that the report did not modify or reserve the treaty. Dawes diary, Jan. 15, 1929, in *Notes as Vice President*, p. 236.

37. *Ibid.*

38. *Congressional Record,* Jan. 15, 1929, p. 1728.

treaty, and not in any sense for the purpose or with the design of modifying or changing the treaty in any way or effectuating a reservation or reservations to the same."[39]

Shortly after four o'clock in the afternoon of January 15, 1929, Senator Borah proposed a vote on the treaty; and the treaty passed, 85 yeas and 1 nay. The lone dissident was Senator Blaine of Wisconsin.[40] Of the nine senators not present for the vote, five were "unavoidably detained," and their colleagues reported that they would have voted yea.[41]

Immediately after Vice President Dawes announced the results of the vote, Senator Brookhart of Indiana arose. "Mr. President," he said, "at this moment I desire to call attention to the fact that the Union of Soviet Socialist Republics and the United States of America are the only two nations that have ratified this treaty and are parties to it, and I hope these two great revolutionary countries will now proceed to outlaw war throughout the world."[42]

39. *Congressional Record*, Jan. 15, 1929, p. 1730. Wrote Elihu Root to Borah, Jan. 17, 1929: "I think the concluding paragraph of your report on the multi-lateral treaty sufficiently saves the treaty from being involved in any confusion." Root MSS. Two international lawyers, Professors Borchard of Yale and Philip Marshall Brown of Princeton, wrote to Senator Bingham that the Senate's explanatory report lacked the force of a formal reservation because it was not communicated. But both professors believed that the report would have a strong "moral" significance. *Congressional Record*, Jan. 14, 1929, pp. 1656–1657.

Kellogg took the attitude that the senatorial report was nothing but a report and had no legal effect whatever. Kellogg to Houghton, Jan. 17, 1929, 711.0012 Anti-War/622. The report, he wrote to Nicholas Murray Butler, "was not adopted by the Senate; it was not attached to the treaty, and the only objection to it is the humiliation forced on me." Letter of Jan. 16, 1929, in N. M. Butler, *Across the Busy Years*, II, 209.

40. He could not approve of the British certain-regions doctrine. Blaine had offered a reservation disclaiming any American recognition of this doctrine on Jan. 3 (*Congressional Record*, pp. 1044–1045). His speech on Jan. 9 was a long tirade against the British Empire (*ibid.*, pp. 1400–1407).

41. Senators who had been most outspoken in criticism of the treaty finally voted for it. When a constituent asked Senator Reed of Missouri about his yea vote Reed is said to have replied: "Do you think I want to be hung in effigy out in Missouri?"

42. *Congressional Record*, Jan. 15, 1929, p. 1731.

Chapter Seventeen: RATIFICATION

AND PROCLAMATION

Success at last had crowned the strenuous campaign to renounce and outlaw war as an instrument of national policy. Peace forces in the United States could look back with pleasure over their recent activities. Only two years before, Frenchmen and Americans had been exchanging insults over who had won the war and who should pay for it. Then, almost miraculously, there came what Aristide Briand later described as his "fragile germ of a suggestion sufficiently discreet, anticipating nothing more than the spontaneous sympathy of the American people." Following an intense campaign by the American peace movement, a campaign strengthened fortuitously by airplane diplomacy, Briand's fragile germ suddenly, on December 28, 1927, burgeoned into gigantic proportions: a treaty to renounce all war as an instrument of national policy. And after much maneuvering and debate the powers had actually agreed to such renunciation, albeit with reservations. In Paris on a memorable day in August 1928 representatives of fifteen nations had solemnly affixed their signatures. The other nations of the world quickly indicated a desire to adhere to this multilateral antiwar treaty. As soon as the United States Senate had advised and consented to American ratification nations from all parts of the globe undoubtedly would be sending to Washington their formal instruments of ratification and adherence. Only ratification by the United States was needed to set off this thrilling chain reaction. And on January 15, 1929, the Senate advised and consented.

I

Two days later President Coolidge signed the American instrument of ratification. The presidential signature was occasion for ceremony. Coolidge signed in the East Room of the White House, surrounded by the Cabinet and members of the Senate, and he used the gold pen of Le Havre.

The ceremony lacked something of dignity. The president became angry at a veteran State Department employee, Sidney Smith, who sought to assist by blotting the presidential signature. Coolidge looked up at Smith and snapped rudely, "Who are you? I don't know you. Go away." [1] Then the foot-long gold pen again ran dry. To complete the signing the president was forced to maneuver a heavy inkwell on to the table. In addition to the above incidents there were the orders and noises of forty or fifty photographers attempting to record the scene for posterity. The photographers impertinently asked the president to "Keep perfectly still" and suggested to Secretary Kellogg, who also signed the instrument of ratification, to "Keep your hand steady." Observing all this with some amusement from a vantage point next to the president, Vice President Dawes concluded that there was no peace during the antiwar ceremony.[2]

When Secretary Kellogg afterward returned to the State Department he confided to Assistant Secretary Castle that it was deplorable the president had lost his temper. "But the funniest thing," Castle wrote later in his diary, "was that the Secretary in telling me got so furious that he trembled all over. He said 'G—— d—— it. The President has no right to lose his temper. If a man can't keep his temper he had better not hold public office.' " [3]

1. Motion picture cameras recorded all this, and Assistant Secretary Castle's diary relates that someone had to attempt to have the episode cut out of the film, "as the President's face looked like murder." Castle diary, Jan. 17, 1928.

2. Dawes diary, Jan. 17, 1929, in *Notes as Vice President*, pp. 240–241.

3. Castle diary, Jan. 17, 1929.

II

Once the Senate had given its advice and consent to the pact of Paris, and President Coolidge had signed the American instrument of ratification, there remained only the question of when the other fourteen signatories would themselves ratify the treaty, thus bringing it into force. The Coolidge Administration, and especially Secretary of State Kellogg, was anxious that the other ratifications all should arrive before March 4, 1929, when the administration went out of office. Australia, Canada, Czechoslovakia, Germany, Great Britain, India, the Irish Free State, Italy, New Zealand, and the Union of South Africa deposited their ratifications at Washington on March 2.[4] The remaining nations were tardy. Ratifications arrived late from Poland (March 25) and Belgium (March 27). Nearly a month later came France's instrument (April 22). There still was lacking ratification by the Government of Japan.

The Japanese were perplexed by a phrase in Article 1 of the treaty according to which the signatories professed to sign the treaty "in the names of their respective peoples." This was contrary to the Japanese Constitution: the emperor signed treaties by himself and not in the name of his people. Secretary Kellogg reassured the Japanese that "in the name of" was synonymous with "in behalf of," and therefore could cause no harm to the imperial prerogative.[5] The Japanese Privy Council nonetheless debated the matter most thoroughly. The debate led to such violence that one privy councilor was compelled to resign for being rude to an old man.[6]

Kellogg, embarrassed by requests from other powers as to when the treaty would come into force, finally intimated to the Japanese ambassador that he might have to propose the signing of a protocol

4. So also did the United States. Depositing was a formality, and the American Government politely had waited until other nations were ready.

5. Kellogg to Chargé Neville in Japan, July 6, 1928, *FR: 1928*, I, 104–105.

6. Memorandum by Castle of a conversation with the Japanese ambassador, Katsuji Debuchi, May 15, 1929, 711.9412 Anti-War/126.

which would put the treaty into effect as between the powers which had ratified. The secretary added that he did not wish to do this unless it were absolutely necessary.[7] But not until over six months after the American Senate had ratified the treaty did the Japanese Government, July 24, 1929, deposit its ratification in Washington.[8]

While aged privy councilors debated in Tokyo, State Department officials in Washington had no opportunity to rest. The mere clerical labor of bringing a multilateral antiwar pact into force was extremely heavy. According to the pact's Article 3, the American Government had to furnish each of the fifteen governments named in the preamble of the treaty, and also every government subsequently adhering to the treaty, with a certified copy of the treaty and of every instrument of ratification or adherence.[9] Department officials estimated that this obligation would necessitate more than 4,000 separate copies, each one certified by actually signing the document.

Thus in the spring of 1929 the State Department found itself bogged in clerical labor—making copies of antiwar documents and duly certifying them. Not so the European foreign offices. Other problems demanded the attention of the Quai d'Orsay, No. 11 Downing Street, and the Wilhelmstrasse.

In England, late in May 1929, No. 10 Downing Street received a new occupant. In the parliamentary elections the Conservatives had met defeat at the hands of Ramsay MacDonald's Labor party,

7. Memorandum by Assistant Secretary Nelson T. Johnson of a conversation between Kellogg and the Japanese ambassador, Mar. 7, 1929, 711.9412 Anti-War/92.

8. The Japanese accompanied their ratification with the following "Declaration": "The Imperial Government declare that the phraseology, 'in the names of their respective peoples,' appearing in Article I of the Treaty for the Renunciation of War, signed at Paris on August 27, 1928, viewed in the light of the provisions of the Imperial Constitution, is understood to be inapplicable in so far as Japan is concerned." *FR: 1929*, III, 255.

9. "It shall be the duty of the Government of the United States to furnish each Government named in the Preamble and every Government subsequently adhering to this Treaty with a certified copy of the Treaty and of every instrument of ratification or adherence. It shall also be the duty of the Government of the United States telegraphically to notify such Governments immediately upon the deposit with it of each instrument of ratification or adherence."

and Arthur Henderson replaced Sir Austen Chamberlain. French officials in Paris feared Henderson would not cooperate with France on the Continent in the friendly fashion of Sir Austen. Meanwhile there were ominous rumblings in Germany where the liberal parties were losing ground to the Catholic Center and the Prussian Conservatives; Stresemann's policy of fulfillment was slipping toward disaster. All this while a committee of economic experts, headed by the American financier Owen D. Young, prepared a new plan for German reparations payments, a complicated proposal already known as the Young Plan. Acceptance of this plan, it was understood, would raise the exceedingly delicate question of Allied evacuation of the Rhineland.[10]

But times generally were good on the Continent, and in the British Isles, and in the United States—since March 4 under the guidance of President Herbert Hoover and Secretary of State Henry L. Stimson.[11] In America especially, almost everyone was happy. Business was good. The stock market was booming.

To the average person and even to close students of international affairs, war during these piping times seemed, if not altogether unthinkable, at least a long way off. There might be obscure squabbles in some remote corner of the globe. Amanullah, the Padishah of Afghanistan, could fight for possession of Kabul. But the chances of a great European war such as broke out in 1914 appeared small indeed. Frank H. Simonds, surely a distinguished observer of international realities, wrote for the *Review of Reviews* during the summer of 1929 that "Nothing seems more assured today than two decades of freedom from any general European conflict." [12]

Such was the prospect when the Imperial Japanese Government signified its intention of depositing in Washington, July 24, 1929, its instrument of ratification of the antiwar treaty. Secretary of

10. The Allies had decided this at Geneva, Sept. 16, 1928, when they agreed to revision of German reparations.

11. Actually Stimson did not take office until Mar. 28, 1929, for he had to return from the Philippines (whence he had gone as governor general). Kellogg served during the interim.

12. Frank H. Simonds, "The Fifteenth Anniversary," *Review of Reviews,* *80* (August 1929), 62.

State Stimson quickly set about preparing a suitable ceremony—
for this would be the final ceremony in connection with the pact
of Paris. Japan would be the fifteenth, and last, of the signatories
to ratify the pact.

III

Henry L. Stimson looked forward to the approaching ceremony
with pleasure. A handsome, capable man with graying mustache
and ascetic forehead, thoroughly patrician in appearance and
tastes,[13] the new secretary of state looked upon the world of early
1929 and pronounced it good: it was peaceful and two great English-
speaking powers ruled much of it. Secretary Stimson was very glad
to help bring into force an antiwar treaty which might maintain
this excellent situation.

For the ceremony of proclamation he invited the Washington
representatives of all the signatory and (as of July 24, 1929) adhering powers,[14] a total of forty-six states. Former Secretary of State

13. A Yale man, Stimson had a penchant for fellow Yale men, preferably
members of Skull and Bones.

14. Fifteen signatories and the following thirty-one adherents: Union of
Soviet Socialist Republics (Sept. 27, 1928), Ethiopia (Nov. 28, 1928), Afghanistan
(Nov. 30, 1928), Dominican Republic (Dec. 12, 1928), Austria (Dec. 31, 1928),
Siam (Jan. 16, 1929), Albania (Feb. 12, 1929), Kingdom of the Serbs, Croats,
and Slovenes (Feb. 20, 1929), Liberia (Feb. 23, 1929), Panama (Feb. 25, 1929),
Portugal (Mar. 1, 1929), Spain (Mar. 7, 1929), Cuba (Mar. 13, 1929), Rumania
(Mar. 21, 1929), Denmark (Mar. 23, 1929), Norway (Mar. 26, 1929), Lithuania
(Apr. 5, 1929), Sweden (Apr. 12, 1929), Estonia (Apr. 6, 1929), China (May 8,
1929), Egypt (May 9, 1929), Nicaragua (May 13, 1929), Iceland (June 10, 1929),
Turkey (July 8, 1929), Netherlands (July 12, 1929), Guatemala (July 16, 1929),
Bulgaria (July 22, 1929), Hungary (July 22, 1929), Peru (July 23, 1929), Latvia
(July 23, 1929), Finland (July 24, 1929).
The following states later transmitted their instruments of adherence:
Persia (July 25, 1929), Greece (Aug. 3, 1929), Honduras (Aug. 5, 1929), Chile
(Aug. 12, 1929), Luxemburg (Aug. 24, 1929), Free City of Danzig (Sept. 11,
1929, transmitted by the Polish Government on behalf of Danzig), Costa Rica
(Oct. 1, 1929), Venezuela (Oct. 24, 1929), Mexico (Nov. 26, 1929), Switzerland
(Dec. 2, 1929), Paraguay (Dec. 4, 1929), Haiti (Mar. 10, 1930), Colombia (May
28, 1931), Ecuador (Feb. 24, 1932), Kingdom of the Hedjaz and Nejd (Feb. 24,
1932, invitation to adhere issued after recognition of the Hejazi Government in

Frank B. Kellogg came from his home in St. Paul, and former President Calvin Coolidge abandoned his front porch at Northampton for a few days. Most remarkable of all the guests, however, was a stocky, bustling lawyer from Chicago—none other than Salmon O. Levinson. Secretary Stimson ("Stimmy," [15] Yale '88) had invited Levinson, his old college classmate, as the only unofficial guest.

The guests, official and unofficial, were assembling in Washington for the ceremony of proclamation when word came that Prime Minister Ramsay MacDonald of Great Britain had suspended work on two new cruisers for the British Navy. MacDonald also decided to cancel contracts for, or slow down, other naval construction. President Herbert Hoover responded immediately by holding up construction of three of the American Navy's new cruisers authorized by the recently passed cruiser bill.[16] This Anglo-American demonstration of good will augured well for the future of the antiwar pact. But the Japanese kept on building up to the Washington-treaty allowances.

While Britain and the United States were disarming each other a local war suddenly threatened along the Russo-Chinese border in Manchuria. State Department employees in Washington, busily certifying documents and preparing for the treaty's ceremonial proclamation, must have gasped in amazement when they learned of the billowing war clouds in Manchuria. Perhaps Frank

---

1931), Iraq (Mar. 23, 1932, invitation to adhere issued after recognition of the Iraqi Government in 1931), Brazil (May 10, 1934).

Argentina, Bolivia, El Salvador, and Uruguay did not deposit instruments of adherence.

Andorra, Monaco, Morocco, Liechtenstein, and San Marino received no invitations to adhere.

15. So Levinson affectionately referred to the secretary of state.

16. As passed, Feb. 13, 1929, the bill had authorized construction of fifteen 10,000-ton cruisers—five each in the fiscal years 1929, 1930, and 1931—and one aircraft carrier (in fiscal 1930). The president was empowered to suspend this program in the event of successful negotiations at a naval conference. Of the five cruisers for fiscal 1929, private shipyards obtained contracts for two, and government yards undertook to build the other three. It was on these latter three cruisers that Hoover decided to halt construction.

H. Simonds, whose prediction of "no general European war for twenty years" already was rolling off the presses of the *Review of Reviews*, began to review his previous line of reasoning. The able Mr. Simonds knew full well that these Asiatic affairs had deep meaning for the politics and diplomacy of Europe.

It is not possible within the scope of these pages to investigate the Sino-Russian undeclared war in Manchuria, or even to study the part played in it by the antiwar treaty (to which both China and Russia were parties). Suffice to say that here, in this Manchurian imbroglio over ownership of the Chinese Eastern Railway, lay the seeds of future world disaster. The pact of Paris, although hastily invoked, proved of little value in averting the conflict or in settling it once fighting had begun.[17] Chinese nationalism exhibited in this undeclared war convinced certain Japanese leaders that the time for reckoning with China was at hand. In 1931 there consequently began the fateful "Manchurian affair," forerunner to achievement of *Hakko Ichiu,* or The Eight Corners of the Universe under One Roof. Observing the futility of the League of Nations' Lytton Commission,[18] certain ambitious individuals in Europe took hope and began to develop their own Hakko Ichiu.

But we must return now to a scene in Washington, on a summer day in 1929, where representatives of most of the nations of the world had gathered in the East Room of the White House to see the president of the United States proclaim a solemn treaty against war.

17. For this there is the authority of Assistant Secretary of State Castle, who wrote in his diary, July 23, 1929: "The Secretary has been appealing to China and to Russia through France, basing his action on the Kellogg Pact. One reason for this was to prevent declaration of war on the day the pact is declared effective—tomorrow. It may have a definitely good effect if the world can be made to believe that, through respect for the Pact, war was averted. This will not be true but that does not matter if the world believes it true. It will make the Pact a real thing and something to be called forth in similar cases in the future."

18. A commission of inquiry set up by the League. After investigation in China the commission brought in the famous Lytton Report, a model of judicious reasoning. The League, however, did little toward putting an end to the Manchurian affair, other than advising League members not to recognize the puppet state of Manchukuo.

President Herbert Hoover declared the antiwar treaty in force at 1:22 P.M., July 24, 1929. "I dare predict," he said, "that the influence of the treaty for the renunciation of war will be felt in a large proportion of all future international acts." [19]

"The Kellogg Pact party today at the White House was a great success," wrote Assistant Secretary Castle in his diary.

The only slip being that the President, who was nervous, made his speech a minute sooner than he should have and, therefore, the radio people did not get the microphones on the table so that he could be heard all over the country. In addition, since his voice was not on the air, the two announcers at the back of the room felt they must keep on talking and that caused a certain confusion of sound. The cameras, etc. were bad, but since the whole purpose of the thing was publicity it was all right. The East Room looked very well and all the seating went smoothly. Representatives of all nations which had ratified were there and the rest came for luncheon. Kellogg was much affected. The luncheon table, horse-shoe shape, was attractive and the food was good. We all had coffee on the piazza afterward. Levinson, the only outsider, was rather a blot on the occasion . . . Ted [Marriner] sat opposite him and said he had never heard so much misinformation dispersed in a short time. [20]

Upon proclaiming the treaty, the Government of the United States received congratulations from statesmen the world over. Stresemann cabled that "The Pact, which gives expression to the inmost yearning of the nations, has created a new foundation for the peaceful development of relations between the States." [21] Briand echoed Stresemann's praises: "The Pact, which tenders such precious promises for the future, becomes today part of the law of nations and is the most important contribution thus far made to the cause of peace." [22] Baron Kijuro Shidehara, minister of foreign

19. New York *Times,* July 25, 1929.
20. Castle diary, July 24, 1929.
21. Stresemann to Stimson, July 23, 1929, 711.0012 Anti-War/849.
22. Briand to Stimson, July 25(?), 1929, 711.0012 Anti-War/835.

affairs of the Imperial Japanese Government, declared in similar vein that "the treaty opens a new chapter in the history of international relations." [23]

"The inmost yearning of nations," said Stresemann. "Such precious promises for the future," said Briand. "Opens a new chapter," said Shidehara.

All these statements were correct.

23. Shidehara to Stimson, undated (received July 23, 1929), 711.0012 Anti-War/846.

Chapter Eighteen: CONCLUSION

The Kellogg-Briand Pact was the peculiar result of some very shrewd diplomacy and some very unsophisticated popular enthusiasm for peace.

Although the French Republic had been among the victors of the first World War, France's position in the postwar years was precarious. Germany, vanquished, nonetheless was a nation of nearly twice the population of France. The Ruhr Valley held an enormous concentration of heavy industry, giving Germany a huge war potential. Not without reason the French people felt insecure vis-à-vis their restless neighbors across the Rhine and desired all the guarantees of peace they could get.

The French relied principally upon their army and upon a new postwar series of military alliances. By the spring of 1927 France had alliances with Belgium, Poland, Czechoslovakia, Rumania, and Yugoslavia.[1] The French foreign minister, Aristide Briand, then attempted to bring the world's greatest non-European power, the United States of America, into France's new design for her own security. If Briand could not obtain an outright alliance (such, we recall, had failed to be ratified after Versailles), then perhaps he might at least secure American neutrality in event of another European war. That such was Briand's purpose appears quite evident from the text of his proposed Pact of Perpetual Friendship: this proposition was naught but a negative military alliance.

To the American State Department such a Franco-American

1. Albeit the latter alliance had not yet been signed.

Pact of Perpetual Friendship was impossible, for it would have deeply embroiled the United States in the age-old rivalries and collisions of the European nations. Briand, however, enlisted in support of his pacific-sounding idea the extremely well-organized and vocal American peace movement. Enthusiasts all over the United States began urging the Coolidge Administration to sign with France.

After several months of ingenious inaction the State Department made a counterproposal: a *multilateral* treaty for renunciation of war. This verbal change side-stepped the dangers of Briand's proposed bilateral pact and at the same time placed the American peace enthusiasts—who could not see the difference between a bilateral and a multilateral treaty—on the side of Secretary of State Frank B. Kellogg. Briand, instead of Kellogg, now was embarrassed. He of course did not desire a multilateral treaty. But the French foreign minister—man of peace, "Locarno prophet," [2] holder of the Nobel Peace Prize—could scarcely refuse outright so grand a treaty against war. As Assistant Secretary of State William R. Castle happily wrote in his diary, "We have Monsieur Briand out on a limb . . . I do not think the French will agree [to the multilateral proposal], but I think they will have an awful time not to agree." [3]

The upshot was (1) Briand's attempt unobtrusively to disentangle himself from the Kellogg démarche and when this failed (2) agreement, but with reservations—particularly "self-defense." Meanwhile the American peace movement waged a tremendous campaign. Even Secretary of State Kellogg caught the popular infection and came to envision his counterproposal as a great contribution to world peace. The popular movement for peace in the United States seemed to reach its apogee of success when the Kellogg treaty was signed, ratified, and proclaimed.

The history of the origins of the Kellogg-Briand Pact shows

2. Ambassador Myron T. Herrick's phrase. Herrick to Kellogg, Feb. 28, 1928, Herrick MSS.
3. "After all," concluded Castle, "we have done what we set out to do. We have made a big, peaceful gesture . . ." Castle diary, Feb. 28, 1928.

that American popular understanding of the great problems and policies of post-1918 international affairs was appallingly naive. Moreover, some of America's most respected citizens, possessing the cherished visible signs of education, proved themselves almost as benighted as the public they sought to lead. This is not in any way to belittle the cause in which the public and its leaders worked, nor to question the goodness which filled their hearts. The volunteer diplomats worked long and arduously for what they believed the public welfare. Peace leaders and workers, according to their lights, did their best. This should not be forgotten. The fact remains that Aristide Briand, observing this immature American idealism, was able to manipulate it with astonishing ease for his subtle purpose of "perpetual friendship" between France and the United States.

Public ignorance hence created a serious problem in the conduct of American diplomacy. American diplomats were capable men, well intentioned, as full of good will as the peace leaders and workers who bothered them. But they had to cope with a public opinion whose only virtue often was that it was public and opinionated. The strength, voice, and unintelligence of American public opinion during the twenties forced the State Department into tortuous diplomatic maneuvering—necessitating even the grand proposal of a multilateral treaty against war.

It is impossible within the confines of the present volume to offer any general conclusions about the various "invocations" of the Kellogg pact from the summer of 1929 onward. That is an extremely interesting portion of history which perhaps can be dealt with in another work. The present purpose has been rather to examine the origins—as apart from the later development—of the Kellogg-Briand Pact. These origins illustrate in a unique way the peculiarities, difficulties, and eventual denouement of the Search for Peace after the first World War. They point up the extremely important and grave problems involved in the inevitable interaction, in a democracy, of foreign policy and public opinion. Perhaps therefore one should hope that by the 1950's American public opinion has become truly sophisticated and will give its unwavering support to a realistic American foreign policy.

The Kellogg-Briand Pact

THE PRESIDENT OF THE GERMAN REICH, THE PRESIDENT OF THE UNITED STATES OF AMERICA, HIS MAJESTY THE KING OF THE BELGIANS, THE PRESIDENT OF THE FRENCH REPUBLIC, HIS MAJESTY THE KING OF GREAT BRITAIN, IRELAND AND THE BRITISH DOMINIONS BEYOND THE SEAS, EMPEROR OF INDIA, HIS MAJESTY THE KING OF ITALY, HIS MAJESTY THE EMPEROR OF JAPAN, THE PRESIDENT OF THE REPUBLIC OF POLAND, THE PRESIDENT OF THE CZECHOSLOVAK REPUBLIC,

Deeply sensible of their solemn duty to promote the welfare of mankind;

Persuaded that the time has come when a frank renunciation of war as an instrument of national policy should be made to the end that the peaceful and friendly relations now existing between their peoples may be perpetuated;

Convinced that all changes in their relations with one another should be sought only by pacific means and be the result of a peaceful and orderly process, and that any signatory Power which shall hereafter seek to promote its national interests by resort to war should be denied the benefits furnished by this Treaty;

Hopeful that, encouraged by their example, all the other nations of the world will join in this humane endeavor and by adhering to the present Treaty as soon as it comes into force bring their peoples within the scope of its beneficent provisions, thus uniting the civilized nations of the world in a common renunciation of war as an instrument of their national policy;

Have decided to conclude a Treaty and for that purpose have appointed as their respective Plenipotentiaries:

The President of the German Reich:
  Dr. Gustav Stresemann, Minister for Foreign Affairs;

The President of the United States of America:
  The Honorable Frank B. Kellogg, Secretary of State;

His Majesty the King of the Belgians:
  Mr. Paul Hymans, Minister for Foreign Affairs, Minister of State;

The President of the French Republic:
  Mr. Aristide Briand, Minister for Foreign Affairs;

His Majesty the King of Great Britain, Ireland and the British Dominions Beyond the Seas, Emperor of India:
  For Great Britain and Northern Ireland and all parts of the British Empire which are not separate Members of the League of Nations:
    The Right Honourable Lord Cushendun, Chancellor of the Duchy of Lancaster, Acting Secretary of State for Foreign Affairs;
  For the Dominion of Canada:
    The Right Honourable William Lyon Mackenzie King, Prime Minister and Minister for External Affairs;
  For the Commonwealth of Australia:
    The Honourable Alexander John McLachlan, Member of the Executive Federal Council;
  For the Dominion of New Zealand:
    The Honourable Sir Christopher James Parr, High Commissioner for New Zealand in Great Britain;
  For the Union of South Africa:
    The Honourable Jacobus Stephanus Smit, High Commissioner for the Union of South Africa in Great Britain;
  For the Irish Free State:
    Mr. William Thomas Cosgrave, President of the Executive Council;
  For India:
    The Right Honourable Lord Cushendun, Chancellor of the

Duchy of Lancaster, Acting Secretary of State for Foreign Affairs;

His Majesty the King of Italy:
Count Gaetano Manzoni, his Ambassador Extraordinary and Plenipotentiary at Paris;

His Majesty the Emperor of Japan:
Count Uchida, Privy Councillor;

The President of the Republic of Poland:
Mr. A. Zaleski, Minister for Foreign Affairs;

The President of the Czechoslovak Republic:
Dr. Eduard Benes, Minister for Foreign Affairs;

who, having communicated to one another their full powers found in good and due form have agreed upon the following articles:

ARTICLE I

The High Contracting Parties solemnly declare in the names of their respective peoples that they condemn recourse to war for the solution of international controversies, and renounce it as an instrument of national policy in their relations with one another.

ARTICLE II

The High Contracting Parties agree that the settlement or solution of all disputes or conflicts of whatever nature or of whatever origin they may be, which may arise among them, shall never be sought except by pacific means.

ARTICLE III

The present Treaty shall be ratified by the High Contracting Parties named in the Preamble in accordance with their respective constitutional requirements, and shall take effect as between them as soon as all their several instruments of ratification shall have been deposited at Washington.

This Treaty shall, when it has come into effect as prescribed in the preceding paragraph, remain open as long as may be necessary for adherence by all the other Powers of the world. Every instrument evidencing the adherence of a Power shall be deposited at Washington and the Treaty shall immediately upon such deposit become effective as between the Power thus adhering and the other Powers parties hereto.

It shall be the duty of the Government of the United States to furnish each Government named in the Preamble and every Government subsequently adhering to this Treaty with a certified copy of the Treaty and of every instrument of ratification or adherence. It shall also be the duty of the Government of the United States telegraphically to notify such Governments immediately upon the deposit with it of each instrument of ratification or adherence.

IN FAITH WHEREOF the respective Plenipotentiaries have signed this Treaty in the French and English languages both texts having equal force, and hereunto affix their seals.

DONE at Paris, the twenty-seventh day of August in the year one thousand nine hundred and twenty-eight.

[SEAL] *Gustav Stresemann*
[SEAL] *Frank B. Kellogg*
[SEAL] *Paul Hymans*
[SEAL] *Ari. Briand*
[SEAL] *Cushendun*
[SEAL] *W. L. Mackenzie King*
[SEAL] *A. J. McLachlan*
[SEAL] *C. J. Parr*
[SEAL] *J. S. Smit*
[SEAL] *Liam T. MacCosgair*
[SEAL] *Cushendun*
[SEAL] *G. Manzoni*
[SEAL] *Uchida*
[SEAL] *August Zaleski*
[SEAL] *Dr. Eduard Benes* *

* *FR: 1928*, I, 153–156.

Note on Sources

I. Bibliographical Aids

For the period of the 1920's the best single guide remains William
L. Langer and Hamilton Fish Armstrong, *Foreign Affairs Bibliog-
raphy: 1919–32* (New York, 1933). More recent publication must
be searched out in the quarterly lists of such journals as the *American Historical Review* and *Foreign Affairs*. In a sense a bibli-
ographical aid, because it points to the problems besetting all historians of the years since the first World War, is the brilliant article
by Max Beloff, "Historians in a Revolutionary Age," *Foreign Affairs, 29* (January 1951), 248–262.

II. General Works

There is no good diplomatic history of the twenties, and one must
turn to works of larger scope which deal in part with the period. A
fine analysis of European politics in the twentieth century may be
found in Hajo Holborn's *The Political Collapse of Europe* (New
York, 1951). E. H. Carr, *International Relations since the Peace
Treaties* (London, 1937; rev. ed., 1941) contains a dependable survey. For catching the diplomatic problems of the 1920's in voluminous detail, the best source continues to be the *Survey of International Affairs,* published annually by the Royal Institute and
usually written by Professor Arnold J. Toynbee.

For diplomatic histories of leading European countries during
the twenties it also is necessary to consult larger works dealing with
the entire interwar period. There are not many of these. A very

good monograph is W. M. Jordan, *Great Britain, France and the German Problem: 1918–1939* (London, 1943). Likewise good is Arnold Wolfers, *Britain and France between Two Wars: Conflicting Strategies of Peace since Versailles* (New York, 1940). W. N. Medlicott, *British Foreign Policy since Versailles* (London, 1940) has a competent treatment.

The best introduction to American diplomacy of the period may be found in two short articles: Edward Mead Earle, "A Half-Century of American Foreign Policy: Our Stake in Europe, 1898–1948," *Political Science Quarterly, 64* (1949), 168–188; and Samuel Flagg Bemis, "The Shifting Strategy of American Defense and Diplomacy," in Dwight E. Lee and George E. McReynolds, eds., *Essays in History and International Relations in Honor of George Hubbard Blakeslee* (Worcester, Mass., 1949), pp. 1–14. The Council on Foreign Relations began publication of its annual survey of American foreign relations in 1928. These volumes, under varying editorship, are not always as critical as they might have been; certainly the initial volumes are not up to the high standard of the Royal Institute's *Survey of International Affairs*. The best treatment of American diplomacy during the 1920's is in the pertinent chapters of Professor Samuel Flagg Bemis' excellent *Diplomatic History of the United States* (3d ed., New York, 1950). Herbert Feis, *The Diplomacy of the Dollar: First Era 1919–1932* (Baltimore, 1950) concerns American lending policies during the twenties; the diplomacy of the dollar was, of course, highly important.

Books on international peace are innumerable, but most of them are tracts advocating one scheme or another. Historians have made little effort to study the peace movement. Arthur C. F. Beales, *History of Peace* (New York, 1931) is the only acceptable general account. In this book, however, peace during the 1920's—when the peace movement reached its apogee—received only some twenty-five pages, entitled "Epilogue." Professor Merle Curti has written the only history of the American peace movement. *Peace or War: The American Struggle 1636–1936* (New York, 1936) is heavily weighted in the years 1860–1918; again, the all-important era of the twenties received cursory examination. Denna Frank Fleming, *The United States and World Organization: 1920–1933* (New York,

1936) is a somewhat uncritical account, written largely from secondary works. Jerome Davis' *Contemporary Social Movements* (New York, 1930) has a rather interesting chapter (pp. 747–868) on "The Peace Movement" from a pacifist viewpoint. Devere Allen, *The Fight for Peace* (New York, 1930) is a tract for pacifism; chaotically written, it nonetheless is crammed with important bits of information. Reliable data about peace organizations appear in Florence Brewer Boeckel, *Between War and Peace: A Handbook for Peace Workers* (New York, 1928). Lyman Besse Burbank, "Internationalism in American Thought: 1919–1929," a doctoral dissertation submitted in June 1950 to the faculty of New York University, has value as an introduction to the organized peace movement of the twenties.

III. Special Works

A. MONOGRAPHS

John E. Stoner, *S. O. Levinson and the Pact of Paris: A Study in the Techniques of Influence* (Chicago, 1942) is an excellent account of the Outlawry movement, written almost exclusively from the Levinson MSS in the Library of the University of Chicago. Many of Professor Stoner's judgments would have been different had he extended his research to other sources. The authoritative exposition of Outlawry as a philosophy may be encountered in Charles Clayton Morrison, *The Outlawry of War: A Constructive Policy for World Peace* (Chicago, 1927). Not without interest is Frank B. Kellogg and William R. Castle, "Outlawry of War," *Encyclopedia Britannica*, 14th ed. Typical articles by the Outlawrists are Charles Clayton Morrison, "Briand Opens a Door," *Christian Century, 44* (May 26, 1927), 646–647; John Dewey, "Outlawing Peace by Discussing War," *New Republic, 54* (Feb.–May 1928), 370–371; John Dewey, " 'As an Example to Other Nations,' " *New Republic, 54* (Feb.–May 1928), 88–89; Carrie Chapman Catt, "The Outlawry of War," *Annals of the American Academy of Political and Social Science, 138* (July 1928), 157–163; Raymond Robins, "The Outlawry of War—The Next Step in Civilization," *Annals of the American Academy, 120* (July 1925), 153–156. For a European attempt to trace Outlawry down through international affairs of the

1920's, see Hans Wehberg, *The Outlawry of War* (Washington, 1931); this philosophicolegal analysis envisions Outlawry where there was nothing of the sort.

A considerable number of books have been written on various aspects of the peace movement. The War Resisters' International published *War Resisters in Many Lands* (Middlesex, England, 1928?), a brief account of its activities; on the same subject is Runham Brown, *Cutting Ice* (Enfield, England, 1930). Then there is *Twenty Years of the Foreign Policy Association* (n.p., 1939). Fern E. Stowe compiled a MS "History of the National Council for the Prevention of War," a copy of which may be found in the Swarthmore College Peace Collection. The Carnegie Endowment recently issued "A Brief Review of Thirty-Five Years of Service toward Developing International Understanding," *International Conciliation*, No. 417 (January 1946), 17–39. For other organizations see Marie L. Degen, *History of the Woman's Peace Party* (Baltimore, 1939); Lilian Stevenson, *Towards a Christian International: The Story of the International Fellowship of Reconciliation* (3d ed., London, 1941); Allan W. Eister, *Drawing Room Conversion* (Durham, 1950); Walter H. Clark, *The Oxford Group* (New York, 1951); Charles S. Macfarland, *Pioneers for Peace through Religion: Based on the Records of the Church Peace Union (Founded by Andrew Carnegie) 1914–1945* (New York, 1946). There is material on the Bok Peace Plan in Esther Everett Lape, ed., *Ways to Peace* (New York, 1924). The voyage of the Ford peace ship, the *Oscar II*, is chronicled in Louis P. Lochner, *America's Don Quixote: Henry Ford's Attempt To Save Europe* (London, 1924). No one has attempted to indicate the part which women played in the organized peace movement. Mary R. Beard's *Woman as Force in History* (New York, 1946) virtually ignores the forceful role of women.

Many books have been written on the Kellogg-Briand Pact, all of them during or shortly after its negotiation. The best juridical analysis is David Hunter Miller, *The Peace Pact of Paris: A Study of the Briand-Kellogg Treaty* (New York, 1928); Miller was principally concerned with the few documents published in 1928. James T. Shotwell, *War as an Instrument of National Policy: And Its Renunciation in the Pact of Paris* (New York, 1929) sought to describe the broader meaning of the pact but failed, in the present writer's opinion, to look very deeply beneath the printed and spoken word. Other studies of the Kellogg treaty, all written closely from a few official documents, are Kirby Page, *The Renunciation of War* (New York, 1928); Denys P. Myers, *Origin and Conclusion of the Paris Pact* (Boston, 1929); and J. W. Wheeler-Bennett, *Information on the Renunciation of War 1927–1928* (London, 1928). Signature of the pact in Paris encouraged an epidemic of poor French doctoral dissertations, of which the following are representative: Robert Le Gall, *Le Pacte de Paris* (Paris, 1930); Cécile Balbareu, *Le Pacte de Paris* (Paris, 1929); P. Kostoff, *Le Moratoire de guerre* (Paris, 1930); Spyros Calogeropoulos Stratis, *Le Pacte général de renonciation à la guerre* (Paris, 1931).

For acute contemporary criticism of the pact, see Edwin M. Borchard, "The Multilateral Treaty for the Renunciation of War," *American Journal of International Law, 23* (1929), 116–120; and Franklin D. Roosevelt, "Our Foreign Policy: A Democratic View," *Foreign Affairs, 6* (July 1928), 573–586. The first effort to get beneath the published documents was Drew Pearson and Constantine Brown, *The American Diplomatic Game* (New York, 1935), chap. i, "The World Renounces War." Written with considerable error and not a little bombast and sensationalism, this account contains an impressive residue of fact.

There are many monographs on the League of Nations, but the best is Alfred Zimmern, *The League of Nations and the Rule of Law: 1918–1935* (London, 1936; 2d ed., 1939). Very good is C. K. Webster and Sydney Herbert, *The League of Nations in Theory and Practice* (London, 1933). For one of the most important origins of the League, see Ruhl J. Bartlett, *The League To Enforce Peace* (Chapel Hill, N.C., 1944). Professor Harry R. Rudin's definitive *Armistice 1918* (New Haven, 1944) provides the immediate setting out of which the League emerged. Then there is David Hunter Miller's *The Drafting of the Covenant* (2 vols., New York, 1928). W. Stull Holt, *Treaties Defeated by the Senate* (Baltimore, 1933), and Thomas A. Bailey, *Woodrow Wilson and the Great Betrayal* (New York, 1945) explain the League's rejection in the United States. Worthy of note is the little book by J. Paul Selsam, *The At-*

tempts To Form an Anglo-French Alliance: 1919–1924 (Philadelphia, 1936). Much debate has arisen over exactly why the League failed to avert the second World War, and certainly one excellent reason is set down in William W. Kaufmann, "The Organization of Responsibility," *World Politics, 1* (July 1949), 511–532. Professor Kaufmann contends that responsibility should go only to those nations capable of exercising it—whereas the League (and also the United Nations) gave responsibility of sorts to the small powers. The result was failure because the small powers could not be responsible. (Nor *would* the large ones, I might add.)

A very important aspect of post-1918 international relations was the naval question—the size of navies, the scope of wartime belligerent and neutral rights and duties. The naval question had deep roots in prewar days. E. L. Woodward, *Great Britain and the German Navy* (Oxford, 1935) analyzes one of the prime causes of the first World War. American naval policy in the postwar years is well treated in George T. Davis, *A Navy Second to None* (New York, 1940). Edwin M. Borchard and William P. Lage, *Neutrality for the United States* (New Haven, 1937; rev. ed., 1940) surveys the neutrality question, much alive during the twenties; written during the mid-thirties when conditions had greatly changed, this volume presents strict neutrality as an essential of American life.

American foreign policy in other particular aspects is dealt with, excellently, in Samuel Flagg Bemis, *The Latin American Policy of the United States* (New York, 1943), and A. Whitney Griswold, *The Far Eastern Policy of the United States* (New York, 1938). For Far Eastern policy, see also the very competent monograph by Dorothy Borg, *American Policy and the Chinese Revolution: 1925–1928* (New York, 1947).

B. BIOGRAPHIES AND AUTOBIOGRAPHIES

David Bryn-Jones, *Frank B. Kellogg: A Biography* (New York, 1937) has a valuable memorandum on the Kellogg-Briand Pact, written by Kellogg himself. Professor Bryn-Jones received Kellogg's active assistance throughout this biography. No one can study Kellogg's career without reference to Professor Bryn-Jones' authoritative work.

There is no adequate biography of Briand. Georges Suarez, *Briand: Sa vie, son oeuvre, avec son journal et de nombreux documents inédits* (Paris, 1938–41) has appeared in five volumes; but, because of the death of Suarez, will not go beyond the year 1923. The extremely important period from 1923 to Briand's death in 1932 thus is not covered. Unlike his contemporary in French political life, Raymond Poincaré (who burned nearly all his papers), Briand saved almost everything. Suarez reported that Briand kept many secret papers in an iron box (so also did Briand's illustrious predecessor, Théophile Delcassé). At the beginning of the recent war the papers were at Cocherel, Briand's summer house in Brittany.

The Stresemann papers (see below, pp. 279–280) are best for the activities of that statesman. There is a recent biography by Walter Görlitz, *Gustav Stresemann* (Heidelberg, 1947), based on these papers. Antonina Vallentin, *Frustration: Or Stresemann's Race with Death* (London, 1931) is a rather unreliable fictionalized account but of some interest because of the authoress' personal acquaintance with her subject.

For Sir Austen Chamberlain there is Sir Charles Petrie, *The Life and Letters of the Right Hon. Sir Austen Chamberlain* (2 vols., London, 1940), a collection of sketchy extracts from letters and a diary, interlarded with explanatory editorial comments. The Chamberlain diary contained some devastating appraisal of the Kellogg pact. Sir Austen's reminiscences on various international and other subjects—unfortunately not including much on the Kellogg treaty—are in his *Down the Years* (London, 1935).

The best biography of President Calvin Coolidge is Claude M. Fuess, *Calvin Coolidge: The Man from Vermont* (Boston, 1940); appropriately, it contains only perfunctory reference to the Kellogg pact. For understanding Coolidge the man, the best source is *The Autobiography of Calvin Coolidge* (New York, 1929), supported with the observations in Irwin Hood (Ike) Hoover, *Forty-Two Years in the White House* (Boston, 1934); Edmund W. Starling and Thomas Sugrue, *Starling of the White House* (New York, 1946); Duff Gilfond, *The Rise of Saint Calvin: Merry Sidelights on the*

Career of Mr. Coolidge (New York, 1932); and, especially, William Allen White, *A Puritan in Babylon* (New York, 1938).

Colonel T. Bentley Mott, *Myron T. Herrick: Friend of France* (New York, 1930) is very slight on the 1920's. Claudius O. Johnson, *Borah of Idaho* (New York, 1936), an almost official biography, is written mainly from the Borah MSS now in the Library of Congress, and consequently has the strength and limits of those MSS. Sir Esme Howard, *Theatre of Life* (2 vols., Boston, 1935–36) has a few interesting pages on the Kellogg treaty. Hugh R. Wilson, *Diplomat between Wars* (New York, 1941) offers a breezily informal, often informative account of life in the State Department during the period 1925–27; it also relates the history of the 1927 Geneva Naval Disarmament Conference. There is nothing about the Kellogg pact but some information on the Search for Peace during the 1920's, especially the World Court, in Philip C. Jessup, *Elihu Root* (New York, 1938), Vol. II. For interesting and often acute contemporary biographical sketches of American political leaders, see Walter Lippmann, *Men of Destiny* (New York, 1927). A similar but much less successful effort is Oswald Garrison Villard, *Prophets, True and False* (New York, 1928). Unreliable, but provocative for its gossip about Washington diplomatic personalities, is Drew Pearson and Robert S. Allen, *Washington Merry-Go-Round* (New York, 1931).

As for leaders in the peace movement there is, first of all, Nicholas Murray Butler's delightful *Across the Busy Years* (2 vols., New York, 1939–40). Jane Addams recorded her activities in *The Second Twenty Years at Hull-House: With a Record of a Growing World Consciousness* (New York, 1930); Miss Addams' war work appears in her *Peace and Bread in Time of War* (New York, 1922). There are two Addams biographies: James Weber Linn, *Jane Addams: A Biography* (New York, 1935), and Winifred E. Wise, *Jane Addams of Hull-House* (New York, 1935). Mary Gray Peck, *Carrie Chapman Catt: A Biography* (New York, 1944) was written partly from Mrs. Catt's memory—not always reliable. The world of statesmen and scholars would appreciate a biography of Professor Shotwell.

IV. Newspapers and Periodicals

The New York *Times* is extremely useful for recent American history for two reasons: its admirable coverage, and its equally admirable index. During negotiation of the Kellogg-Briand Pact the *Times* carried dispatches from its Paris correspondent Edwin L. James which often reflected the viewpoint of the French Foreign Office. The *Times* also usually printed reports of presidential and Department of State press conferences. Frequently, of course, the *Times* obliged Dr. Nicholas Murray Butler by publicizing his activities.

The London *Times* was consulted at various points where information offered by the New York *Times* seemed unnecessarily bare. Almost always the New York *Times* reported European affairs better than did its London opposite. I did not undertake the enormous task of hunting through files of Continental newspapers. On important occasions during negotiation of the Kellogg-Briand Pact, the London *Times* or the New York *Times* or the State Department made systematic surveys of foreign press opinion. Foreign public opinion moreover was relatively unimportant, compared to American opinion, in negotiation of the pact.

Especially useful periodicals were the *American Journal of International Law* and the *British Year Book of International Law*. On a more popular level were articles in *Foreign Affairs* and its British counterpart, the *Journal of the Royal Institute of International Affairs*.

V. Printed Sources

Documents relative to general diplomatic history of the 1920's may be found in appendixes or documentary annexes to the Royal Institute's annual *Survey of International Affairs*. The only comparable American collection is the documents printed in the Carnegie Endowment's monthly *International Conciliation*.

Upon signature of the Kellogg-Briand Pact in August 1928, several of the signatories issued collections of exchanged notes.

The German, French, British, and American publications were virtually identical. The French *Pacte général de renonciation à la guerre comme instrument de politique nationale: Trente pièces relatives à la préparation, à l'élaboration et à la conclusion du traité signé à Paris le 27 août 1928 (6 avril 1927–27 août 1928)* (Paris, 1928) contained two or three cables between Briand and Claudel, but these were not very informative. All of these exchanged notes published by the various nations, together with much new and highly important material, appear in *Foreign Relations of the United States* for the years 1927 and 1928. German, French, and British archival papers relating to the Kellogg-Briand Pact have not similarly been re-examined and representative portions of the papers printed.

A convenient guide to parliamentary debates on the Kellogg-Briand Pact was Malcolm W. Davis and Walter H. Mallory, *A Political Handbook of the World: Parliaments, Parties and Press as of January 1, 1928* (New Haven and Cambridge, Mass., 1928); first published in 1928, this handbook has passed through many subsequent editions. Parliamentary debates consulted were the *Congressional Record, House of Commons Debates, Verhandlungen des Reichstags,* and debates of the French Chamber of Deputies. The German and French debates had little to do with the Kellogg-Briand Pact. The *Record* has the important debate on American ratification. The Commons debates are interesting for various interpellations during negotiation of the pact.

The League of Nations published annually, under slightly varying titles, verbatim records of its Assembly and committee meetings.

The League's *Treaty Series* printed the original texts—and, when necessary, English translations—of all registered treaties. A specialized treaty collection is Max Habicht, *Post-War Treaties for the Pacific Settlement of International Disputes* (Cambridge, Mass., 1931).

Few personal papers of statesmen and other participants in the Kellogg pact have been published. Most notable of the published papers of course is Eric Sutton, ed. and trans., *Gustav Stresemann: His Diaries, Letters, and Papers* (3 vols., London, 1935–40). This collection prints memoranda, letters, speeches, and press conferences, with commentary by the editor. The Stresemann papers offer an excellent view of German diplomacy during the twenties. The only other published collections worthy of notice are *The Collected Papers of John Bassett Moore* (7 vols., New Haven, 1944), which has some trenchant criticisms of the Kellogg pact by Judge Moore; and Charles G. Dawes, *Notes as Vice President: 1928–1929* (Boston, 1935), the vice president's diary from June 27, 1928, to March 6, 1929, useful for its account of the Senate's advice and consent to the Kellogg treaty.

Peace organizations themselves rarely bothered to issue yearbooks or other documentary publications. The only available material concerns the Carnegie Endowment: its annual *Year Book*, published since 1911; also its *Manual of the Public Benefactions of Andrew Carnegie* (Washington, 1919). Worth some mention is the British National Council for Prevention of War, *Peace Year-Book* (London, 1921, 1927, 1929), presenting cursory glimpses of the peace movement in various European countries.

VI. Manuscript Sources

A. ARCHIVES

The basis of the present study was the voluminous records of the Department of State, now deposited in the National Archives in Washington. The Kellogg pact material comprises several entire files. Ancillary files have other valuable documents. In stressing the value of the archives one should not however offer the impression that the documents printed in *Foreign Relations* were relatively insignificant, or that the compilers of *Foreign Relations* suppressed important material. The State Department has been eminently fair in its publications, but it can print only a limited number of documents. The American archives are now (1952) open, under certain restrictions, for investigation of material dating to the year 1937.

Archives of the Weimar Republic, captured by the American Army during the second World War, in a few years may also be opened. The British Foreign Office archives of the interwar period are now being studied by Professors E. L. Woodward and Rohan D. Butler; but there is no assurance that publication of the several new post-1918 series of *Documents on British Foreign Policy* will be followed by opening the archives beyond 1901, their present dateline. The Quai d'Orsay records are closed beyond the year 1876.

B. PERSONAL PAPERS

Of great value was the detailed diary of William R. Castle, assistant secretary of state for Western European affairs during negotiation of the Kellogg pact. For the period of the negotiations the diary has several hundred typescript pages.

The Salmon O. Levinson MSS (University of Chicago Library) are a huge collection of 40,000 letters and over 100,000 pieces of various sorts. Levinson saved everything. These manuscripts are of high importance for the Kellogg-Briand Pact and the peace movement generally during the twenties.

The papers of Senator William E. Borah, now in the Library of Congress, have a significant amount of material on the Kellogg pact and related subjects. Borah's interests were wide.

The Calvin Coolidge MSS (Library of Congress) are a very large collection which has to be consulted through an inadequate card file. Coolidge rarely committed himself on paper, and most of this material is interesting for what people told Coolidge rather than for what he replied. Occasionally, however, the presidential personality peeps through the answers, and these glimpses well reward much search. It is obvious from the Coolidge collection that the president had little faith in the Kellogg-Briand Pact.

The William Howard Taft papers (Library of Congress) contain little on the Kellogg treaty, although during the 1920's Taft's political interests were exceedingly wide: his curiosity about political affairs was insatiable.

The papers of Elihu Root (Library of Congress) are not especially interesting for the period of the twenties. But although the correspondence during this era is mostly personal, there are occasional letters from important individuals which are worth search. Root, in reply, frequently made no carbons.

Dr. Nicholas Murray Butler's papers, now gathering dust up near the dome of the Low Memorial Library at Columbia University, are a vast collection of mostly trivial correspondence. It is reported that a secretary to Dr. Butler, shortly before the latter's death, went through the papers and pulled out and burned many letters. Some of the most important folders of correspondence are empty; and each empty folder has a peculiar crayon "X" mark. There nonetheless remained a few letters of exceptional interest relative to the Kellogg-Briand Pact.

The papers of Myron T. Herrick (Western Reserve Historical Society, Cleveland, Ohio) are in considerable disorder, and Herrick's correspondence while home in Cleveland on leave is not here. There is not much on the Kellogg pact, or even generally on Herrick's second Paris ambassadorship, 1921–29.

Senator John J. Blaine was the only senator to vote against the Kellogg treaty. His papers, now in the library of the State Historical Society of Wisconsin, reveal virtually nothing that was not already known about his position on the treaty (Blaine voted against the pact because he considered it recognition of the British Empire).

Mrs. Jessie Jack Hooper, a prominent clubwoman of Oshkosh, Wisconsin, was international relations chairman of the General Federation of Women's Clubs. In this capacity she advocated signature and ratification of the Kellogg treaty. Her correspondence (State Historical Society of Wisconsin) indicates in great detail that the treaty provoked nation-wide interest and had a large following in Midwestern states.

The American ambassador to Germany during negotiation of the Kellogg pact, Dr. Jacob Gould Schurman, left many of his papers to the Collection of Regional History, Cornell University. For the period of Schurman's Berlin embassy there is very little in the Cornell collection except clippings of newspapers and drafts of speeches.

The Carter Glass MSS (Library of the University of Virginia) have virtually nothing on foreign relations, although the senator was very outspoken in his opinion of the Kellogg pact.

The papers of John Bassett Moore, presently under the personal supervision of Karl T. Frederick of New York City, reflect Judge Moore's slight interest in the Kellogg-Briand treaty.

Miss Emily Greene Balch has deposited some of her papers in the Swarthmore College Peace Collection. These illustrate the 1927–29 activities of the Women's International League for Peace and Freedom, of which Miss Balch was president of the American Section.

The papers of Hannah Clothier Hull also are at Swarthmore. Mrs. Hull was active in the peace movement.

The Jane Addams MSS at Swarthmore are disappointing for the 1920's. Miss Addams was very careless with her correspondence. The Swarthmore collection however does offer piquant details both of the general functioning of the international WILPF and the organization's special concern with the Kellogg treaty.

Mrs. George H. Moses of Concord, New Hampshire, kindly searched through the senator's papers for material touching the Kellogg pact, but discovered nothing of special interest.

The office files of several American peace organizations are now deposited at the Swarthmore College Peace Collection. These files are essential to understanding the fervor and method by which peace groups worked. Especially valuable were the files of the National Council for Prevention of War, the Women's International League for Peace and Freedom (American Branch, and International Office), and the Women's Peace Union of the Western Hemisphere.

A very useful source for President Calvin Coolidge's opinions on various subjects, including Outlawry of war, is the voluminous verbatim transcript of Coolidge's press conferences. For over twenty years this transcript reposed in a nailed-up wooden box at The Forbes Library, Northampton, Massachusetts. The present librarian, Lawrence E. Wikander, obligingly opened the box, and the transcript now is available to interested students.

Index